Irangeles

Protest rally against the Iran-Iraq war
after the escalation of the "war of the cities."
March 1988.

# Irangeles
## Iranians in Los Angeles

*Edited by*
**RON KELLEY**

JONATHAN FRIEDLANDER, CO-EDITOR

ANITA COLBY, ASSOCIATE EDITOR

PHOTOGRAPHY BY RON KELLEY

*Gustave E. von Grunebaum Center for Near Eastern Studies*
*International Studies and Overseas Programs*
*University of California at Los Angeles*

UNIVERSITY OF CALIFORNIA PRESS

BERKELEY    LOS ANGELES    OXFORD

University of California Press
Berkeley and Los Angeles, California

University of California Press, Ltd.
Oxford, England

© 1993 by
The Regents of the University of California

Library of Congress Cataloging-in-Publication Data

Irangeles : Iranians in Los Angeles / edited by Ron Kelley ; Jonathan Friedlander, co-editor ; Anita
    Colby, associate editor ; photography by Ron Kelley.
        p.   cm.
    Includes bibliographical references and index.
    ISBN 0-520-08008-4 (cloth : alk. paper). — ISBN 0-520-08009-2 (pbk. : alk. paper)
        1. Iranian Americans—California—Los Angeles—Ethnic identity.   2. Iranian Americans—
    California—Los Angeles—Social conditions.   3. Iranians—California—Los Angeles—Ethnic
    identity.   4. Iranians—California—Los Angeles—Social conditions.   I. Kelley, Ron.
    II. Friedlander, Jonathan.   III. Colby, Anita.
    979.4'94004915—dc20                                                                    92-26401

Printed in the United States of America

9  8  7  6  5  4  3  2  1

The paper used in this publication meets the minimum requirements of American National
Standard for Information Sciences—Permanence of Paper for Printed Library Materials,
ANSI Z39.48-1984. ⊗

The publisher gratefully acknowledges the contribution provided by the General
Endowment Fund of the Associates of the University of California Press.

*The photographs in this book are intended as an exploration, not of individuals, but of Iranian
culture as a whole. No person's character, actions, motivation, relationships, worldview, values, or
personal qualities should be construed from any photograph herein. Those photographed at political
demonstrations and other gatherings should not be presumed members—or even supporters—of any
organization. Nor should it be assumed that everyone in the photographs is Iranian.*

# CONTENTS

# ACKNOWLEDGMENTS

A large number of people cooperated with us in the formation of this volume. Much thanks to all those cited in the text and/or photographed, many of whom offered considerable help and hospitality. The editors would like to acknowledge the steadfast support and commitment to the project at UCLA by Georges Sabagh, Director, Center for Near Eastern Studies, and John Hawkins, Dean, International Studies and Overseas Programs. A grant from the Cultural Affairs Department of the City of Los Angeles provided partial support for the preparation of the photographs. Special thanks to Lynne Withey, Stephanie Fay, and the University of California Press. The following individuals are among those who shared their knowledge, lent their advice, or provided important support: Ali and Mindy, Behzad Allahyar, Elizabeth Dourley-Ashabi, Maziar Behrooz, Jane Bitar, Carolisa Brenner, John Brumfield, Isaac Cohen, Bob and Azar Edinger, Sholeh Ehtesham, Germán Esparza, Payam Farrahi and family, Steve Gold, Latifeh Hagigi, Richard Hovannisian, Lisa Janti, Nikki Keddie, Manoot Khodabakshian, Azadé Kian, Tony Lee, Pari Mirhashem, Michael Morony, Mary Murrell, Mohsen Naderi, Youram Nassir, Abdullah Nazemi, Mahmoud Omidsalar, Jacqueline Orozco, Sia Ostovany, Glaiol Panbechi, Rubina Peroomian, Alice Petrossian, Sheila Pinkel, Kamash Pourki, Marina Preussner, Mashyat Ramani, Sohrab Riahi at Sayeh Film, Yona Sabar, Ramin Sadr, Shirley Schwartz, the Tabatabai family, Barbod Taheri, Shohreh Zandieh, Hossein Ziai, Sherifa Zuhur, and others who prefer to remain unnamed.

# INTRODUCTION

Since United States immigration laws were liberalized in the 1960s, the racial and cultural "face" of America has changed significantly. Once the destination of mostly European immigrants because of a "national origins" policy that decidedly favored them, the United States in recent decades has received immigrants from over a hundred countries, many in the Third World. The size, diversity, settlement patterns, and cultural histories of these groups have been subjects of increasing discussion and sources of controversy among American government administrators and the popular media. Cubans and Haitians have made dramatic escapes from their homelands, for example, and have captured national attention. The Cuban refugees have been welcomed here whereas the Haitians have faced confinement and deportation. Immigration is also attracting increasing public attention in Germany, France, and other European countries as well as in the Middle East.

According to official immigration figures 6 million legal and an estimated 2 million illegal immigrants came to the United States in the 1980s. They represent one of the largest influxes in American history, second only to the 8.8 million foreigners who reached American shores during the first decade of the twentieth century. Immigrants accounted for more than one-third of America's total population growth in the 1980s, and today foreign-born residents make up about 7 percent of the U.S. population. Among the new arrivals are legal residents (Asians, Latin Americans, and Caribbean peoples account for over 70 percent of this category), refugees (more than 100,000 in 1989 alone), and increasingly large numbers of undocumented aliens (with immigrants from Mexico representing over 90 percent of those apprehended in the last decade).

The most common destination for new arrivals has been California, particularly the Los Angeles metropolitan area. According to some estimates, one-third of today's Los Angeles population is foreign-born. By the early 1980s *Time* magazine was heralding Los Angeles as the new Ellis

Island, home to a purported 2 million Mexican Americans, 200,000 Salvadorans, 200,000 Iranians, 175,000 Japanese, 150,000 Chinese, 150,000 Koreans, 150,000 Filipinos, 130,000 Arabs, and sizable numbers of Israelis, Colombians, Hondurans, Guatemalans, Cubans, Vietnamese, Samoans, and East Indians (from India, Pakistan, and Bangladesh), among others. Responding to the changing needs of the city and its immigrant population, Los Angeles Mayor Tom Bradley proposed a pilot program that would provide people telephoning city agencies with interpreters in any of 140 different languages.

The steady influx of immigrants to Los Angeles continues, giving rise to questions about social and cultural assimilation, language rights, and the economic and political ramifications of the permanence of their stay here. For example, how will the increasing cultural diversity affect social and political stability? (The tension between Korean grocery shop owners and African-Americans in predominantly black neighborhoods is often cited as a negative example.) Are immigrants a disproportionate burden on public aid and school agencies? Or, in the broader economic picture, are they largely beneficial? A *Los Angeles Times* article entitled "L.A.'s Turn as Urban Laboratory" (December 11, 1991) notes that "economists are using Los Angeles to study the way Korean entrepreneurs do business. Medical researchers are examining the cancer patterns and chest pains that afflict racial and ethnic subgroups. Sociologists are dissecting everything from the settlement patterns of Yemeni immigrants to the way Iranians set up local economic networks based on their religion." The advantage of studying Los Angeles, claims a UCLA demographer, is that there one can understand urban processes "in a nutshell."

Immigration issues give the Los Angeles media a steady source of material. From January 1990 to September 1991, for instance, the *Los Angeles Times* ran seventy articles on some aspect of immigration to the city. The article under a front-page headline in July 1991, "Jet-Age Immigrants Are Swamping I.N.S. Facilities," described a 300 percent rise since 1987 in the number of undocumented aliens who, having paid thousands of dollars for false travel documents, flew direct to the United States from countries like Sri Lanka, Pakistan, and China. Nearly 70 percent of them arrived in Los Angeles.

An appellate court in July 1991 overruled a Los Angeles judge's 1988 ruling that immigrants have the same free-speech rights as American citizens. The U.S. Justice Department had appealed the 1988 decision, seeking to deport seven Palestinians and a Kenyan who it claimed—despite their denials—were members of the Popular Front for the Liberation of

Palestine. Lawyers for the government argued that national security interests outweigh the rights of resident aliens.

The unusually fragmented forty-sixth congressional district of Los Angeles, which includes parts of Koreatown, Chinatown, the Armenian community of East Hollywood, Little Salvador, and a sizable Filipino neighborhood, illustrates some of the challenges of political assimilation. Public school children there speak nearly fifty languages, including Thai, Spanish, Portuguese, Tagalog, Laotian, Korean, Khmer, Hindi, Italian, Vietnamese, Amharic, and various Chinese dialects. Although the population of the district is 360,000—mostly immigrants—only 63,000 are registered voters. Of these, less than 15 percent are expected to vote in the next congressional election. Although whites account for about 15 percent of the district's population, they are expected to constitute about 60 percent of those voting. The issue of political representation may become increasingly heated as minority populations struggle for influence in twenty-first century California.

This book addresses an important piece of the complex mosaic of immigrant Los Angeles—a sprawling metropolis shaped by a preoccupation with the present and the future, a city of illusion, superficialities, and artifice, rarely concerned with the preservation of its past. Among its hundreds of thousands of newcomers, Los Angeles has the largest concentration of Iranians outside Iran. Most of them came to the United States to escape the consequences of the 1979 Islamic revolution in their homeland. Ironically, during the "hostage crisis" of that same period, when the American embassy staff were detained in Iran, Iranians in the United States often faced extraordinary American resentment and hostility as scapegoats for international tensions. Other than a vague appreciation of the Shah as a loyal U.S. ally, few Americans knew anything about Iran and its people. To this day, only a small number of Americans realize that Iranians in this country are not, ethnically or religiously, a homogeneous group. Instead, each one among a range of Iranian subgroups in the pan-Iranian community transposed to America has its own distinctive history, culture, and contributions to make to American society.

This volume explores Iranian life and activity in the Los Angeles metropolitan area. Our intent is to reveal the variety and complexity of Iranian identity, focusing on class, politics, gender, religion, and subethnicity—all in the context of Iranian history and American culture. Originating as a photography project, the work quickly expanded to include interviews and a range of informed commentators analyzing the local community. The breadth of content and the variety of approach herein are considerable, and the blend of photography and diverse texts provides a multifaceted portrayal. We expect this volume to interest scholars, "Iranophiles," and photographers but have labored to make it accessible to a popular audience as well. We hope it will improve Americans' understanding of the diverse Iranian community in Los Angeles and even help to illuminate the complex issues surrounding the revolutionary formation of the Islamic Republic of Iran.

RON KELLEY

JONATHAN FRIEDLANDER

PART I

PRELUDE TO MIGRATION

FIGURE 1. Woman at the Islamic
Center of South Bay, Lomita.

FIGURE 2.   Pro-Shah demonstrator.
September 1987.

# NATIONALISM AND SOCIAL CHANGE
# IN CONTEMPORARY IRAN

*Mehrdad Amanat*

The history of exile in Iran goes back at least to the eighth century, when a group of Persian Zoroastrians in search of religious freedom left Iran to form their own community in India. Since then, Persians have frequently migrated to escape religious persecution and political oppression or to seek economic opportunities. Throughout the nineteenth century, thousands of Iranians immigrated to the Russian empire looking for work in the oil fields of Baku or trading in the newly annexed areas of southern Russia. Other, smaller-scale, immigrations by Iranian Jews and Christians to North America took place around the turn of the century, and large numbers of Jews immigrated to Israel during the post–World War II period. The mass emigration from Iran since the outbreak of revolutionary upheavals in 1978, however, differs in size and character from any prior movement of the Iranian population.

Iranian immigrants residing in the West today differ profoundly from their nineteenth-century counterparts. Highly educated, professional, and entrepreneurial, this group clearly reflects the social, cultural, and economic changes that have taken place in Iran during the twentieth century. They are, for the most part, products of the Pahlavi era (1925–1979) and belonged to Iran's newly formed, predominantly secular middle class. Most Iranians in Los Angeles can be understood in this context.

The development of secularism in Iran can be traced back to the nineteenth century, when reform-minded Iranians, some with ties to indigenous messianic movements and others influenced by the West, called for radical social and political change. With their nation suffering economically and militarily at the hands of Western powers, these reformers had become increasingly conscious of Iran's steady decline. They objected to the arbitrary powers and excesses of their own country's local governors, tribal leaders, and landed aristocracy as well as the clergy and the royal family. Extremist and revolutionary elements called for the downfall of the ruling Qajar dynasty (1796–1925), while moderate groups argued for equal

FIGURE 3. Pro-Islamic Republic march
through Westwood. July 1988.

FIGURE 4. Man in an Ayatollah
Khomeini costume at a West Hollywood
discotheque on a regularly scheduled
"Persian Night." Halloween, 1989.

### 1921

Coup d'état against weakened Qajar monarchy led by a journalist, Sayyid Ziya Tabatabai, and an army officer, Reza Khan.

### 1921–26

Reza Khan, in a bid for supreme power, ousts Tabatabai and arranges his own election by the Constitutional Assembly. He names himself Reza Shah, King of Kings, and establishes the Pahlavi dynasty.

### 1927–40

Reza Shah pursues an avid campaign of secularization. Revolts by Muslim clerics are brutally repressed. Central government imposes its authority throughout the country. The wearing of the veil is banned, Muslim leaders are forced to shave their beards, and men are forced to wear Western attire. For the first time in Persian history, all citizens are required to have birth certificates and last names.

### 1941

British and Soviet troops invade Iran. Reza Shah, who had been attempting to lessen British and Soviet influence in Iran by developing ties with Nazi Germany, is forced to abdicate. His son, Mohammad Reza, is acceptable to Allied powers and is sworn in as new Shah.

Marxist, pro-Soviet Tudeh party established.

treatment of citizens, the establishment of the rule of law, and the expansion of public education. Both groups opposed the orthodox Shi'i clergy's control of the intellectual sphere and its resistance to innovation and dissent.

Unlike mainstream Sunni Islam, in which the clergy's role and authority have been limited, Shi'i Islam's religious establishment maintained a great deal of power. Besides controlling educational institutions and much of the administration of justice, clerics also enjoyed a great deal of political independence. Historically, they were recognized as the most qualified interpreters of Islamic law. Unlike Sunnis, Shi'is relied on the opinion of living clerics, who were regarded as models for emulation. The clerics' political independence was further enhanced during the eighteenth century, when the central Shi'i leadership moved to Iraq and thereby freed itself from Iranian state influence. In Iraq, the leading clerics received large sums from religious taxes collected and sent to them from Iran and elsewhere. They used much of this money to support a large network of religious leaders, scholars, preachers, and students who at times posed a serious challenge to state authority in Iran.

During the Constitutional Revolution of 1905, a group of merchants who resented the state's arbitrary rule joined reform-minded intellectuals to demand a parliamentary style of government. Some leading clerics, lacking a clear understanding of the ideals of the modernists, also participated in the revolution, hoping to establish Islamic law in the country. Because of their great influence over the general public, the clergy helped the revolution succeed. Later, however, as conservative clerics began to recognize the anti-Islamic goals of the constitutional movement, such as equal treatment of minorities and the adoption of a Western-style civil code, they turned against it and joined the Shah in a counter-revolution. Nevertheless, the trend toward secularization was well under way, leaving conservative religious factions with little political influence for the next seventy years.

Although the Constitutional Revolution of 1905 fulfilled many of the ideals of the reform-minded intellectuals—the constitution guaranteed individual rights and freedoms for all citizens—it was soon followed by foreign invasion, counter-revolution, parliamentary factionalism, and political stagnation. Frustrated by the slow rate of change, the reformists sought alternatives. The idea of an "enlightened" autocrat, who would establish stability and security with a strong army, suppressing tribal and separatist armed insurgencies while introducing reforms from above, appealed to moderate and radical reformists. The devastation and chaos

**1951**

Mohammad Mossadeq, the popular prime minister, leads the National Front, a social-democratic organization, to power. When the Persian oil industry is nationalized, Britain invokes an economic boycott.

**1952**

Iran's economy is weakened. The Tudeh party gains strength, and the United States fears growing Soviet influence in Iran. Mossadeq and the Shah struggle for power.

**AUGUST 1953**

The Shah attempts to dismiss Mossadeq, but the prime minister resists. The Shah flees Iran but the army returns him to power in a coup organized with U.S. and British covert support.

**1957**

The secret police organization SAVAK is instituted, with technical assistance provided by CIA and FBI advisors. By the 1970s SAVAK employs between 3,120 (government's figure) and 30,000 (opposition estimate) people. Many more act as informers. The number of those imprisoned, tortured, or killed is impossible to verify. (In 1977 the Shah admits to 3,200 political prisoners; the opposition claims up to 100,000.)

**1962**

Beginning of the Shah's White Revolution, a series of reforms intended to expedite the country's development and modernization programs. Changes include land reform, nationalization of forests, and women's suffrage.

created by World War I and the terrible famine that took the lives of thousands of Iranians made this notion of a strong reformist leader even more attractive.

When an army officer, Reza Khan—later known as Reza Shah Pahlavi—led a successful coup in 1921, many thought that he was the leader who would bring order and progress to the country. Helped by other army officers and supporters and using intimidation and shrewd parliamentary tactics, he managed to quell his opponents, consolidate power, and declare himself Shah.

The rise of the Pahlavi dynasty can be seen as a culmination of trends in the history of modern Iran. The Shah shared an interest in secularism, political reform, and rapid social and economic change with many constitutionalists. And he would have been unable to implement far-reaching changes without the cooperation and active participation of a large group of reform-minded intellectuals. But many of his supporters who admired his enthusiasm for rapid change and were willing to accept his disrespect for the constitution as part of the formula for the enlightened autocrat, themselves became victims of his arbitrary rule.

Reza Shah put an end to the excesses of tribal chiefs, the corrupt clergy, and the landed aristocracy. His development of such institutions as the secret police, however, gave the state greater control over public life and facilitated the suppression of all political opposition. Reza Shah's rise to power marked the end of Iran's first experience in parliamentary democracy and the beginning of a centralized Iranian state, complete with a modern army and an effective state bureaucracy. The process involved an extensive program of reform and development affecting all spheres of urban life. Components of the Shah's reform program included improved communication networks, Iran's first railroad, a modern judiciary, a national registry for documents and property, a national educational system of state-run elementary and secondary schools and the country's first university, and a system of public health care. The establishment of the first national bank and the introduction of modern industries proved major steps in the country's economic development. The growing educational network trained a new professional class needed to run the expanding bureaucracy.

Other measures, including changing the country's name from Persia to Iran, were designed to improve Iran's image in the West. The name Iran was adopted in 1935 to identify the country with the so-called Aryan race and to convey an aura of progress. To change the country's image, the state banned veiling for women and enforced a Western dress code that made

FIGURE 5. Pop singer Faramarz Asef at a political rally.

FIGURE 6. Young man outside a San
Fernando Valley nightclub that has
a weekly "Persian Night."

1963
The cleric Ruhollah Khomeini agitates against the Shah's regime, particularly against secularization and foreign influence in Iran. Riots after his subsequent arrest are violently suppressed. Government claims 200 killed; the opposition claims thousands murdered.

OCTOBER 1964
Iranian Parliament approves bill that extends diplomatic immunity to American military advisors in Iran, their staffs, and families. Ruhollah Khomeini foments unrest against the bill. Within days he is arrested again and exiled to Turkey.

OCTOBER 1965
Khomeini continues his exile, now in the holy Shi'i city of Najaf, Iraq, condemning the Shah's regime and policies: the imprisonment of religious leaders, university students, and other oppositional groups; the practice of torture; the suppression of basic freedoms; and the lavish lifestyle of the Shah and the ruling class.

FEBRUARY 1971
First major guerrilla operation against the Shah's regime by leftist Feda'iyan organization.

OCTOBER 1971
At an estimated cost of $200 million, the Shah celebrates the twenty-fifth centenary of the Persian Empire in air-conditioned tents in the desert near Persepolis, one of the most lavish displays of wealth and pageantry in history. Food and artisans are flown in from France and Switzerland; dignitaries from around the world attend. The event becomes a symbol of decadence for Iranian opposition groups

some traditional women stay home for years. Like traditional clothing, the veil was seen as a cultural eyesore, antithetical to the state's modernist self-image. That the ban on veiling was a first step in bringing women out of the home and into the modern work force was secondary, even incidental.

A new secular, reformist, and nationalist political culture was established to replace Islam as the state's main source of legitimacy. For the first time in the history of Islamic Iran, the ruler was not claiming the protection of Islam as the justification for his rule. Instead, the Shah, influenced by ideas of Persian nationalism, deliberately identified Iran with pre-Islamic symbols and glorified the achievements of the ancient Persian Empire. The invading Arab armies of the seventh century were now blamed for imposing their religion on the "pure Persian race," destroying its superior culture, and causing several centuries of political and economic decline. This view ignored the invading Arab governors' lack of interest in converting the local population; at times these governors had even discouraged conversion to Islam, which called for the equal treatment of all Muslim believers. Mass conversions to Islam became widespread only in the tenth century.

This nationalist view of history is not unique to modern Iran. In reaction to Western superiority, in an attempt to form a national identity, and as a manifestation of old hostilities, Arabs, Turks, and Persians blamed one another for their shortcomings. In the case of Iran, Arab and Islamic influences became a convenient explanation for Iran's economic backwardness. Reacting to the Shi'i clergy's control over the country's intellectual life as well as to what were perceived as archaic elements in twentieth-century Shi'ism, some extremists and secular reformers went so far as to advocate a complete break with Islam and Islamic tradition. Others called for the abandonment of the past and the adoption of a Western orientation. Still others attacked Persian poetry and mysticism as the sources of popular apathy toward progress and called for a campaign against them. After World War II, many Soviet-style socialist intellectuals wanted to do away with traditional Persian culture. These attempts to deny the nation's Islamic past, however, did not go very far. The memory of Iran's pre-Islamic past was too vague to replace thirteen centuries of Shi'i Islamic history and to erase their effects on Persian culture and society. Nonetheless, a new cultural separation grew between those who subscribed to a Westernized worldview and those who advocated traditional Islamic religious values and practices. This growing cultural division in Iranian society paralleled widening socioeconomic divisions.

Persian nationalism helped restore a sense of pride and self-confidence in Iranians whose contact with the West had revealed the extent of their own who cite country's widespread social problems, including illiteracy and poverty.

MAY 1974
Secretary General of Amnesty International notes, "No country in the world has a worse record on human rights than Iran."

1975
Shah abolishes political parties and establishes a single party, Rastakhiz (Resurgence), loyal to the regime.

1976
International Commission of Jurists in Geneva, after hearing reports by former prisoners subjected to SAVAK torture, declares, "There can be no doubt that torture has been systematically practiced over a number of years against recalcitrant suspects under interrogation by SAVAK."

JANUARY 1977
President Carter's human rights pronouncement on Iran pressures the Shah, implying that countries guilty of human rights violations may not get U.S. aid.

MAY 1977
Fifty-three lawyers address a letter to the Imperial Court demanding an independent judiciary.

JUNE 1977
Dr. Ali Shariati, a prominent critic of the Shah's regime, an influential theorist of a progressive Islamic movement, and a veteran of eighteen months in the Shah's prisons, dies in London. Although the reported cause of his death was a heart attack, the circumstances are widely perceived as suspicious.

country's backwardness. These upwardly mobile and educated Iranians saw themselves as inheritors of a civilization at one time superior to that of the West. The Shah's nationalist pride made him resent British officials who treated Iran as another colony. Nationalism also meant a commitment to national unity and, at least in theory, a rejection of age-old ethnic hostilities and parochial differences.

In an ethnically diverse nation where many languages and dialects were spoken, the promotion of the Persian language and Persian literature in the expanding educational system enhanced the sense of nationhood. One by-product of the nationalist political culture was the drive toward ethnic conformity and the denial of ethnic diversity. The use of ethnic dialects was discouraged, Western-style dress was enforced, and peripheral cultural differences were downplayed in favor of the state's hand-picked uniform culture and language. The boundaries of mainstream middle-class culture precluded provincial dialects and customs. Along with widening social and economic differences, ethnic divisions created new tensions between Tehran's urban culture and that of the provinces.

Pastoral nomads in particular came under enormous state pressure to settle and assimilate. The tribes, which historically had enjoyed a great deal of political autonomy, were perceived as a threat to the authority of the central government. Moreover, pastoral nomadism was seen as a backward way of life, contrary to the modern image projected by the state. Therefore, over the years, tribal nomads either settled or became increasingly isolated from the nation's social and economic center.

World War II and the Allied occupation of Iran in 1941 led to the fall of Reza Shah and the installation of his son, Mohammad Reza Shah. The collapse of the much-vaunted armed forces to a great extent discredited the state and impugned the claim that modern Iran would recapture the glories of ancient Persia. Many secular-minded Iranians looked for a new definition of nationalism.

The short-lived period of parliamentary government that followed the war was marked by a new type of nationalism, embodied in the charismatic leader Premier Mohammad Mosaddeq and the oil nationalization movement of 1951–53. In 1951 the Iranian government nationalized the oil industry and abrogated the Anglo-Iranian oil treaty of 1933. Iran's objectives were to increase oil revenues and to assert Iranian independence by standing up to a world power and rejecting British dominance of Iran's political and economic life. The British responded by organizing a Western boycott of Iranian oil.

Many of the newly politicized members of the middle class rallied support for Mosaddeq's brand of nationalism. A combination of internal

FIGURE 7. Woman at a Moharram
gathering, commemorating the death of
the Imam Husain, in a rented hall at
Bellflower High School.

FIGURE 8. Wedding reception at a
home rented for the ceremony. 1989.

Forty prominent writers and intellectuals write to the Iranian prime minister to protest censorship and the suppression of intellectual freedom.

FALL 1977
Formation of the Iranian Committee for the Defense of Freedom and Human Rights, the Association of Iranian Lawyers, the National Organization of University Teachers, and other advocacy groups.

NOVEMBER 1977
Some 8,500 Iranian students demonstrate in Washington, D.C., against the Shah's visit. Ayatollah Khomeini's son, Mostafa, dies. Opposition groups suspect SAVAK involvement.

JANUARY 1978
Government-controlled daily newspaper *Ettelaat* in Tehran publishes an article impugning and ridiculing Khomeini. Subsequent riots in Qom and other cities, in which hundreds are killed, begin the cycle of protests that empower the revolutionary forces.

FEBRUARY 1978
First major riot in Tabriz: 27 killed, 262 wounded.

AUGUST 1978
Rex Cinema in Abadan burns down. Locked exit doors contribute to the deaths of 477 people. Controversy over responsibility, but widespread popular opinion blames agents of the Shah's regime.

SEPTEMBER 7, 1978
"Black Friday" massacre. Government troops fire on thousands of demonstrators violating martial law at

weakness, fragile coalitions, and foreign intervention, however, ended this nationalistic experiment. As the financial strain of the boycott became apparent, Mosaddeq began to lose the support of the parliamentary coalition that had assisted his rise to power. In 1953 a CIA-sponsored coup toppled his government and handed Reza Shah's son, the young Mohammad Reza Shah, the instruments necessary for autocratic rule. The oil industry resumed operation, dominated by several European and American oil companies.

Many Iranians, weary of the country's increasing politicization, the daily demonstrations, and the fighting in the streets, were relieved to see political stability return. Others were left with a bitter taste as a foreign power—this time the United States—again defeated an attempt at economic independence and self-rule. Disillusionment gave way to apolitical apathy, which continued through the mid-1970s.

Foreign intervention has been a major theme in the history of modern Iran. Because of its strategic value, Iran was caught in the expansionist rivalry between Tsarist Russia and the British Empire. Throughout the nineteenth and the first half of the twentieth century, Iran faced repeated political intrigues, military threats, and invasions, making many Iranians suspicious of the intentions of foreign powers. At times, this suspicion has given way to fatalism or a tendency to see conspiracies in all aspects of Iran's political life. These reactions may be the natural outcome of years of repressive rule and the lack of popular control over—or participation in—ongoing political events. Such thinking remains evident in popular theories that explain the Iranian revolution of 1979 as a British or American conspiracy.

The 1953 coup was a turning point in Iran's relations with the United States. Prior to World War II the United States had played virtually no role in Iranian politics and was looked on as a potential ally. The help provided by American financial advisors was appreciated, as was American assistance in establishing modern schools and hospitals. During the crisis of 1945, when the Soviets refused to withdraw their forces from Azerbaijan, the United States played an important role in restoring the province to Iran. But after the 1953 coup, many Iranians viewed the United States, not as a politically neutral and progressive force, but as an interventionist and imperialist power. Nonetheless, contrary to the image often portrayed in the American media, Iranians' pro-American sentiments remained strong and their fascination with American culture continued (and still continues in some sectors). For example, Iranians felt a widespread sense of sorrow at the assassination of John F. Kennedy, expressed in popular songs lamenting his death. That Iranians of various social and ideological backgrounds,

Jaleh Square in Tehran. Government claims 122 dead and 2,000–3,000 wounded; opposition claims up to 3,000 killed.

OCTOBER 1978
Strikes in public sector, then oil industry, customs department, post office, factories, banks, and newspapers. Ayatollah Khomeini continues to influence the course of protest from exile. Pressure by the Shah's regime on Iraq results in the directive that Khomeini leave that country. Aides convince him to move to France, where he is afforded worldwide media exposure, granting 120 interviews in his first four months in Paris.

NOVEMBER 1978
Hundreds of thousands march in Tehran in support of Khomeini. Strikes spread throughout the country.

JANUARY 1979
Facing continuing unrest, the Shah leaves Iran. Shahpour Bakhtiar accepts the post of prime minister from the Shah providing authority is granted to a Regency Council. Bakhtiar dissolves SAVAK and grants freedom to the press. American general Robert Huyser flies to Iran to investigate the feasibility of an army coup. Three days after the Shah's departure, a million people demonstrate against the new prime minister as the Shah's appointee. Within the month, Bakhtiar resigns and his cabinet collapses.

FEBRUARY 1, 1979
Khomeini returns to Iran, greeted by millions in the streets of Tehran. He appoints Mehdi Bazargan prime minister.

including supporters of the Islamic Republic, still immigrate to the United States, moreover, indicates that the regime's anti-American propaganda has not been entirely successful.

After returning to Iran in 1953, the Shah expanded the security agencies developed under his father to suppress his opponents. The leftist Tudeh party (which drew its support from the intelligentsia and the urban working class, moderate nationalists, and reform-minded intellectuals) and, in later years, two guerrilla organizations, the Marxist Feda'iyan and the Islamic Mojahedin, were among the chief targets of repression. Throughout the Pahlavi era, the state's intimidation and co-option of the political leadership of the professional middle class left its members little opportunity for political organization or action. At the same time, the traditional and religious groups had relatively more freedom. The bazaar merchants, for example, not only benefited from the country's economic prosperity in the 1970s but maintained a good deal of political independence, with the guilds being permitted to elect their own elders. The age-old connection between the mosque and the bazaar continued to survive.

Although the government influenced or controlled a large part of the clerical class, some clerics remained independent. Finding left-wing opposition more threatening, the Shah at times encouraged religious elements, hoping they would act to stem the growth of communism. A more populist, Westernized, and somewhat politicized version of Shi'ism was preached freely, attracting the young and the educated. By the 1970s, the Shi'i clerics and the militant religious organizations affiliated with them proved a much more potent threat to the regime than the less popular militant secular left. Foremost among the religious radicals was the Mojahedin, a guerrilla organization formed in 1965 by a group of university graduates, which conducted guerrilla warfare in the streets of Tehran.

The Shah continued his father's policy of reform and development, focusing on the country's infrastructure. In 1961 he initiated a program of land reform, followed by a series of reforms aimed at rural development and health and education. These reforms, publicized under the grandiose title White Revolution, had only limited success. During the next ten years, government propaganda portrayed revolutions as generally positive social phenomena. By 1973, when oil prices skyrocketed, the government had launched a new propaganda campaign, Toward the Great Civilization, which promised that Iran in a few years would reach a level of industrialization equal to that of Japan, if not greater.

To Iranians experiencing food shortages and lacking utilities, Iran's dependence on the West seemed obvious and the Shah's promises of rapid progress were greeted cynically. The Shah himself, however, seems to have

FIGURE 9. Woman dancing on a table during the pop singer Hayedeh's set at a Persian New Year's concert. March 1986.

FIGURE 10. Traditional Persian
folkdance celebrating the Mehregan
(harvest festival) at the Zoroastrian
Center in Westminster. October 1988.

FEBRUARY 10–11, 1979
The Shah's regime, with its army of 400,000, is overthrown. Military barracks and governmental buildings are overrun. In the following days and weeks *komiteh*s (local revolutionary committees) are formed throughout the country to act as a police force, guard government buildings, search cars, and make arrests. In Tehran alone over 1,500 *komiteh*s are instituted.

FEBRUARY 16, 1979
First four deaths by decree of the revolutionary tribunal. By November over 550 people have been executed, most of them members of the Shah's secret police and military.

APRIL 1979
Government claims 98 percent of voters approve referendum to establish Islamic Republic. Iranian army offensive initiated against Kurds rebelling for autonomy.

MAY 1979
Establishment of Pasdaran Enqelab, the revolutionary guards, in effect a military organization directed by clerics.

AUGUST 1979
Limitations set on the press and political organizations, including the National Democratic, Feda'iyan, Mojahedin, and Tudeh parties.

OCTOBER 1979
Shah admitted to a hospital in the United States for treatment of cancer.

NOVEMBER 4, 1979
American embassy is overrun by armed students and hostages seized. Demand is made that the Shah be returned to Iran to stand trial.

been convinced that his program for instant industrialization would work. He ignored his advisors' recommendations of slower growth and a more thoughtful state spending policy that would take into consideration the country's limited resources and infrastructure. The consequences included rampant inflation, high rates of urbanization, and extreme socioeconomic inequality—many of the factors that fomented the revolution. The Shah responded to the economic problems by establishing strict price controls at the retail level, thereby causing further discontent among shopkeepers, bazaar merchants, and industrialists.

The Pahlavi era was one of great social transformation. Ethnic, religious, and geographical allegiances gave way to class distinctions and a national identity. Aristocratic privilege was replaced with new measures of social status, such as educational level and influence in state agencies. Rapid urbanization and higher levels of education were accompanied by increased economic stratification. A new class was formed of professionals, army officers, bureaucrats, and entrepreneurs with values and beliefs different from those of their fathers and with expectations of a more open society.

Traditional and religious groups saw in the social changes excessive Westernization and a lack of respect for Islam. By the 1970s, a new generation of intellectuals with little faith in the state's brand of nationalism and its secularist reforms favored a return to their Islamic roots. Influenced by anti-imperialist ideas regarding economic dependency, they also rejected any modernization programs that followed the Western model of economic development. In 1978, when the revolutionary forces were growing rapidly, many younger intellectuals, at least superficially, found a good deal in common with the Islamic opposition and were attracted to the idealized image of a holy man. For them the Ayatollah Ruhollah Khomeini symbolized the unique indigenous identity that had somehow been taken from them, while the Shah stood for concessions to Western powers. Thus came about an ironic allegiance between intellectuals, who rejected Western economic dominion, and the religious opposition, who objected to Westernization for cultural and religious reasons. The religious opposition also criticized the Shah's regime for its close ties to the West, for placing members of religious minorities in key governmental positions, and for what they saw as moral decadence—for example, sexually explicit films and the media's anti-clerical bias.

The rise of social and economic grievances coincided with a number of external political developments, including the Carter administration's campaign for human rights. The Shah, who felt dependent on U.S. support, nervously initiated liberalizing measures to improve relations with the new Democratic administration. Professional and human rights groups took

NOVEMBER 6, 1979
Powerless, Mehdi Bazargan
government resigns. Revolutionary
Council takes control.

NOVEMBER 14, 1979
Carter administration freezes official
Iranian assets in the United States
totalling $6 billion.

JANUARY 1980
Abol Hassan Bani Sadr elected first
president of the Islamic Republic, but
control of parliament is wielded by
rival, Ayatollah Beheshti.

APRIL 1980
Islamic cultural revolution is instituted.
Beginning of the Islamization of
universities. Left-wing political
organizations are given three days to
leave the campuses. Clashes at colleges
leave over 20 people dead. Universities
are ultimately shut down for two years.

JUNE 1980
Khomeini publicly denounces the
Mojahedin, a popular organization
combining Islamic and socialist
principles.

MID-1980
Leftist Feda'iyan organization splits:
"minority" faction opposes the
Khomeini regime; "majority" faction
supports the Tudeh party's position that
the Khomeini government deserves
support for its uncompromising stand
against U.S. imperialism.

JULY 1980
Shah dies in Egypt.

SEPTEMBER 22, 1980
Iraq, perceiving its neighbor's
vulnerability, invades Iran. Iranians
rally to defend the homeland. This
bitter and bloody war will last eight
years.

advantage of the relaxation of police controls to demand a more democratic system of government. The increasingly radicalized religious opposition, however, quickly organized a series of demonstrations throughout the country, demanding no less than the downfall of the Pahlavi regime. The ensuing violent clashes between demonstrators and the army and police led to a large number of deaths in 1978, the Shah's departure in January 1979, and the downfall of the Pahlavi regime in February 1979.

Subsequently, a group of middle-class professionals, many with ties to traditional religious families, formed the moderate, nonclerical, provisional government of Mehdi Bazargan. Its agenda included ending the revolutionary chaos, establishing a Western-style parliamentary democracy, and implementing a program of economic reconstruction. This process was steadily undermined by radical clerics supported by Khomeini, the Mojahedin, radicalized intellectuals, and the Left, who favored continuation of the revolution. They established autonomous revolutionary organs in all governmental agencies, challenging all spheres of governmental authority. By ordering the execution of many accused of supporting the old regime, the revolutionary tribunals created a state of terror in which the firing squad, the seizure of private property, and a disregard for civil liberties and freedom of expression became the norm. Many on the Left, in the Mojahedin, and among the radicalized intellectuals supported Khomeini's hard-line measures and accepted the executions as part of the revolutionary process.

The turning point for the Bazargan government came when a group of "students of the Imam's line" occupied the U.S. embassy and took its staff hostage. Frustrated by its inability to control the situation and by Khomeini's support for the students holding the embassy, the Bazargan government resigned, giving the upper hand to the radical clerics. What became known as "the hostage crisis," one of the most publicized political events in U.S. history, lost its political significance in Iran a few days after the hostages were taken, when the Bazargan government was removed from power and Iran broke all ties with the United States. The price Iran would pay for taking the hostages—its economic and political isolation in the international community—was hidden by the theatrics of parades and demonstrations where U.S. flags and effigies of Uncle Sam were burned.

The election of French-educated Abol Hassan Bani Sadr as Iran's first president raised the hopes of the professional middle class for stability and security. Instead, the new president, who lacked both the political network and the cunning of his clerical rivals, fell into the trap of competing for popularity and political control with the newly established Islamic Republican party (IRP) and its united front of cleric supporters throughout

FIGURE 11.  Young men cruising Rodeo
Drive in Beverly Hills. 1986.

FIGURE 12. Iranian women talking to
an Eastern European immigrant on a
bus in Westwood, 1988.

**JANUARY 1981**
American hostages in Iran released on
the day Ronald Reagan is sworn in as
president. Mojahedin begins armed
insurrection.

**JUNE 1981**
Bani Sadr is deposed as president after a
power struggle with the Islamic
Republican party, goes into hiding,
joins forces with the Mojahedin. In July
he escapes with the leader of the
Mojahedin, Mas'ud Rajavi, to France.
Announcement of the National Council
of Resistance to overthrow Khomeini.

**JUNE 28, 1981**
Huge explosion at Islamic Republican
party headquarters, attributed to the
Mojahedin, kills 100 important party
leaders, including party's founder,
Ayatollah Beheshti. Assassinations of
religious and governmental officials
loyal to the Islamic regime accelerate in
key Iranian cities.

**AUGUST 30, 1981**
Explosion at the prime minister's office
kills President Raja'i and Prime
Minister Mohammad Bahonar.

**OCTOBER 1981**
Ali Khamene'i elected president after
surviving an attempt on his life.
Amnesty International cites over 3,350
government executions in Iran since the
beginning of the revolution.

**DECEMBER 1981**
To curb revolutionary tribunal excesses,
Ayatollah Khomeini orders courts to
stop unlawful arrests and imprisonments
and the unwarranted confiscation of
property and bank accounts.

**1982–83**
New waves of repression. Some
estimate that 5,000–10,000 people,
many supporters or suspected

the country. Bani Sadr failed to bring the independent revolutionary organs under control, and the reign of terror spread. Summary executions were no longer reserved for supporters of the old regime but expanded to include drug dealers, women accused of adultery, and members of the Baha'i leadership.

As one of the foremost beneficiaries of the oil boom, the professional middle class had witnessed the country's rapid change with little interest in the political process. Years of suppression of all political activity had left this group of Iranians with few avenues of expression. The traditional groups, in contrast, had maintained their guilds, trade associations, and religious organizations. They were also closely tied to the Shi'i clerical establishment, which for years had its own reasons for discontent. This alliance successfully brought about Iran's first clerical government.

Although nationalist and leftist intellectuals participated in the early stages of the revolution, the dominance of the religious groups soon became obvious to the other contenders in the power struggle. The heavy-handed suppression of all opposition by the Islamic Republic left no room for political debate and forced a large number of political activists into exile. This process accelerated after the mass assassination of the leaders of the IRP in 1981 and the regime's increasingly violent reaction to all political opposition.

Intellectuals who had sympathized with or participated in the revolution in hopes of a more democratic society and a more equal distribution of wealth saw the Islamic Republic as a more repressive version of the old system. Although the Shah's regime tolerated little political opposition, it did not generally intervene in people's private lives. The Islamic Republic exerted a more pervasive influence on people's lives through such measures as a ban on alcohol and the prohibition of popular music. All music with women's singing was also banned for fear of arousing men.

Many secular Iranians were shocked and confused. Those whose search for an indigenous identity had led them to support the religious elements felt a painful sense of alienation and betrayal as they realized the breadth of the gap that separated them from the religious clergy. In fact, however, this wide cultural division had existed in Iranian society ever since the Constitutional Revolution had introduced secularism as an alternative to Shi'i Islam.

Nowhere is this cultural gap more evident than in the treatment of women in the Islamic Republic. Just as secularists had seen the elimination of the veil as a means of bringing Iran into the Western twentieth century, the clerics saw the control of women's appearance as fundamental to the integrity of Islam. Both the secularists and the clerics were forceful in supporters of the Mojahedin, are executed. Opposition claims that regime holds up to 40,000 political prisoners.

MAY 1982
Parliament approves a new law that judges must be *mojtahed*s, religiously trained experts in Islamic law.

JUNE 1982
Khomeini calls for the overthrow of Saddam Hussein.

AUGUST 1982
Sadeq Qotbzadeh, Khomeini's former foreign minister, executed for plotting against the Islamic Republic.

1983
Iranian troops embark on major offensives, driving into Iraq to overthrow Saddam Hussein. Human-wave attacks directed at fixed Iraqi positions. Iranian troops cross defensive "killing zones," fields sown with millions of landmines.

1984
Twelve thousand clerics sent to the front; 700 ultimately killed.

JULY 1984
Vigilante patrols instituted to combat forbidden, un-Islamic, behavior.

FEBRUARY–MARCH 1985
Acceleration of the "war of the cities" in the Iran-Iraq war. Iraq rains bombs and missiles on 40 Iranian population centers (including Tehran) and increases gas and chemical attacks on Iranian troops at the front.

SEPTEMBER 1986
In a ten-minute broadcast pirated onto Iranian national television, Reza Shah, the late Shah's son, encourages citizens to agitate against the Islamic government for a constitutional monarchy.

implementing dress codes. Neither understood the personal dimension of the issue. The strict enforcement of the dress code under the Islamic Republic was probably as intrusive and painful for the independent women of the 1980s as unveiling had been for the traditional women of the 1930s.

After some seventy years of state-sponsored secularization, those with secular or anti-clerical views were suddenly at the losing end of power relations in Iran. But unlike the traditional religious groups, who had had no choice but to stay in Iran during the decades of secularist rule, the Westernized middle class, many with contacts in Europe and America, had a clear alternative to what seemed to them a return to the archaic past.

The so-called cultural revolution of 1981–82 effectively closed down all of the country's universities and led to the dismissal of many of the country's educated elite from their academic positions. Highly skilled professionals, excluded from the work force, soon sought employment abroad. Like the Shah before them, the Islamic government used schools and the state-controlled mass media as its most important instruments for ideological indoctrination. Many families feared the influence of state propaganda on their young children. These fears became particularly acute after the outbreak of the Iran-Iraq war and the government's attempts to recruit teenagers through ideological persuasion as well as the military draft. For families who saw no justification for continuing the war, the possibility of their youngsters' being drafted was itself an incentive to leave the country. Subsequent air attacks on large cities created a state of terror among the urban population and further increased the rate of migration.

Iran's religious minorities are well represented among immigrants. In part this can be explained by their relative social mobility during the Pahlavi era. Though they made up less than 2 percent of the total population, minorities were a significant part of the modern middle class. Their disproportionate representation in higher income levels can be explained to some extent, in the case of the Baha'is, by their higher level of education and, in the case of the Jews, by their historical engagement in trade. Like minority groups elsewhere in the world, they worked hard, once opportunities became available, to make up for years of social and economic deprivation.

In a way, many of the upwardly mobile minority groups became victims of their own success. Faced with discrimination and limitations on their choice of occupations, many non-Muslims saw education as one way of achieving social mobility. As far back as the mid-nineteenth century, minority groups sought outside help to start modern schools. Jewish schools were established by the Alliance Israelite, Zoroastrian schools began with help from Indian coreligionists, and Baha'i schools sought help from

FIGURE 13.   Argument at a pro-Shah
rally. March 1986.

FIGURE 14. Audience uproar in response to the
lack of seating for a Persian New Year's concert
at the Bonaventure Hotel, Los Angeles. Fire
marshals ultimately shut down the celebration
because of overcrowding. March 1987.

NOVEMBER 3, 1986
Iran-Contra affair made public as *Al-Shiraa*, a Lebanese weekly newspaper, reports that the U.S. government—in direct contravention of the Reagan administration's stated policy—sold weapons to Iran to gain the release of American hostages in Lebanon. Within the month it is further revealed that proceeds from the Iran arms sale had been channeled to the Nicaraguan resistance fighters at a time when U.S. military aid to the Contras was prohibited by Congress.

JULY 31, 1987
Over 400 Muslim pilgrims, mostly Iranians, killed by security forces in Mecca during demonstrations against the Saudi government.

FEBRUARY 1988
New acceleration of the "war of the cities." For the first time Iraq uses enhanced Scud missiles to strike Tehran, at one point hitting the capital 17 times in 24 hours.

JULY 1988
A U.S. Navy warship, in the Persian Gulf to protect oil tankers, mistakenly fires at an Iranian passenger plane, killing 290 people.

AUGUST 1988
Iran-Iraq war ceasefire. Over 1 million Iranian and Iraqi dead and 2 million wounded—one of the bloodiest and most brutal wars in history.

FEBRUARY 10, 1989
Following riots in Pakistan and other countries against Salman Rushdie's novel *The Satanic Verses*, Khomeini issues a death sentence for its author, who is accused of writing against Islam.

JUNE 3, 1989
Death of Ayatollah Khomeini at age 87.

American converts. Perhaps the most important contribution was that of Christian missionaries. Forbidden to convert Muslims, they concentrated their efforts on Jews and other Christians. Later, their schools served as an example for a state-run network of public schools.

By the 1920s, when the expanding state bureaucracy needed trained personnel with a knowledge of foreign languages, graduates of these new schools promptly filled many high-status positions. Other minorities benefited from the expansion of international trade, and still others made advances in technical and professional areas. When Iran's first university opened in 1936, non-Muslims took advantage of the equal opportunities for higher education and social mobility. This trend accelerated in the 1970s, when a few non-Muslims rose to become upper-class industrialists closely tied to the Shah and the royal family.

The history of Iran's religious minorities is filled with episodes of discrimination, persecution, forced and voluntary mass and individual conversions, and spontaneous and cleric-instigated mob attacks as well as occasional periods of relative calm and prosperity. During the nineteenth century, when the power and independence of the Shi'i clergy had been fully established, religious minorities were often used as scapegoats by ambitious clerics, who instigated riots to show their power over the weak central government or to extort money for protecting the community.

The outbreak of revolutionary upheavals brought a return of some of these old discriminatory sentiments to Iran. Baha'is in particular have been persecuted, with executions and imprisonment, confiscation of property, and expulsion from state agencies all matters of course. For those who could afford it, exile became an attractive alternative. Thousands of Muslims also left either because they feared being associated with the Pahlavi regime or with other opposition groups or because they wanted basic freedoms.

After years of living abroad, many Persians have given up hope that political conditions in Iran will change and are beginning to see themselves as permanent residents in America. The majority, with their middle-class background, education, prior contact with the West, and knowledge of English, have begun to assimilate socially and economically. The process of cultural absorption, however, will not be as easy.

FIGURE 15.  Woman at a Mojahedin meeting showing scars from torture on the soles of her feet. She claims the torture was inflicted by agents of the Islamic Republic. 1986.

*Interview*

Maryam is the pseudonym of a thirty-six-year-old woman, imprisoned and tortured for leftist political activity under the Shah and the Khomeini regime. She answered questions in Persian, and her husband, also imprisoned and tortured under the Shah, or a friend translated her responses into English; the translation is transcribed here as Maryam's own voice. Neither Maryam nor her husband or friend gave a real name; all fear reprisals against themselves, friends, or relatives. After rolling down her socks to show the evidence of torture on her foot, Maryam declined to have the foot photographed, concerned that the configuration of the scars might identify her.

RON KELLEY:     How were you first arrested?

MARYAM:     As a young intellectual I was interested in achieving social and political progress in my country, so I was reading books to learn more about society. In about 1971 I started getting in touch with other students at a university that was the center of intellectual and political debate and discussion. Many students were politically active against the Shah's regime. In 1976 I was arrested.

Q:     What were the circumstances of the arrest?

MARYAM:     We were holding an ordinary meeting, discussing how to organize our group. The main issue was how we could work as a team without being known to the police and SAVAK, which was very effective against political groups. We were not involved in guerrilla warfare, but we did believe in a mass movement, political activity, organizing. Because we knew a lot of people and had a lot of connections, one of the main issues of the meeting that night was how to survive if any one of us was captured by the police. If anyone was caught, there should be a way to prevent our passing on information to the secret police when they used torture. We even discussed using cyanide, killing ourselves to save others, if we were captured.

31

Q:          This is what you were discussing when you got caught?

MARYAM:     Yes. One of our members had been captured two days earlier. Our phones were tapped, but we didn't know it. After I walked into the meeting house, SAVAK came out of hiding and surrounded us. They came in with machine guns and told us to put our hands up against the wall and started searching bags and wallets. By walkie-talkie they told their officer in charge, "We've got them." So they took us all to prison, separately, so we couldn't talk and coordinate what to confess.

Q:          How many people were captured?

MARYAM:     Four: the owner of the house—the leader—and three others. The members had a safety code: they would telephone before coming to the house. I had called, and everything was supposedly fine. No one knew the house was under surveillance. SAVAK had information about the owner of the house, but not about me. For some time they had been watching this house so they could catch the whole group.

            After I was captured, I was put into an isolation cell for fifteen days before they started torturing me. In those first two weeks they were trying to get enough information from the main man to bluff others into confessions. After fifteen days they took me to a man named Azadi; he was one of the main torturers in the Shah's time. He said, "You had better tell us everything because we know everything." And I kept saying, "I don't know anything. I just went to visit that man's sister. I don't know anything about the political activity in that house." I denied everything. So they decided to torture me.

HUSBAND:    They had a special torture room at that center.

MARYAM:     They tied me to a bed and started hitting me with a cable, something like an electric wire. Another one of their famous torturers was named Hosseini. He and another man would question me, and if I didn't answer, he would start hitting me. When he got tired, he would hand the cable to the other man. He would sit on my face so I couldn't breathe while the other guy was hitting me on the bottom of my feet. Every time I passed out, they would pour water on my head. When I started screaming, they'd stuff dirty socks in my mouth. After a while I had been hit so much that my foot swelled up and turned black. Then they made me walk so they could get me ready for more torture. They hit me so much that I didn't feel anything at the end—again and again, cutting through skin to flesh and blood. This time it was more painful than the first time. You can see my foot. I had to have surgery to repair it.

HUSBAND: Let me explain. They beat the bottom of the foot because that is one of the most sensitive parts of the body. They had found that beating the prisoner there would exert the most pressure and would also cause the least obvious damage. But if they continued too long, the foot would swell so much that they couldn't continue or all the tissues would rupture and bleed. So they hit for a while. Then they made the prisoner walk or jump or run to reduce the swelling. Then they started again.

MARYAM: They put rags in my mouth. I was supposed to raise my finger if I wanted to confess. Every five minutes or two minutes or every second they stopped the torturing, which would give me energy to endure another time. The people they tortured couldn't see anybody or anything. Before the guards brought you into the torture room, they blindfolded you. You couldn't even see the tools they used. After the first torture, they took me back to my cell. One of my feet was injured seriously, and the other was badly swollen. For three days they left me alone. But then they brought me back, and this time they told me to sit on a chair. I had heard that when they tell you to do this, they pull out your fingernails. So I sat down, terrified. And they said, "Stand on the chair, not sit." So I stood, and they tied me to the ceiling by cable and kicked the chair away. Then they started whipping me while I hung by my hands. This torture wasn't as bad as the first one because my clothes absorbed some of the blows.

HUSBAND: When they had whipped the feet, they were not covered.

MARYAM: This time they had someone from my political group in the room with me; he was a relative. So they started telling him as they tortured us, both of us blindfolded, that if he didn't give them information, they would rape me. This is a cultural thing in Iran. To get to a man, they threaten a woman, someone related to you, a family member. They torture your wife or sister or other relatives. People who could handle the physical torture themselves broke down when a relative was tortured. So the torturers were talking to each other: "Go and take her clothes off. Put her on the bed and rape her." And my relative was moaning, "No, don't do that." So they put me on the bed and started hitting me. And I was screaming. They wanted to make it sound as if they were raping me.

Throughout the torture I had to analyze what sort of information my torturers had. If I could figure out what they knew, then I could confess and confirm what they already had.

HUSBAND: Tell him how you made contact with members of your group in prison.

MARYAM: We had a code to communicate with each other in the bathroom. On the walls. We used this to let one another know what information SAVAK already had, so the prisoners could play with them to get less torture or prove they're not really political. If SAVAK believed you, they would ease up on the torture. Unfortunately, they found out I was communicating with other prisoners. I don't want to say how I communicated with them, but SAVAK apparently knew. So this time when they tortured me, I was already badly injured. One of my veins was torn apart, and they broke a bone. One man slapped me in the face for an hour and a half. He did it so many times that I didn't feel anything anymore. And he started bothering me. He didn't rape me, but he started touching me. Because of all the slaps, both of my ears were torn inside and injured. After this new torture, I couldn't walk. They took me around and displayed me to new prisoners to show that this was going to happen to them if they didn't cooperate. At this point, they wanted to make me confess so they could determine my sentence in court. And because of this new charge of political activity in prison, they told me that I had to suffer some torture every day. But it didn't turn out that way; it was off and on for a few months.

Q: How did you finally get out of prison?

MARYAM: Because the political situation in the world changed. President Carter came to power in the United States. His administration pressured the Shah to be more democratic. I had been in prison for about five months under torture, and when I heard I would be going to court, it was very good news. I knew I would leave the torture chamber and go to court, and they'd tell me the kind of sentence I'd get. But the real reason that they let me go to court was that SAVAK had had a tip, and they were going to arrest another big group of people. So they wanted to clear out the prison to get ready for the new prisoners. A lot of people. They told me that my charge was being a member of a communist group and trying to organize and advertise this ideology. They sent me to another prison and my file to court. They said the charge against me was very serious, and they were going to request my execution. I was given a choice: go through with the inevitable sentence of death or collaborate with them and they would go easy on me in court. I continued to tell them I was guilty of nothing, but I was worried that if they really knew anything about me, it meant death. Those caught in political activities were often charged with attempting to overthrow the government.

I had two court sessions. The first sentence was eight years in prison, but the second one, with Jimmy Carter as president, was four. I was in prison for two and a half years until the revolution started, the prison system broke down, and everybody got out. During the uprising the Shah started releasing some of the prisoners and making some reforms.

Q:     How did you come to be imprisoned by the Khomeini people?

*(By request, the tape recorder is turned off as Maryam discusses with the others how, given the current situation in Iran, she can answer the question without revealing information that could harm her or her relatives. She decides she must leave out the details of her ultimate departure from prison under the Islamic Republic.)*

MARYAM:     I'll explain generally. In the beginning, after the revolution and the overthrow of the government, Khomeini's regime could not arrest a lot of people because of the democratic atmosphere after the revolution. As time passed by and the regime started establishing its army and the Revolutionary Guards, however, they attacked political activists and developed a plan to fight the different groups. They went through a long process of checking all the political activists in the Shah's time. All the files of SAVAK were turned over to SAVAMA, the new name for the secret police. They checked to see what all those people were doing now and jailed them if the government thought they could cause trouble. They arrested a lot of people for questioning and imprisoned them. That's how I ended up in prison a second time, now under Khomeini's regime. They knew I was in prison during the Shah's time, so when they checked SAVAK's list of suspected activists, they found my name and put me back in prison.

HUSBAND:     They didn't have any specific evidence to start with. They just presumed that former political prisoners had not given up their beliefs and ideas. So they started to investigate them.

MARYAM:     Because some of the investigators under Khomeini's regime had been student activists against the Shah, they knew the tactics of opposition groups during the Shah's time. They used that experience to pursue suspects. They knew that a lot of activists from the Shah's time would continue their work. I don't know how they started following me, but when the Mojahedin started its uprising—an armed struggle—the regime became very sensitive. I was approached on the street. They searched me and asked me some questions. I thought that was all. I was going to go and get a cab, but they said, "No, wait. We have sent for a car to take you. You are coming with us." So they put me in the car and told me to put my head down so I wouldn't see where we were going. And they took me to an organization called the Committee. I was there for one night. The next day they took me to Evin Prison. My first observation was that the prison wasn't as organized as during the Shah's time. It was like an office, all these rooms. And I could hear the crying and moaning and screams from the prisoners. Like SAVAK, they blindfolded me, and I couldn't see anything except, if I dared, the floor. They put my head down on my knees, and I waited for my name to be called. At night prisoners just lay down to sleep wherever they were; we weren't taken to a cell or anything. All kinds of people were arrested, just for questioning. They didn't know one another or why they had been brought there. They couldn't talk; everybody just sat there blindfolded.

HUSBAND: There was a long hallway, a corridor with rooms for the Islamic investigators and torturers. The people who were arrested sat in the corridor all day, blindfolded, their heads at their knees. The Islamic investigators called them into the rooms to be beaten. At night, they were given a very thin military blanket and slept on concrete till morning.

MARYAM: When they took people into the rooms, you could hear them asking all kinds of questions: "Give me your contact. Who are you working with? What kind of political group do you belong to?" After that, you could hear silence for a minute or two, then noises of torture, screams. For three days I waited, listening to that.

HUSBAND: She could figure out that the prisoners were fainting after torture. One of the guards brought a doctor with a stretcher, and they carried the prisoner out of the room. When you can hear the screams of the other prisoners, it is even worse than being tortured. When you are tortured you know what's going on; it seems much less than what you imagine when you hear someone else being tortured and screaming.

MARYAM: They brought a lot of people and just dumped them there in the hallway, as if they were delivering boxes or something. They piled them up together; people couldn't even get up to move to another space to get more comfortable. And you could always hear the noises of torture, bodies carried out, and so forth. All these noises were worse than being tortured yourself. Under SAVAK your mind was busy with your pain and you could handle it. But now you thought about what would happen to you. You get to the point where you think you're losing your mind. That's how I felt. On occasion I didn't even know how to go to the bathroom. I would just sit there. It affects you psychologically so that you can't handle it.

HUSBAND: She lost her mental and psychological stability, and when they called her to go to the bathroom, she didn't know what to do. She went to the bathroom, where you're supposed to urinate or whatever. They wouldn't take you again till six to ten hours later. But she forgot what was going on and she sat with her clothes on and didn't do anything. She was lost.

MARYAM: When I came out, I noticed that my pants were wet.

HUSBAND: She was in this situation for three days. After that they took her from the hallway to a room where all the prisoners were sitting. Again they were blindfolded.

MARYAM: While I was in prison under the Shah and being tortured, I had self-confidence and pride because of my belief in the political struggle. There wasn't any time when I'd lose my mind or feel weak or unconfident. But under Khomeini's people, during those three days, even though I wasn't being tortured I sometimes felt I was losing my mind. I was so disillusioned. I felt worse than when I was under torture during the Shah's regime.

HUSBAND: Let me elaborate on something. During the revolution the release of political prisoners was one of the demands of the demonstrators; it was called for everywhere when all the service employees went on strike, when all the workers in different industries went on strike, when all the university students or high school students went on strike. The public believed that under the new government we would not have political prisoners. And for a while the Khomeini regime didn't have any. They didn't make many arrests. But after 1981, when the Mojahedin used guns and declared war against the Khomeini regime, this situation changed completely, creating confusion throughout society. People saw that under Khomeini people were arrested with even less evidence than under the regime of the Shah. Those who were arrested experienced questioning and torture that they hadn't expected. They didn't believe it would happen so soon.

MARYAM: There's a point I'd like to emphasize in this comparison of the means of torture during the Shah and Khomeini regimes. The Shah was as bad as Khomeini in torturing people, but the Shah wasn't facing a lot of prisoners and an uprising. And he was also more experienced, more knowledgeable, and more organized than Khomeini's people. Khomeini's torturers just hit you anywhere, because the only thing they were after was information. They had arrested so many people that they didn't have time to develop official plans to torture them. The Shah thought you had to keep prisoners alive in the process of torturing them. Khomeini's people didn't need that, didn't have time, and didn't have the technique or experience. The Shah's experts when they tortured you, for example, would hit on the bottom of the feet in a specific spot that they knew would give more pain but wouldn't tear you apart. But Khomeini's people just hit you. All over.

OK. After three days, my questioning started. They took me to a room and started pushing and kicking me. And they gave me all kinds of forms to fill out. I kept saying, "I haven't done anything." After a while they brought a supposed informer in and tried to create the illusion that he had political information about me. Supposedly, he had already confessed everything, and his bluff was so good that I almost felt that maybe they had found out something. And they said, "OK, now that we know you are guilty, tell us everything else you know; if you don't, you have to write that you were not part of any group activity. But if you were in this group, and we have documents that prove it, we will kill you right now." In that spot, for a moment, I almost believed that this guy had really confessed about me. The pressure was so great that I was ready to die. But I decided to take a chance and just write down that I didn't do anything, and if they had proof, then, OK, I'd die. So I wrote down that I hadn't been in any groups or political activities. And I signed it. After that they said, "OK. Bring the firing squad." And they brought a gun and put it to my head and made it seem as if they were going to shoot me right then. I was to the point where I didn't even care. Then they took me to a room under the main torture area. You could hear all the noise upstairs of people being hit and dropping on the floor, screaming. There were some old women around me, mothers of Mojahedin members. They couldn't handle hearing what they thought was their son or daughter being tortured above them. They started screaming and crying and hitting themselves. Imagine. You are involved in thinking about your own preservation and suddenly you see someone else's mother screaming and crying. Twenty-four hours a day. In this room they took off my blindfold, and I could see everybody. There were over a hundred people in a room six by six meters. It was so bad that at night when you wanted to sleep, you couldn't sleep face down or up. You had to sleep sideways so you could fit among all the people. But even if you did that, some still had to sleep standing up and leaning against the wall. So we took turns each night, standing against the wall, trying to sleep.

HUSBAND:    There were five rooms, six by six, and there were two smaller rooms, three by six.

MARYAM:    In all there were about six hundred and fifty people in these rooms, and there were four toilets for them all. Whenever you wanted to go to the bathroom, you had to stay in line for an hour and a half. Sometimes people needed to go to the bathroom so urgently that they begged those in line: "Please, let me go to the bathroom." And everybody was so . . . They wanted to stay in line. They'd say, "Oh, no, she's lying." And this creates a situation . . . I mean, what kind of life is this? You can't trust anyone. Most of these people were political, idealistic, you know? But there they lived just fighting for their own life. Each prisoner was in a bad situation; they were very depressed. And the place where they executed people was next to the rooms where we were living together. We could hear the execution process. They would call the names and we would hear them going to their execution. You could hear the machine guns; they created an echo in the room.

HUSBAND:    Like the sound of an avalanche.

MARYAM:    You could hear the final shot. You could count how many were executed that way. This created such a terrible mood; it was always in your mind. And besides this, there were some people among the prisoners who were collaborating with the government. You couldn't trust any other prisoner. Everyone was watching everyone else. You couldn't discuss anything. And when the authorities said it was time to pray, everyone had to pray the way they wanted you to, even if you didn't believe. You had to show that you believed; otherwise they punished you. Or they took you to the Islamic ideological lecture. You had to go. We couldn't express our true feelings to anyone because we were so afraid. All of this created an atmosphere of such dejection that we thought, even if we get out of prison, there's nothing left to live for after this. They destroyed our dignity, our pride, everything we'd fought for, all the beliefs we'd had. During the Shah's time, we'd go to prison and handle all the torture, but we couldn't find our way here because everybody was afraid and we had lost our humanity. You're less than an animal in this situation.

FIGURE 16. Monir Nahid and her only
remaining son, Farhad Rashidian. Mrs. Nahid
is holding a 1979 *Paris-Match* photograph of
agents of the Khomeini regime executing
alleged Kurdish resistance fighters. Two of the
blindfolded prisoners in the photograph,
including the wounded man lying on the
ground, are her sons. 1988.

# Interview

Farhad Rashidian is a Kurdish political refugee. Since coming to Los Angeles he has worked as an accountant and a taxi driver.

RON KELLEY: You had been in the construction business for two years, and the revolution happened just when you were becoming successful?

RASHIDIAN: Right. We had finished a small project and were in the middle of the rest; eight roads and two buildings were half-finished when the revolution happened. Three of my partners, with a seventy-five percent share in the business, left the country in the first weeks of the revolution with their personal belongings and assets. They sold their apartments, cars, everything. They took money from the company and came to the United States. In the first weeks they got green cards, permission to work and live here legally. I stayed in Iran and was punished as a Kurd. The punishment was directed against the Kurdish Democratic party, which is the biggest organized group in Iranian Kurdistan fighting against Khomeini's regime for Kurdish self-determination. The KDP took some of our equipment in Kurdish areas, machines we were using for road building—bulldozers, tractors, graders, and other things. Of course they couldn't take the asphalt plant. They didn't need that. But they needed tractors to pull cannons, to put them in position to shoot Iranian troops. So they got us involved. Our office was in Tehran. We were in the middle of Khomeini's people, but our equipment was mostly on the Iran-Iraq border. The KDP took over some of our Landrover cars. And, most important, they took fifteen tons of dynamite. Fifteen tons! We used dynamite for breaking the mountains for roads; they used it against the Revolutionary Guards and the Iranian army. So here I was, accused of helping the Democratic party—the guerrillas—against Khomeini and the Revolutionary Guards! That's why they arrested me;

the government took our asphalt plant and about fifteen of the big trucks we had for carrying the stuff. We had so many things!

Q:    So during the revolution both the Kurdish Democratic party and the Khomeini regime took things from you?

RASHIDIAN:    For almost two years they took everything we had. About eighty million dollars' worth—all paid off. First the Kurds took them and then the Khomeini government.

Q:    Your business partner who remained in Iran was Kurdish too?

RASHIDIAN:    He wasn't Kurdish, so he didn't have as much of a problem as I did. He had financial problems, but not political problems. Of course, ten percent of what the government took belonged to him, but nobody arrested him and accused him of having helped the Kurdish guerrillas against the Khomeini regime. I was accused, for the same reasons my brothers were killed: I was a Sunni Muslim; I was Kurdish. And because my two brothers were killed by Khomeini's regime, they assumed I was involved.

They had every reason to assume I had given the dynamite to the Kurdish Democratic party. Sometimes they arrested me twice a week. The Revolutionary Guards used to come to my office to take me in for questioning. Then they released me. The next week, again. I have a heart condition. And a broken heart from the loss of my brothers. You can imagine how difficult it was. After eighteen years, I had built up this corporation—buildings, an asphalt plant, and so much besides. They took everything! When I came to your country I had seven dollars left. Because of my health problems, I had wanted to come here for a checkup several years ago, but I was not allowed. The authorities wouldn't let me leave the country. I had a doctor's letter saying that I needed medical attention, but they wouldn't let me go. Finally I collected what I had left—about twenty thousand dollars—and I gave it to the Iranian authorities as a bribe. And they let me leave. I had nothing left after eighteen years. Everything you can imagine, I had—money and apartments and cars. But I lost it all. I lost my family, my brothers; I had sacrificed for them for twenty years. I spent a lot of money to raise them well. They were successful in their lives; they were going to college. They had it all. I lost both of them. I lost all my things, because the Kurds needed them. And the Khomeini regime took the rest. I was assumed to be an anti-revolutionary.

Finally, I came here with nothing, empty-handed. I started all over again for three thirty-five an hour. After a year, my heart condition got worse. I went through a second open-heart surgery here. That surgery was a year and a half ago. But here they helped me a lot. They didn't take any money; they didn't demand it from me, even though the operation cost a hundred nineteen thousand dollars! They didn't demand a penny. In my old life a hundred nineteen thousand dollars would have been a piece of cake. It wasn't really much. But here, they asked if I could pay twenty percent of that. I said, "No, I can't even pay ten percent." Ten percent would be about twelve thousand dollars. How could I possibly pay twelve thousand dollars? I had been robbed in Iran! Because I was a Kurd. If I had not been a Kurd, I could have kept my corporation. But because of my nationality, I lost that. Everything.

Q: Tell me about your brothers.

RASHIDIAN: In 1978 the revolutionary movements began. Leftists, rightists, and religious people all started to take part in demonstrations against the Shah. Our family were not Shi'i Muslims. My brother Hassan was a metallurgy student, but he spent most of his time in political activities in those years—anti-Shah and Kurdish movements in Kurdistan. In the eighth month after the revolution, Hassan was trafficking armaments, guns and rockets, from one part of Kurdistan to the other, and, by coincidence, my other brother—the smaller one, Shahyar, was in that region. He went to see Hassan. He had a few days' vacation. So he was with Hassan when he was trafficking guns, and they got caught by the Revolutionary Guards and other forces the new government had sent to Kurdistan to keep the people quiet. They got caught, and after five days they were executed. Both of my brothers. There was no trial, no right of defense, no lawyer, nothing you are familiar with in your country. My mother met one of them—Shahyar, the smaller one—the day before his execution. She asked him, "What's going on here? Have you been questioned?" My brother said that the Shi'i Muslim official in charge of the trial had asked him three questions: "What's your job?" Shahyar said, "I'm a college student." "What's your religion?" "I'm Sunni Muslim." "And what's your nationality?" "I'm Kurd." And that religious person, who was in charge of the trial, said, "Each of these answers is enough reason to kill you. You have given all three." The trial had taken five minutes. All he asked was these three questions. Then he ordered both of my brothers, and nine other people who had been captured with them, to be executed.

FIGURE 17. Newly arrived refugees
beginning a temporary stay at a motel in
Van Nuys. 1989.

# Interview

Sue Kelly is Volunteer Resource Coordinator of the Refugee Resettlement Program, Immigration and Refugee Division, Catholic Charities, Archdiocese of Los Angeles.

RON KELLEY:  How do refugees get to America?

SUE KELLY:  Refugees entering the United States have to come through an agency like ours, which is recognized by the U.S. State Department. We provide the core services for legal refugees mandated by the State Department, Justice Department, and the Immigration Service. If you enter this country as a refugee, you first sought asylum in a country other than your home country, and you applied to resettle permanently in a third country. Many "countries of first asylum" allow almost no one to resettle permanently. They're very generous and allow people to come, and they care for them, but no one can stay. That each of those countries operates differently colors the perception and expectations of the refugees when they then reach the country of permanent resettlement.

Germany is considered an extremely humanitarian country in the way they treat refugees. They provide them with adequate housing; they provide them with money for food. But they do not allow them to work, and they do not accept them as permanent residents. Germany since the Second World War can't turn down anybody who asks for political asylum. Refugees have to agree to leave Germany, to settle in another country. But life is very nice in Germany. You don't have to do much. To get refugees to leave this nice, idyllic life, German government workers lead them to believe that life in the United States will be even better than what they have experienced in Germany. When they arrive in the United States, they discover that someone in authority has lied to them, and they take out all their anger and frustration on the person at the refugee resettlement agency and on their caseworker, who is not a government employee but is the last stop.

Everyone will deny that this occurs. The policy of other countries that are considered less humane may, in the long run, be better for refugees—for example, Greece. You apply for asylum, fine; you get it. You're allowed to work, and you must provide for yourself financially. You don't become dependent on anyone else. Your level of expectations has not been raised, so you don't have a huge letdown and depression.

All refugees are dealt with the same way. But they consistently arrive here with expectations that cannot be met. And our agency has to deal with the consequent depression.

Q:      Are you talking here about political refugees?

KELLY:   There is a great deal of difference between refugees and immigrants. Refugees have been persecuted or fear being persecuted for their ethnicity, their religion, or their political viewpoint. They are considerably sadder than immigrants. Why? Because most refugees can never go home again. If you're an immigrant, you haven't burned your bridges. In most instances you can go home. If you can get enough money together to travel, you can go visit grandma. If you come with immigrant status, you haven't left your country illegally, you're not on a list someplace, and you haven't burned your bridges. Most refugees can never go home again, even if they become citizens and have an American passport. There's an inherent danger in returning home.

Q:      Is it any easier for refugees to come here than for immigrants?

KELLY:   Well, there's a quota. A quota for refugees is voted each year by the United States Congress. This year it's approximately ninety-two thousand, divided by geographical areas, based on the number waiting and so forth. A fixed number of refugees are allowed to come in. Some private individual must cover the cost of their transportation and guarantee that they will not become public charges for a period of time. Immigrants who come to this country legally are not eligible for any public assistance during the first three years they are here.

Q:      How many refugees has this organization settled over the last ten years or so?

KELLY:   Last year, 1988—our year runs from October 1 to September 30—we settled more than five thousand.

Q:      Do you have any idea what percentage was Iranian?

KELLY:      I think we had seven to eight hundred Iranians last year, just through this agency in Los Angeles. I don't know what other agencies did.

Q:      I found you through an Iranian refugee relief organization. What is their relationship to you?

KELLY:      They are what is known as a mutual assistance association. They work with agencies like us, providing extra things in the community. There are many of these associations—Vietnamese, Cambodians, Afghans . . . We can call on a mutual assistance association, saying, "OK, we're going to take on this refugee case, but we need your help to help them."

Q:      So what happens to people who come off the plane? They don't know English, and they don't have any friends here. What happens to them?

KELLY:      They do have friends because the mutual assistance association fills that void; they will not be alone. In some instances, it turns out that though we don't know it, arriving families have friends here. The friends don't come in and fill out a form, but through the grapevine they find out that their friends are here. And they show up and take them away. This happens about fifty percent of the time. The mutual assistance association and this agency and others provide support for those who don't have friends. We recruit volunteers. That's what I do. For four years before I came to work here, my husband and I provided long-term housing in our home for refugees who had no one. We resettled thirty-five people out of our home in a nine-year period. They lived with us, at least a month and at most a year. And my husband and I have a daughter.

Q:      Have you ever had any Iranians live with you?

KELLY:      Yes, I have.

Q:      Any thoughts on that?

KELLY:      Well, the hardest people to place as refugees are single males under the age of thirty. They have no intrinsic value to anyone. They're difficult—their nationality doesn't matter. They think they know everything; you can't tell them anything. They don't cook and they don't clean because in the societies they come from, males don't do these things.

Q:    They're pretty macho?

KELLY:    Oh, they're all macho: "I'm tough. I survived." So older women who will take a family or a single female won't take single males. My family and I would take them. Unless there are at least three together, they can't survive. The government doesn't provide enough money for people to live alone. They can't make it, not in L.A., not with what rents are.

A total of five men lived with us, not all at the same time. Persians—all very charming, and I still see most of them. The first three came at Christmas in 1983. They arrived on short notice, less than twenty-four hours. (Just after Thanksgiving we'd had a lot of refugees coming through, always on short notice.) All three were musicians. One had been with the Tehran Philharmonic in an administrative role; he was a talented musician and composer, who arrived with two of his apprentices. They had been in Spain for a long time.

Single refugees are at the end of any list. Families and family reunification take precedence—it doesn't matter what country you're going to—over all other categories. So single people wait longest, in any country of first asylum, for permanent resettlement. The norm for them is anywhere from two to four years unless someone comes forward to say, "I claim this person." "He's my brother." "He's my cousin." "He was a friend." You know, "I'll take him."

Q:    What were their perceptions of America when your guests arrived here?

KELLY:    When they got here, they were impressed at how big it is. How you can get publications in almost any language. Video, music. One of the men was Iranian Armenian, and all his life he had had to hide being Armenian. When he got to L.A., he discovered that being Armenian is OK here, and the governor is Armenian, and all of a sudden, instead of saying he was Iranian, he said, "I'm Armenian." He came here when he was about eighteen. The first day he ventured out by himself—I live in Hollywood, a predominantly Armenian community—he came back and said, "It's not a crime to be Armenian in California, you know? I'm really a big deal." George Deukmejian was just about to be installed as governor for the first time, and I had a couple of commemorative copies of the announcement of his inauguration, the invitation. He sent one to his parents in Tehran—they had it framed and hung on the wall. An Armenian is elected to a big-time post in the United States! They wrote me a very nice letter in English—they used an English-language dictionary to show their appreciation that I had taken in their son. He had an aunt and uncle who lived here, but he arrived on such short notice that they were unable to help. They didn't have space for him to sleep. They were already ten people in a two-bedroom house. Adding one more was impossible. They would pick him up on the weekends to do things, but he needed a place to sleep.

Q:      There's a stereotype in L.A. that most, if not all, Iranians are wealthy. What is your experience with the people you run into?

KELLY:      Most Iranians who come here are from rather affluent backgrounds. It doesn't necessarily mean they're affluent when they get here, but they bring with them the reactions and experiences of people who were rich. They're unlike Eastern Europeans, who, even if they're bourgeois, know how to do everything. They can fix the vacuum cleaner. They make it work because they know they're not going to get a new one. For Iranians, this isn't true. The women always had help in the house. Most of them don't know how to cook, don't know how to sew, don't know how to take care of children, because they always had someone else do these things for them. So now they don't have the life skills to survive here. And they're not going to have a maid and a nanny and a cook and a housekeeper. So all of a sudden they have difficulty adjusting to their life. And they keep talking about what their life was. Well, nobody cares what their life was. Everybody starts here with a clean slate. You are no better than I am, or the man who lives down the street, or the Mexican or the Korean or the Japanese. Everybody starts the same way here. And you'll only be as good as what you do. You can't influence people by saying, "I was important" because nobody cares!

Q:      You run into this kind of thing a lot?

KELLY:      Oh, we see it all the time!

Q:      In the Iranian community more than any other?

KELLY:      Yes, because if you were poor where you came from and now you're a poor refugee here, the emotional transition is less difficult than that from rich to poor.

Q:      So there's more disillusionment?

KELLY:      Yes. If they were educated in the United States and graduated here, they can get copies of their papers. So if they were doctors and went through medical school here, they're probably going to be able to practice here because they already meet all the requirements. But if they went to medical school in Iran, they're not going to be able to practice here—not until they do their residency all over again and take the licensing exam in English. That's the law. They cannot be accountants, lawyers, engineers, or architects. They may have worked in TV, or they may have been high school principals. They cannot do those jobs here. To make the transition in a short time is impossible. It takes five or more years for them to gain English skills and be able to take the test, get the license. And if they are already forty-five years old, they will be fifty before they can practice. Well, they can't wait. So they take whatever job they can get. That's an entry-level, minimum-wage job. And a lot of these men, particularly, cannot adjust emotionally to this situation.

Q:     We're still talking about Persians?

KELLY:     Yes, particularly Persians. They are unhappy because they're not fulfilled in what they're doing. So they go home and they're angry with their wife and their kids because those are the only persons they have . . . The wives are angry with them because they are not providing for them in the manner to which they have been accustomed. And life is hard. She has to learn to cook, to budget, to keep house. They live in an apartment, which is not what they're used to but what they can afford. And that means it's not in a particularly nice neighborhood; they don't have fancy furniture. She has to do everything herself. Persian women are used to very fashionable clothes and makeup. They can't afford them anymore. If they've come with jewelry, often the jewelry has to be sold to provide what's needed to start over.

Q:     Where do these people live? Can you generalize?

KELLY:     A lot of them live in the west San Fernando Valley. There are a lot of low income apartments in Canoga Park, Reseda—that area—where they have managed to settle. And this is hard for them, so you have a lot of mental depression in the community. Anybody who is thirty-five and under has a far better chance of surviving—of being flexible and adaptable to this new set of circumstances. Each year past thirty-five becomes harder and harder. Little kids are totally bilingual within six months; they go to school, they absorb like a sponge, they have no problems. They make friends. But grandma, who's fifty-five, has nobody to talk to. All of a sudden she has to do what she considers menial labor all the time—the cooking, the cleaning. She's never done this before. For a while I gave cooking lessons here. I'm not a professional, but I have cookbooks from everywhere. They knew what the food was supposed to taste and look like, but they didn't know how to get there. They didn't know American measurements. "You go and buy the rice."

Q:    So there is a class difference between Persians and all the other ethnic groups here?

KELLY:    Yes. In most of the world, Eastern Europe for example, there is no help at home. I mean, grandma or maybe an aunt might help out, but everybody has to learn how to do things. Iran made the transition from Middle Eastern country to westernized country in a very short time. And a large population—a third of Iran—had been educated and had lived this wonderful life. And then there were still peasants. The gap between the two populations grew and grew and grew, fostering this hatred between the two groups. We're talking about living a lifestyle in Iran that is very foreign to Americans. Few people are that rich even in wealthy families in the United States. I'm talking about the Kennedys and the Rockefellers and people like that. Everybody learns how to cook, starting when you're about five years old. You learn to take care of yourself, even if you don't have to do it all the time. You know how to do your laundry and cook and clean your house. Because you may marry somebody who can't provide this lifestyle. But labor was so cheap in Iran that you could hire one servant for each room in the house, and that servant's responsibility was just that room. And you would throw parties and read books and go to school. Iranian women were very well educated.

Q:    Have you gotten this information from your clients or from your own studies?

KELLY:    From my own observations in working with these people.

Q:    And your office here must deal with their dissatisfaction?

KELLY:    Oh, yes. They express it vehemently! "Why? Why? What has happened to me?!" And we have seen a lot of mental health problems. My mother has an apartment building in North Hollywood. The apartments are large, and she has found that refugees and immigrants make very good tenants. They just want to be left alone. They keep things clean, you know. So we had a family come in—they didn't have anybody. He had been a high school principal in a small town in Iran. The husband and wife had a college-age son and a daughter. The wife had been a hairdresser, and she busied herself to get her new life started here. She was considerably younger—about fifteen years younger than her husband. He got a job in a gas station, but he simply could not adjust to the fact that . . . I mean, he was the principal of a high school in a small Iranian town. It was a big deal. He was important, respected by everybody in the town. Now he's pumping gas, and he knows that he will never regain his level of . . . Even after two years, he simply just couldn't adjust.

Q:     Is it fair to say that it is more difficult for you and your people to work with people from Iran than other immigrant groups?

KELLY:     They are one of the most difficult. Class enters into it, and expectations. Other groups are difficult, but they are one of the most difficult.

Q:     So your organization essentially sponsors them economically?

KELLY:     We have a contract with the U.S. government. These are federal refugee funds. We had an incident Monday. And this is typical of Iranians. We have to make arrangements for apartments before the people actually arrive, and we pick out apartments that they can afford. Now what they can afford is not going to be what they perceive that they need. There's a big gap. We don't rent the apartments for them, but we make the arrangements for the apartment to be available for them to rent. They sign the rental agreement. With Iranians, we have found that most of the time they will not accept these arrangements. Period.

Q:     What are their options? What options do they think they have?

KELLY:     They think they have the right to pick out something they have been used to. So used furniture is not what they want. They want new furniture, something they pick out. And we try to collect things—we go to a great deal of trouble. If somebody's bought a new bed and the old bed isn't ripped or terribly stained, we will take the mattresses, we will take the furniture. Table and chairs, a couch, a coffee table, mattresses to sleep on. Sometimes we get new linen. We go to our churches; we run drives to collect clean linen, blankets, household items, pots and pans. Typically, Iranians will not accept any of this. If it's been used by somebody else, they don't want it. So they refuse our services, and then they're on their own.

Q:     In your experience, are there any Iranians who come to this country who are poor to begin with? Do you ever run across such people? Do any peasants come here?

KELLY:     Yes, a few. But from Iran, the two places you can escape to, by land, are Pakistan and Turkey. Those are the only two options by land. The other way is to get on an airplane. To get on an airplane out of Iran means buying an airplane ticket, getting a visa. It takes a great deal of cash to pay the bribes that allow you to get on the airplane and leave.

Q:     What happens to individuals who get to Turkey and Pakistan and want to go to the United States?

KELLY:     They are put into camps. These are very definitely Third World countries, and what happens in Turkey is that they're wandering around, their money gone, they're considered vagrants. They might get picked up and put in prison in Turkey. Turkey is afraid of Iran. They share a common border, but their relationship is not what you would call even polite. So there's a camp there. The Turks provide the minimum needed for subsistence. The camp is tense. So the Iranian community here tries to send financial assistance to the camps; they try to check the prisons and make sure that if somebody's been picked up they haven't committed any crime other than not having the proper papers. Most of us know a Turkish prison is not a wonderful place.

   In Pakistan you're on your own. You can work. Pakistan allows people to work, but Pakistan can hardly feed its own population, let alone feed and care for a huge refugee population—close to five million Afghans and close to a million Iranians.

Q:     So an Iranian over there starts thinking he or she wants to get to this country . . .

KELLY:     It takes money. A friend of mine, who used to work here, had been a military officer. He was tipped off that he was going to be arrested. He had enough time to flee, but his wife and kids were left behind. He communicated with them. His father-in-law then put together the equivalent of about fifty-three thousand dollars, which is what it took to get those three people out of Iran. Bribes and so forth. That was a fortune, even by Iranian standards. They all reached Turkey, but without much money. And he had information. As a former military officer, he had a lot of information to offer to the Western world on how things worked in Iran, who was doing what, and so forth, so he was moved along rather rapidly in his resettlement. He moved from Turkey to Germany and, within six months, to the United States. Because he had something to bargain with. But he didn't have any more money. That had all been used up in getting his family out of Iran.

Now for peasants who decide that it's time to leave there's a land route. But Iran is very big: from Tehran, it's fifteen hundred miles to Pakistan and a long way to Turkey. Now, if they're going by car, they need gasoline, food, places to stay. They don't take on that trip without preparations. They might not be killed by the military, but they might die from the elements if they're not properly prepared. To be prepared they have to collect all these things. Well, then the authorities notice. Why is this person collecting gasoline and water and food and all these things? Everything is rationed and controlled by the military government. Those who become obvious to the authorities can be picked up even if they weren't on the list. They probably will be picked up because they've made it apparent that they want to leave. And that's against God.

Q:     Is the Iranian business community here interested in helping their own people?

KELLY:     Those who have come and have made it generally say that newcomers are too arrogant; they don't want to work hard. This backlash happens in any community. Those who have been here twenty years say the newcomers are lazy. This happens across the board. So you have to remind them: "Remember what it was like when you came, and give this person a chance." And it's hard. We do have a lot of employers who consistently give work to refugees, but the refugees have to be flexible. They have to be willing to take the swing shift, the night shift, Saturdays, Sundays. And the refugees are not going to be able to finish school and then go to work. They have to work and go to school at the same time. This means they're not going to have a lot of free time. And they keep saying, "But I really need to go to school." But most American kids who go to universities work and go to school at the same time. That's the norm. Immigrants who come with no English work and go to school at night. That's the American experience. They don't get to choose one or the other. And it's hard for them to accept not having the luxury of doing what they want, which they have always been able to do if they came from a particular class.

PART II

IDENTITY AND DIVERSITY

FIGURE 18. Pacific Palisades Park, Santa Monica, a favorite spot for a Sunday stroll for Iranians living on the West Side of Los Angeles.

# BEYOND NATIONALITY: RELIGIO-ETHNIC DIVERSITY

*Mehdi Bozorgmehr, Georges Sabagh, and Claudia Der-Martirosian*

Located immediately south of the UCLA campus, Westwood Village is one of the few havens for pedestrians in Los Angeles. Its movie theaters, fast-food restaurants, and fashionable stores lure tourists and Los Angeles residents alike. It is also one of the most expensive places to live and own a business in Los Angeles. A change in Westwood Boulevard becomes apparent a short distance south of the village: Persian script appears on storefronts, and from Iranian restaurants the distinctive aromas of food permeate the air. Welcome to Little Tehran, as this neighborhood is called by some Iranians and the media.

Little Tehran is only part of the picture of a highly diverse Iranian community in Los Angeles. In fact it is more correct to talk about Iranian communities in Los Angeles. These correspond to distinctive religio-ethnic Iranian subgroups such as Shi'i Muslims, Armenian and Assyrian Christians, Jews, Baha'is, Kurds, and Zoroastrians. Distinctions within the Iranian communities are not readily apparent to outsiders, and some subgroups would be completely overlooked if we were to base our image of Iranians on a stroll along Westwood Boulevard. Although Iranian Jews are the most entrepreneurial of all Iranian subgroups, few Jewish-operated businesses are located here. Similarly, although Armenian Iranians constitute a large segment of the Iranian population of Los Angeles, few live in this part of the city. One would have to venture to other areas of the metropolis, such as downtown Los Angeles, to notice a Jewish Iranian presence, or go to Glendale to find Armenian Iranian businesses.

The call for sensitivity to ethnic diversity, often heard in multiethnic settings such as Los Angeles, usually stops at the level of nationality. Interest in ethnic diversity, though, should not ignore internal ethnicity, that is, the presence of ethnic groups within an immigrant group. Indeed,

This essay is based, in part, on research supported by grant #SES-8512007 from the National Science Foundation.

immigrants themselves often identify with both their ethnic and national origins. When asked about their primary ethnic identity, minorities from Iran typically identify themselves in terms of their religion or ethnicity as well as their nationality, whereas Muslims identify mainly with being Iranian. More than other Iranian minorities, Armenian Iranians consider themselves Armenian only, and none perceive themselves as Iranian only.

Internal ethnicity raises important questions. How different are Iranian ethnic and religious subgroups from one another and, by implication, from Iranians as a whole? Is Iranian identity overshadowed by ethno-religious identity, or vice versa? In answering these questions, we present a profile of Iranians in Los Angeles and also highlight differences between Muslims, who were the majority population in Iran, and other Iranian subgroups who were religious minorities in their homeland.

With Muslims accounting for approximately 98 percent of the population, Iran is a religiously homogeneous country. The Iranian revolution and the establishment of the Islamic Republic forced many of the country's religious minorities into exile. Los Angeles, with the largest Iranian concentration in the United States, has attracted the full range of religious minorities from Iran in sizable numbers. Other large Iranian communities in the United States, such as those in Washington, D.C., and in New York, are more homogeneous than the community in Los Angeles. Whereas some Americans who have migrated here from other states have chosen Los Angeles for its pleasant weather, most Iranians have come to Los Angeles to be near their family and friends.


SOURCES OF INFORMATION

This article draws on a survey we conducted in late 1987 and early 1988, supplemented by 1980 Census data. Though the survey is more up-to-date than any accessible governmental sources on Iranians, its strength lies not in its relative recency but in the detailed questions it asked. Unlike the U.S. Census, moreover, our survey distinguishes among the four largest Iranian subgroups—Muslims, Armenians, Jews, and Baha'is. The survey gathered data on all members of nearly seven hundred Iranian households: about two hundred each Muslim, Armenian, and Jewish households and about one hundred Baha'i. These numbers do not correspond to these groups' actual proportion of the population. Instead, minimum requirements for statistical analysis dictated the sample sizes. The survey and Census data are further augmented by data from the U.S. Immigration and Naturalization Service (INS) on the patterns and trends of Iranian migration to the United States as a whole. The INS data, however, are even

FIGURE 19. *Ghadam zadan* (strolling).
Iranian men and women strolling along
Ocean Avenue, Santa Monica. 1986.

less useful than the Census data in identifying Iranian ethno-religious subgroups.

## BACKGROUND AND ORIGINS

According to the Iranian census taken in 1976, two years before the Islamic revolution, religious minorities, excluding Baha'is, made up less than 1 percent of a total population of 34 million. With the unofficial population estimate of Baha'is added, the religious minorities still made up less than 2 percent of the total. There were about 100,000 Armenians and 62,000 Jews in Iran in 1976. According to religious minority community estimates, the number of Armenians was over twice the official figure (around 250,000), and the number of Jews was slightly higher than the official figure (about 80,000). Estimates of the number of Baha'is in Iran prior to the revolution range from 300,000 to 400,000.

The social class of Iranian subgroups in Los Angeles is much higher than that of these same groups in Iran. The fathers of Iranians interviewed in Los Angeles had a high level of education, including informal schooling. The major differences were between the Muslim majority and the three religious minorities. The fathers of Muslims were the most highly educated, and the fathers of Armenians the least. The most striking occupational difference is in the rate of self-employment. Almost all the fathers of the Jewish respondents were self-employed, compared to less than half the fathers of the Muslim respondents and slightly more than half the fathers of the Armenians and Baha'is. Clearly, the tradition of entrepreneurship was very strong among Jews but not as strong among other religious minorities, including Armenians, who are commonly perceived as entrepreneurial.

That the vast majority of Iranians in Los Angeles are from the capital city of Tehran facilitates interaction among Iranians in general and within Iranian subgroups. Regional diversity among Iranians in Los Angeles is less important than religio-ethnic diversity.

Among Iranian heads of household in Los Angeles, over two-thirds held full-time jobs in Iran. The vast majority of them were concentrated in the top occupations—Armenians in construction and services, Jews in wholesale and retail trade, and Baha'is and Muslims in public administration. As we shall see, these differences in the social origins and personal backgrounds of Iranian subgroups directly affect the economic adaptation of Iranians to the United States and their socioeconomic status here.

Friendship ties, participation in ethnic organizations, religious observance, and language are indicators of ethnicity for each subgroup. Iranians

FIGURE 20. Picnicking family eating
seeds and nuts, a favorite Persian snack.
Santa Monica, 1986.

place a premium on friendship and treasure close friends. Given that friends spend a considerable amount of time together, the ethnicity of friends strongly reinforces one's own ethno-religiosity. All four subgroups chose their close friends from among their coreligionists. Remarkably, although the population of Armenians in Tehran was much smaller than that of Muslims, a larger proportion of Armenians than Muslims had coreligionists as close friends in Iran.

In general, participation in voluntary organizations was uncommon in pre-revolutionary Iran, partly because the regime feared organized opposition. Yet religious minorities were allowed to establish and actively participate in their own ethnic organizations. Over half the Armenians and Baha'is in Los Angeles but only one-fifth of Jews and Muslims belonged to organizations in Iran. Most Baha'is belonged to religious associations, such as assemblies and committees. Conversely, Armenians participated more in social or cultural organizations. By and large, members of these organizations were members of the same religions.

Strictly speaking, in Iran, Baha'is and Muslims are religious groups, whereas Armenians and Jews are both religious and ethnic groups. Before leaving Iran, all three religious minorities were more religiously observant than the Muslims. Iranian Muslims in Los Angeles were highly secular even before emigrating, and Baha'is were more observant than Jews and Armenians.

In summary, Iranian religious minorities in Los Angeles had distinctive social ties in the homeland that set them apart from one another. They brought these minority identities to Los Angeles, where they have intensified since the Islamic revolution in Iran. Among Muslim Iranians, however, who for the first time have become a minority in Los Angeles, the opposite is true.

FIGURE 21. Mohammad Shadadi, a board member of an Iranian refugee relief organization, and his Japanese-born wife. One of their daughters married an Italian, another an American, and the third an Englishman. Mr. Shadadi's wife speaks fluent Persian. Brentwood, 1989.

FIGURE 22. Jimmy Sedghi, who once ran as a Republican candidate for the U.S. Senate, and his ninety-three-year-old mother at their home in Westwood. 1989.

## MIGRATION

Large-scale migration from Iran to the United States is very recent. Immigration and Naturalization Service data show two migration waves since 1950, one before and one after the Iranian revolution of 1978–79. These waves reflect a change in both the tempo of Iranian migration and the type of migrant. INS records show that about 35,000 immigrants came to the United States from Iran during the first wave (1950–77) and about 104,000 during the second (1978–86). The increase in Iranian migrants, gradual in the 1950s and 1960s, accelerated after the oil boom in 1974. Iranian migration to the United States rose markedly during the revolution, until 1980, the year after the closure of the American embassy in Iran. Since that time

FIGURE 23. *Above*: Wedding anniversary
party at a private home in Hermosa Beach.
The woman in the background, in Persian
dress, is serving tea in a traditional manner.

FIGURE 24. *Opposite, above*: Iranian mother
following the custom of serving candy to
her family, minutes after the countdown
to the Iranian New Year on Persian TV.
Reseda, March 1990.

FIGURE 25. *Opposite*: Rosh Hashana
(Jewish New Year) celebration at a Jewish
home in Tarzana. September 1989.

FIGURE 26. Jewish wedding at the
Valley Cultural Center in Reseda. The
couple are being married under the
traditional *hupa*, or wedding canopy.
1989.

migration from Iran has dwindled because of the difficulty and cost of obtaining a U.S. visa.

Before the revolution, the vast majority of Iranian migrants to the United States were college and university students. Student migration from Iran increased in the 1970s, when the booming Iranian economy enabled more students to study abroad. After the Iranian revolution some students returned to Iran, but many remained in this country because of uncertainties associated with the revolution. Some were later joined here by exiled family members. Disproportionately large numbers of these exiles were members of religious minorities. Most came from the professional and entrepreneurial classes of Iran. A combination of affluent and skilled exiles and former college students accounts for the unusually high socioeconomic status of Iranians in the United States.

Although overall less than one-third of the Iranians now in Los Angeles arrived before the revolution, the patterns of migration differ among the various subgroups. A larger share of Muslims and Baha'is came before the revolution, while a larger proportion of Armenians and Jews arrived after it had occurred. The timing of Baha'i migration, which may seem puzzling because the persecution of this group intensified after the revolution, can be explained by the number of Baha'i students who came to the United States before the revolution.

Almost half the Iranians in Los Angeles had a visitor's visa when they last entered the United States; another quarter came as students; the rest arrived as immigrants. Student and visitors' visas were common in part because Iranians had only limited chances of obtaining permanent visas. Until recently, few Iranians arrived under the family preference provision since few of those already here were naturalized citizens. As the number of Iranians with American citizenship rises, this option will become more feasible. After the revolution many Iranians obtained visitors' visas in hopes of subsequently changing this status to one of permanent residency. Almost all have done so. Whereas a large proportion of Muslims entered the United States as students, a higher percentage of other religious minorities arrived as visitors, some of whom were granted political asylum. Iranians constitute the preponderance of those in the United States who have been granted asylum. To seek political asylum, individuals must first arrive in the United States; to apply for political refugee status, in contrast, they must file an application from overseas. Muslims are much less likely either to enter the United States as refugees or to apply for political asylum than are the three Iranian religious minorities, who are in a better position to prove fear of persecution upon their return to Iran. But Iranian Muslims are more likely than other Iranians to gain permanent resident status by occupational preference, investor's exemption, or marriage to a U.S. citizen.

Less than half of all Iranians in Los Angeles arrived alone in the United States; almost one-third arrived with a spouse. One in ten was assisted by governmental and international organizations that aid in refugee resettlement. Once more, a major difference exists between the Muslim majority and the three minority subgroups. Family migration and organizationally assisted migration are more prevalent among Armenians, Baha'is, and Jews than among Muslims. The explanation for these differences again lies in differences in the status of migrants themselves—as exiles or immigrants. Political refugees often require organizational assistance. Family migration, more common among exiles and political refugees than among economic immigrants, increases the likelihood of permanent settlement in the United States. That nearly all Armenians and Jews and two of three Baha'is consider themselves permanent settlers here, as compared with only half the Muslims, reflects the religious minorities' fear of persecution in Iran. Of course, the plans of all those who come hinge, to a large degree, on the current regime in Iran. Recently the Iranian regime has relaxed its policies toward its nationals abroad and has even encouraged repatriation. In response, some Iranians are returning to visit Iran; whether they will choose to repatriate remains to be seen.

POPULATION SIZE

The number of Iranians in Los Angeles is a subject of intense controversy. Iranians themselves continually speculate about their numbers. The American mass media often quote the highest numbers, which are generated within the Iranian community; community members, in turn, cite journalistic accounts as authoritative. Even academics sometimes quote the exaggerated numbers, as if these increase the significance of their research. Iranians are not unique among immigrant groups in overstating their population, but their reasons for doing so differ from those of other groups. Whereas other immigrant groups seeking political and economic clout in America exaggerate their numbers to win the support of politicians, Iranian exiles or political refugees have an additional motive for exaggerating: large numbers of political refugees confirm the community's dissatisfaction with the revolutionary regime.

The most remarkable features of the numbers game are the range of estimates and the speed at which the numbers are inflated. According to the Iranian media, there were 200,000 to 300,000 Iranians in Los Angeles in the

FIGURE 27. Zoroastrian wedding in
Westminster. The bride and groom
are led around the fire urn by the
Zoroastrian religious leader, the *mobed*.
Another feature of Zoroastrian weddings
is the symbolic tying together of the
couple by the priest as they sit beside
each other. 1988.

FIGURE 28.  Armenian wedding couple
preparing to walk down the aisle at
St. Mary's Apostolic Church in
Glendale. 1988.

mid-1980s. Our research-based estimates of the Iranian population in Los Angeles range from 53,000 to 74,000 for 1986, much smaller than those of the community and the mass media.

A Los Angeles Iranian magazine recently reported that, according to the 1990 Census, there are 1.8 million Iranians in the United States, a third of whom live in Southern California. This report is astonishing, not for its claim that 0.6 million Iranians live in Southern California, but for its anticipation of Census data not yet released. When released, however, the 1990 Census is unlikely to resolve the discrepancy between official and unofficial figures. The Iranian community will probably dismiss as inaccurate any count much smaller than its own. But even if the Census has undercounted Iranians, its figure will be more accurate than any the community proposes based on unknown sources.

In 1980 Armenians made up about one-quarter of the Iranians in Los Angeles. The number of Baha'is, Jews, and Muslims will remain unknown since the Census collects data on ancestry but not religion. Our survey returns indicate that Muslims are the largest Iranian subgroup, followed, in order, by Armenians, Jews, and Baha'is. Assyrians, Zoroastrians, and Kurds are smaller subgroups, whose size is unknown.

EDUCATION AND OCCUPATION

Iranian immigrants in the United States are highly educated, with 40 percent in 1980 holding a bachelor's or an advanced degree. This percentage is twice that among all other foreign-born immigrants arriving between 1970 and 1980 and two and a half times that among the native-born U.S. population. The level of education among Iranian subgroups differs greatly, however. Given that many Iranian Muslims came to the United States initially as students, it is not surprising that most Iranian Muslim heads of household in Los Angeles have at least an undergraduate degree; about 40 percent have graduate degrees. By contrast, about half the Baha'is and Jews and one-third of the Armenians have completed at least four years of college. Armenians tend to be less well educated than other Iranian subgroups in Los Angeles, but they have a higher level of education than many other immigrant groups.

Education is one of the best predictors of occupational level. Iranian heads of household tend to be managers, executives, and professionals (doctors, dentists, lawyers, teachers, etc.) or to have technical, sales, or administrative support jobs. Only one in ten holds a blue-collar job. These occupations are less prestigious than one might expect from the educational backgrounds of Iranians, an anomaly partly caused by the high level of self-employment among Iranians on the whole and in some subgroups in particular. The overall rate of self-employment among Iranians in Los Angeles is over 50 percent, or about six times that among native-born Americans. Iranian Jews have an 82 percent self-employment rate, the highest among any new immigrant group in the United States. Self-employment among Iranians in Los Angeles creates an ethnic economy outside the general labor market. Higher income and the possibility of advancement are the main reasons Iranians give for going into business for themselves. Factors facilitating Iranian entrepreneurship, especially among minorities, include tradition, capital brought over from Iran, education, and knowledge of English.

An appreciable proportion of Iranian entrepreneurs have partners and co-owners, many of them relatives and Iranian coreligionists, suggesting that ethno-religious diversity also plays a decisive role in economic activity. In fact, self-employed Iranians hire Iranian coreligionists more than either other Iranians or the general population. Iranians from each religio-ethnic subgroup operate partially separate ethnic economies instead of an all-encompassing Iranian economy.

The most common Iranian Jewish businesses are wholesale and retail trade, particularly apparel and jewelry. These traditional ethnic niches account for about half of the industries in which all Iranian Jews can be found. Not surprisingly, Iranian Jewish businesses are concentrated in downtown Los Angeles, the heart of jewelry and garment districts, whereas most Muslim businesses are in the western sections of Los Angeles. Armenian Iranians operate their businesses in Glendale, where they also live. They are involved in finance, insurance, and real estate as well as repair services, following a long-standing tradition of artisanship among them in Iran. Both Muslims and Baha'is are concentrated in construction and the manufacturing of durable goods, but Baha'is are also employed in health and legal services. Baha'i businesses are more scattered than those of the other three subgroups in Los Angeles.

Iranians from all ethnic groups are prominent in construction, especially in Iranian neighborhoods. The construction business is attractive to Iranians for several reasons. First, even with the economic and political uncertainties in Iran, investment in hard assets such as real estate was relatively safe. Because most Iranians benefited from skyrocketing prices in Tehran real estate prior to emigration, they have pursued this type of investment in the United States. Second, the huge Los Angeles construction industry was booming in the mid-1980s. Finally, although construction requires more capital than other businesses, such as retail stores,

FIGURE 29. Traditional setting of
symbolic foods and decorations at a
Muslim wedding held in the Irvine
Hilton Hotel. 1989.

some Iranians were able to bring enough capital from Iran to invest in this economic activity.

RELIGIO–ETHNIC AND NATIONAL IDENTITY

The exile experience has fostered a strong devotion to the homeland among many Iranians in Los Angeles. Forging and maintaining an Iranian identity is inherently problematic, however, in view of the ethnic and religious fragmentation of this population.

Typically, ethnic populations maintain their identity and resilience through residential concentration, religious observance, marriage and friendship ties, language, and participation in organizations. There is a clear distinction between Armenians, who live mainly in Glendale, and other Iranians, who reside in other parts of Los Angeles. The geographical distribution of the other three Iranian subgroups is less distinctive than that of Armenians, who live near one another. Baha'is are concentrated in West Los Angeles and Santa Monica, Muslims in Santa Monica and Palms, and Jews in the more affluent neighborhoods of Westwood and Beverly Hills.

Iranian minority subgroups are more religiously observant than the Muslim majority. Almost 80 percent of Muslims never follow the Islamic practices of daily prayers, fasting during Ramadan, and so forth, partly because of their secular background and partly because of disenchantment with the role of Islam in Iran. In contrast, less than 10 percent of Armenians, Baha'is, and Jews are nonobservant. A mere 2 percent of Muslims, compared with over one-third of Baha'is, about one-fourth of Jews, and one-fifth of Armenians, always observe their religious practices.

Endogamy, in this case marriage to an Iranian coreligionist, helps to maintain ethnicity in the household. Iranian children in endogamous households are more likely to speak their mother tongue (Persian or Armenian) than children raised in exogamous homes. Iranian subgroups tend to be endogamous, partly because most immigrants were married in Iran. The range of endogamous marriage is from over two-thirds, among Baha'is, to the vast majority, among Jews. Armenians and Jews are the most endogamous, Baha'is and Muslims the least. Baha'is intermarry more frequently with other Iranians, Muslims with Americans. Muslim intermarriage with Americans can be attributed to the comparative youth of Muslims among the Iranian subgroups as well as the larger proportion of Muslims who came to the United States as students.

Insofar as friendship is voluntary, social ties are a powerful indicator of ethnic attachment. Close friends who are co-ethnics are likely to reinforce ethnicity. Moreover, the ethnicity of children's close friends provides a clue to generational changes in ethnicity. Adult Armenians and Jews are more likely than either Baha'is or Muslims to associate with Iranian coreligionists. Like their parents, Armenian children are much more likely to interact with Armenian Iranians than with other subgroups. Jews show a similar, though weaker, tendency. Muslim and Baha'i children are much less likely to choose Iranian coreligionists as close friends. Iranian coreligionists constitute a majority at the parties, weddings, and other celebrations attended by Armenian and Jewish respondents. This proportion is twice as high as that reported by Baha'is and Muslims.

Social interaction with coreligionists has varied from Iran to the United States. Muslims are expected to interact less with Iranian Muslims in the United States than they did in Iran. But Iranian ethno-religious minorities continue to interact at the in-group level. Because patterns of interaction varied in Iran, they could be expected to vary in the United States. Armenian Iranians interact with their coreligionists as much in the United States as in Iran, and Baha'is somewhat less. Surprisingly, Jewish Iranians interact with their coreligionists more in the United States than they did in Iran.

Although Iranians in Los Angeles are not extensively involved in voluntary organizations and associations, some subgroups are more active than others. The proportion of Armenians and Baha'is belonging to organizations is larger than that of Jews and Muslims. A comparison of the social ties of Iranian subgroups in Iran and in the United States shows that some changes have taken place; among Muslims and Baha'is, these changes are drastic. Although in Iran Muslims and Baha'is interacted mostly with coreligionists, in the United States they no longer do. Slight changes in the ethnic composition of formal networks for Armenians and Jews in the United States have increased both groups' interaction with coreligionists here.

In a pattern closely reflecting the current friendship patterns discussed above, Iranian Muslims, Baha'is, and Jews in Los Angeles speak mostly their mother tongue, Persian, with close friends in Los Angeles, whereas Armenian Iranians speak Armenian (they are also proficient in Persian). Muslim and Baha'i Iranians, who associate more with non-Iranians (including Americans) in Los Angeles than do Jews and Armenians, are more likely to speak English with close friends.

Among Baha'is and Muslims the use of Persian has declined as the use of English has increased. Not surprisingly, the patterns of English language use indicate that ethno-religious ties are weaker among Muslims and Baha'is than among Armenians and Jews.

How well do Iranian subgroups retain their ethnicity? This question can be answered in relation to the following indicators: ethnic identity, religiosity, endogamy, family ties, social ties, and preference for ethnic organizations. The ethnicity of Armenians and Jews is stronger than that of the other subgroups; that of Muslims is the weakest. The ethnicity of Baha'is is somewhat weaker than that of Armenians and Jews from Iran but stronger than that of Muslims. In sum, the subgroups who were minorities in Iran retain their ethnicity in the United States more tenaciously than the subgroup that was the majority in Iran.

Parental preferences vis-à-vis the ethnicity of children's spouses suggests a possible shift in the ethnicity of social ties. Given the strong role Iranian parents play in selecting mates for their sons and especially for their daughters, the parents' desire for endogamy is a reasonable predictor of the outcome. Although almost all Iranians want their children to marry coreligionists, a larger share of Baha'is and Muslims than of Armenians and Jews have no preference. Iranian Jewish parents, among whom endogamy is more prevalent than it is in the other three groups, prefer Iranian Jews as spouses for their children; as a second choice these parents prefer Jews of any background rather than non-Jewish Iranian mates for their children. Similarly, Armenians interact extensively with other Iranian Armenians and hence desire either Iranian Armenian or non-Iranian Armenian spouses for their children. In either case, the order of preference is first and foremost to have an Iranian coreligionist in-law; second a coreligionist; and only third, an Iranian of a different ethnic and religious background.

CONCLUSION

Although Iranians in Los Angeles have much in common, the community's distinctive subgroups differ in history, background, characteristics, and adjustment to American society. These differences, obvious enough to Iranians, may not be apparent to outsiders. Because discussions of the group as a whole can conceal important differences between subgroups, any discussion of identity, ethnicity, and ethnic change for future generations must be attentive to the subgroups.

Informal and formal social ties in Los Angeles tend to reinforce separate Armenian, Baha'i, Jewish, and Muslim identities rather than an all-encompassing Iranian national identity. Armenians and Jews, who have maintained their ethnicity, have resisted the pressures of assimilation more than Baha'is and Muslims. Few Iranian immigrants socialize mostly with Anglo-Americans. Yet a number of Muslims and Baha'is have a fairly wide social network that includes both Iranians and non-Iranians. The Baha'i experience is to be expected in view of the universalistic outlook of this religion, which is conducive to integration. In none of the four subgroups is association with non-Iranian coreligionists extensive, despite large non-Iranian Armenian, Jewish, Baha'i, and Muslim communities in Los Angeles. The process of absorption into the wider religio-ethnic group takes time. But the evidence regarding Armenian children's best friends and Armenian parents' desired spouses for their children as well as this subgroup's distinctive language suggests that Armenians may be absorbed more quickly than either Baha'is or Jews. Iranian Muslims, given their strong identification with nationality rather than religion, are unlikely ever to become integrated into the non-Iranian Muslim community in Los Angeles. Iranian subgroups in Los Angeles cling, to varying extents, to the pattern of social ties that existed for them in Iran. Only time and further studies will determine whether future generations maintain these ties.

SUGGESTED READINGS

Bozorgmehr, M. "Internal Ethnicity: Armenian, Baha'i, Jewish, and Muslim Iranians in Los Angeles." Ph.D. diss., University of California, Los Angeles, 1992.

Bozorgmehr, M., and G. Sabagh. "High Status Immigrants: A Statistical Profile of Iranians in the United States." *Iranian Studies* 21 (1988): 5–36.

———. "Survey Research among Middle Eastern Immigrant Groups in the United States: Iranians in Los Angeles." *Middle East Studies Association Bulletin* 23 (1989): 23–34.

———. "Iranian Exiles and Immigrants in Los Angeles." In *Iranian Refugees and Exiles since Khomeini*, edited by A. Fathi, 121–144. Costa Mesa, Calif.: Mazda Publishers, 1991.

Der-Martirosian, C., G. Sabagh, and M. Bozorgmehr. "Subethnicity: Armenians in Los Angeles." In *Comparative Immigration and Entrepreneurship: Culture, Capital, and Ethnic Networks*, edited by I. Light and P. Bhachu. New Brunswick, N.J.: Transaction Publishers, forthcoming.

Light, I., G. Sabagh, M. Bozorgmehr, and C. Der-Martirosian. "The Four Iranian Ethnic Economies in Los Angeles." *Israel Social Science Review*, forthcoming.

Sabagh, G., and M. Bozorgmehr. "Are the Characteristics of Exiles Different from Immigrants? The Case of Iranians in Los Angeles." *Sociology and Social Research* 71 (1987): 77–84.

———. "Secular Immigrants: Religiosity and Ethnicity among Iranian Muslims in Los Angeles." In *Muslim Communities in America*, edited by Y. Haddad, forthcoming.

FIGURE 30. Iranian, Iraqi, and other
Shi'i Muslims at prayer in a rented
elementary school cafeteria in Downey
during Ramadan, the month of fasting
throughout the Muslim world.
April 1990.

# ETHNIC AND RELIGIOUS COMMUNITIES FROM IRAN IN LOS ANGELES

*Ron Kelley*

## Muslims

"I'm an atheist, but I still consider myself a Muslim." The homesick Iranian scholar who made this statement one morning in Los Angeles was not talking about religion, but rather about culture—the values, mores, and lifestyle of Iran. In her homeland, Islam was both a national faith and a shaping force in day-to-day existence. Transposed to Los Angeles, she quickly became aware of how differently she was accustomed to perceiving life and human relations. Compared with the closely knit family life and warmer social interactions in Iran, life in the United States seemed cold and callous. Western friends here were transient, elusive, and unreliable. Even the intellectual community in America was somehow more provincial, more limited than that of Iran. During the Desert Storm bombings of the Iraqi people, she was shocked—so soon after the Iran-Iraq war—to discover that she identified with the Iraqis, members, like her, of an Islamic culture.

Although she never actively practiced Islam, she argued that its influence was everywhere in her Iranian past as a far-reaching system of morals, values, and mutual expectations. Although the majority of Iranians in Los Angeles still consider themselves Muslims, most are secularized. Religious Muslims espouse a specific belief system based on the Quran and the teachings of the prophet Mohammad. Asked whether an atheist can be a Muslim, the religious people brushed off the question as ridiculous: "The terms are mutually exclusive." Only one local religious leader was open enough to respond to the theological question "Who is a Muslim?" with "A Muslim is whoever thinks he's one. It's between him and God."

There are two major branches of Islam: Sunni, the larger branch, and Shi'i, the smaller one, to which most Iranian Muslims belong. Sunnis and Shi'is share some fundamental beliefs, including the acceptance of Mohammad and the Quran as the holy word of God, daily prayers, fasting, charity, and—for those who can afford it—pilgrimage to Mecca. But important

INTERVIEW

. . . . . . . . . . . . . . . . . . .

*Venus, aged twenty, and her
husband, Soheil, in his early thirties,
are practicing Muslims living in
Torrance, California, who have been
out of Iran for a decade.*

. . . . . . . . . . . . . . . . . . .

RON KELLEY:
What is it like, as a woman, to practice
Islam in this country?

VENUS:
I started wearing the *hejab* [traditional
Muslim head covering] about two or
three years ago. I wasn't married. I was
home, and my mom used to tell me
about Islam, and I was in an Islamic
environment. I really liked it because
deep down inside . . .

You know, I'd have fun. I'd go out.
But I'd never go to a discotheque. I
never went to bars or anything like
that. If I went anywhere, my brother
escorted me. I didn't go to my prom
because my dad was very strict. He's
not religious, but he'd never allow us to
go, under any circumstances. My mom
started talking to me about Islam, and I
felt it was fulfilling my inner needs.

So I put on the *hejab*, and what was
really strange was that my best friends
from college all stopped talking to me.
Just because of that. Because they
thought I was strange or stupid. I
wasn't in Iran; I didn't have to wear the
*hejab*, you know? They stopped talking
to me. They thought I got money to
spy on their organizations for Iran. It
wasn't that way at all! I'm not wearing
the *hejab* anymore, as you see, because I
started working again after I got
married—it's been about seven or eight
months since I stopped wearing it. It's
very difficult. I wanted to wear it at my
last job, and they told me it didn't fit

differences divide them. The key division concerns the succession of leadership in the Islamic world after the death of the prophet Mohammad in
A.D. 632. For Sunnis, the question of Mohammad's successor is answered
in the temporal realm, through a series of worldly leaders, called caliphs.
For Shi'is, Islamic leadership is considered to be not only temporal, but
also spiritual via a succession of twelve holy Imams, each ancestrally linked
to the prophet Mohammad. Shi'is contend that Mohammad desired his
son-in-law and cousin, Ali, to succeed him, and, indeed, Ali did finally
acquire political authority, twenty-four years after Mohammad's death, as
the fourth caliph. Shi'is, however, regard him as the first Imam, clarifier,
interpreter, and explicator of God's law. Shi'is further believe that in the
succession of divinely guided Imams, the last is in occultation and will
return before the day of Judgment.

There are also many other distinctions between Sunni and Shi'i beliefs,
including differences in the proper performance of prayer. Both branches
recognize the Quran and the exemplary behavior of the prophet Mohammad (called *sunna*) as basic sources of Islamic law, but the versions, interpretations, and emphases of these traditions sometimes differ. Citing religious texts, for example, Shi'is sanction *sigheh*, or temporary marriage,
whereby a man and woman agree to a mutually satisfactory financial
arrangement and schedule for conjugal relations, a practice endorsed by the
current Islamic Republic. Sunnis dispute the Shi'i claim that temporary
marriages are sanctioned by Islam. Another distinctive Shi'i religious practice disavowed by Sunnis is *taghiyeh*, which permits a believer to hide or
deny the faith to avoid danger.

The Shi'is, moreover, unlike the Sunnis, have a tradition of intense
ritualized mourning. During the holy month of Moharram, the faithful
gather for ten days to weep and wail in commemoration of the events
leading up to the slaying of the third Imam, Husain, and his band of
supporters in the year A.D. 680. The particularly zealous mourn by beating
and whipping themselves. Husain's battle against overwhelming military
odds to reclaim the lost caliphate is perceived as a selfless struggle for both
temporal justice and religious righteousness. More than any other event in
Shi'i tradition, his sacrifice has fueled the ethos of martyrdom, the ready
acceptance of ultimate personal sacrifice that so befuddled the Western
media in the Iran-Iraq war.

Allegiance to the Islamic faith among Iranians in Los Angeles takes
various forms. Although many in the community only identify with (and
long for) the familiar sociocultural manifestations of Islamic society, others
are active religious practitioners. Of these, a few pray with Muslims from
all over the world at pan-Islamic mosques near their homes. More often,

their dress code. Of course I didn't want to discuss it with anyone. I just felt, OK, fine, I'll just take it off.

Q:
They wouldn't permit it?

VENUS:
No. I had it on, and they asked me, "What is that for?" And I said—what was I going to say? "A fashion statement." Something like that. I wasn't about to . . . you know. They said, "Oh, it's a fashion statement. It's all right to wear it now, but you can't wear it anymore. It's not in our dress code." I didn't have any alternative. I didn't tell my husband; I didn't tell anyone. For a week or two he didn't know that I was going out without covering. That bothered me. Finally, it was killing me inside, so I had to tell him. I'm ashamed of myself. I wish I could know Islam and practice it better than I can now. Hopefully, again, one day, I can wear the *hejab*.

SOHEIL:
If a woman goes to a job interview wearing a *hejab*, that's a serious problem right there. You might as well forget about that interview. They're going to say, "This person is just too unusual."

Q:
Tell me again what you told me earlier about walking down the street here wearing the *hejab*.

VENUS:
A couple of times I was walking down the street, minding my own business, going shopping. And I wanted to cross a street. A man was coming very fast, so I waited to cross. As soon as he saw me, he stopped. And I said to myself,

however, they are members of distinctly Iranian religious societies.

Among the Iranian immigrants living in southern California are a few hundred supporters of Iran's Islamic Republic. What was once a unified community has divided somewhat because of personality clashes, internal politics, and differences in religious opinion.

One group, the Moslem Student Association, Persian Speaking Group, is predominantly an organization of Iranian students and former students who meet regularly at homes and universities for religious, social, and political activities. They hold their largest annual event to mark the anniversary of the institution of the Islamic Republic. Lecturers from the United States and abroad extol the Iranian revolution and the future of the Islamic movement. This event, unlike most others, is conducted largely in English in deference to the few non-Persian-speaking members of the audience. When lectures must be presented in Persian, small radio systems are passed out and a volunteer translator informs the English-speaking listeners of the speaker's salient points. The Moslem Student Association has also staged public protest marches against the Saudi Arabian embassy in Westwood and in support of the Iranian revolution.

A second Iranian congregation attends the religious classes and services of Seyyed Morteza Ghasvini, a Shi'i cleric who fled Iraq, his place of birth, survived an assassination attempt by agents of Saddam Hussein in Kuwait, and immigrated to Iran in the early years of the revolution to partake in its religious revival. Speaking Arabic, Persian, and English, Ghasvini became a judge in the Iranian Islamic legal system and was also a leader at a Tehran mosque. At the invitation of a group of religious Iranian students in Los Angeles and with the encouragement of his peers in Tehran, Ghasvini made his way to America to start an Islamic teaching center. Recently his group purchased a small church in a Hispanic neighborhood in the city of Southgate and renovated it as a Shi'i mosque. The group had held prayers, lectures, and discussions at Ghasvini's home until unsympathetic neighbors called the police to demand the enforcement of local zoning codes. Important religious occasions requiring additional space were observed in local public school halls and cafeterias. During the fasting month of Ramadan, the group gathered in a school hall to pray and share a potluck dinner. Once during a Moharram observance, two hundred people had to move from the Bellflower High School cafeteria to the gymnasium because the cafeteria had been promised to the organizers of a bingo game.

During Moharram, Ghasvini recited the tale of the martyred Imam Husain, a yearly ritual in Shi'i mosques throughout the world. The lights in the room were turned out to enhance the somber mood, and the audience could freely weep and moan in relative privacy. Heads were bowed,

"Oh, good, he wants me to cross." I waved my hand to say thanks. As I was passing his car, he beeped so hard I almost had a heart attack. And he started calling me names. He was laughing and pointing at me as if I were some weird, strange thing from outer space.

Another day when I was walking down the street, people spit at me. And once at a demonstration they poured water on me—I hope to God to this day it was only water. They have nasty attitudes when you walk—especially my own people.

SOHEIL:
Especially Iranians.

VENUS:
Especially Iranians. God forbid if I go to an Iranian restaurant. They all look at me like . . .

SOHEIL:
It's very difficult for a woman wearing a *rusari* [headscarf] to go to an Iranian restaurant here, where most of the people are going to be Iranian.

VENUS:
Oh, they just want to kill you! They look at you and they hate your guts!

SOHEIL:
Most of them are going through a difficult time not being in Iran. They hate the Iranian government. When they see a woman wearing a *hejab* or *rusari*, they think that she's pro-government. There's a lot of friction, mean looks, even words. Generally, I avoid going to Iranian restaurants with her wearing a *rusari* because I don't want to get into a situation like that.

and men and women were encouraged to release their accumulated sense of loss and melancholy. After a period of sobbing and wailing, the men all rose and stood in a group at the front of the hall, rhythmically thumping their chests (*sineh zadan*) in unison, chanting and shouting exaltations to the beloved martyr Imam Husain.

This encouragement of communal expressions of sadness and suffering has few equivalents in modern Western culture. Some have argued that Shi'is promote a self-perception of victimization and oppression, contending that the real starting point for the study of Shi'i Islam is the rejection of Ali's Imamate by Sunnis. In this view, a great psychosocial burden has been passed down from generation to generation throughout Shi'i history along with a tradition of lamentation that pervades the classical Iranian arts, from poetry to traditional music.

Seyyed Ghasvini's missionary projects in the American community have been realized only slowly. He has aided an American convert in securing permission to study Islam in the holy Iranian city of Qom, and has encouraged an African-American Muslim leader to set up a small Shi'i mosque in the local African-American community. His dream is to establish a local Islamic university.

Seyyed Ghasvini's core congregation in Los Angeles is mostly Iranians, Iraqis, and Lebanese, although he is a respected religious leader for other Shi'i groups as well. Religious services are conducted each night in Persian and Arabic. Ghasvini speaks for a while in one language, then the other. Members of the audience respond in their own tongue.

Another site of strict Shi'i religious observance is the predominantly Pakistani Jafaria Hall, a mosque located in a Hispanic neighborhood in Cudahy. Small numbers of Iranians occasionally come here for prayer and other gatherings but find the Urdu language and cultural variations (particularly on important religious nights) obstacles to concentration. Other sites of occasional pan-Shi'i interaction include a Lebanese mosque two miles from Jafaria Hall and an East African mosque in Pico Rivera, which serves mostly Indo-Pakistanis who were raised in Africa before moving to the Los Angeles area. The broad Shi'i community here comes from many nations, and during important times like Moharram local members often segregate along language, ethnic, and/or ideological lines.

Not all religious Muslim Iranians accept the current agenda of the Islamic Republic. In Beverly Hills, for example, Dr. F. Hormozi—founder in the 1960s of the Moslem Brothers of America—opens his home to any visitor on Friday nights for Quranic readings and discussion, as he has done for the past thirty-five years.

Another well-known practitioner of a less restrictive, more adaptive

Islam in California is Mohammad Nemazikhah, a professor of dentistry at a Los Angeles university. A few years ago he and a group of friends, desiring to maintain their Islamic faith, began holding prayer recitals every Thursday night in his home in the San Fernando Valley. Word of this regular religious meeting spread rapidly. Today, on important Ramadan and Moharram nights, over three hundred people follow him in prayer, filling his large home to overflowing.

These weekly gatherings are entirely open. Friends tell friends, and all are invited to Nemazikhah's home for a free dinner, catered by a local Iranian restaurant, and the recitation of Islamic prayers. Nemazikhah is careful to point out that his home is not a mosque and that he makes no pretense of being a religious leader. He merely invites people to gather in prayer, to help them regain something spiritually lost in their transition to America.

The gatherings attract a wide range of visitors. Though non-Iranians are rarely present, it is far from a traditionally Islamic crowd. Older women in classical head-to-toe chadors sometimes attend, but so do fashionably dressed businessmen and women who look as if they had just interrupted a shopping trip. A few women unpack a chador and briefly prostrate themselves in a side room in the prescribed Islamic manner and then pack away the modest gown. Others ignore such traditional prayers and simply await Nemazikhah's recitations.

For many visitors, the Thursday night services provide an opportunity to revitalize their Islamic faith without identifying with the perspectives of the Islamic Republic. In fact, such Muslims note that the American tendency to associate Islam in Iran with hostages, terrorism, and revolutionary excesses has been a major problem in starting a proposed central mosque for Iranians in Los Angeles. Most of the founders of the estimated forty mosques in Southern California established them for communities with a common national, ethnic, language, and cultural background, from Afghani to African-American. Although Seyyed Ghasvini's congregation has recently established a small mosque in the city of Southgate, the group is only partially Persian. Its existence is not publicized, and few local Iranians know its location. Because its members are not highly visible, they are not opposed or harassed by the mainstream Iranian community.

The Iranian Muslim community has tried to develop plans for a mosque that would serve as both a religious and a cultural center for those who do not particularly identify with the Ayatollah Khomeini. But financial backers often withdraw for fear of the negative reaction of the American public to a mosque in Los Angeles built by and for Iranians. In addition, vehemently anti-Khomeini critics in the local exile community express concern that such a project would inevitably attract supporters of the Islamic Republic. The prospect of political conflict at the site of prayer has made potential sponsors wary, at least for now.

Another approach to religious restoration and renewal in the Los Angeles Iranian Muslim community, particularly among the intelligentsia, is the Sufi tradition of ascetic mysticism. From the early history of Islam, Sufi devotees sought to circumvent religious intermediaries, searching for a more personal communion with God through contemplation, discipline, and ecstasy. There are at least three Iranian Sufi meeting places in Los Angeles. In 1990 between three and five thousand people from all over the world reportedly gathered for a Sufi ceremony in the city of Lancaster, a hundred miles north of Los Angeles.

For a recent Eid al-Adha holiday, when traditional Muslims slaughter sheep to commemorate Abraham's willingness to follow God's order to sacrifice his son, one of the local Sufi orders held an observance at their center in Burbank. This group of about a hundred follow the teachings of the order of Oveyssi Shahmaghsoudi, a line of forty-two Sufi masters going back to the prophet Mohammad. All dressed in white, men on the left side of the room, women on the right, the group gathered beneath a chandelier to face a poster-sized, blue-neon-framed color transparency of a revered Sufi master and listen to their local spiritual leader lecture on ego denial and the quest for union with God. Later, as the room was gradually darkened, the speaker led his audience in a cycle of memorized songs, chants, poems, and prayers. The group responded with increasing intensity. People began swaying back and forth, weeping and shouting, releasing an avalanche of unguarded emotions. This contagious rhythmic chanting culminated with the group's joining hands, raising them above their heads, and repeatedly exhorting—in an ecstatic cheer—the name of God, Allah. Then the group quietly sat down, the lights returned, and tea and pastries were served by five male attendants. For fifteen minutes, as the tea was served and the cups gathered up, there was absolute silence. Then, after parting remarks by the speaker, each member of the audience backed away from the altar, accepted a wrapped gift of grapes and cucumbers, and went home.

With these various exceptions, most Iranians in Los Angeles who refer to themselves as Muslims are not religious. But they still consider themselves linked to the Islamic creed, and most follow Muslim traditions, at least to some extent, in marriage and funeral ceremonies. There are, however, no major communal events or organizations around which they unite. In other words, unlike the Iranian minority groups here, the secular Muslims are not a distinct community. Most of the cultural events and

FIGURE 31. Seyyed Morteza Ghasvini at home. Born in Iraq, he
became an active critic of Saddam Hussein's Ba'thist regime. In 1972 he
escaped to Kuwait. After the Iranian revolution, suspected agents of the
Ba'thist regime shot at him as he passed in a car. Fleeing next to Iran, he
became an Islamic judge and the religious leader of a mosque in Tehran.
Meanwhile, his ninety-year-old father, also a Shi'i religious scholar, has
languished in Iraqi prisons for the past twelve years. Seyyed Ghasvini
first visited Los Angeles in 1985 at the invitation of local Muslim
students. With the encouragement of Ayatollah Ali Montazeri (at one
time the heir apparent to the Ayatollah Khomeini), Ghasvini returned
to Los Angeles to set up an Islamic studies center in 1986.

FIGURE 32. Ghasvini presiding over a Moharram congregation of
Iranian, Iraqi, and other Shi'i Muslims at a rented high school hall in
Bellflower. The women behind a curtain in the foreground have
chosen to seclude themselves from the male congregation. Later, the
lights were dimmed, and Ghasvini recited the story of the martyrdom
of Imam Husain in A.D. 680, eliciting communal weeping. July 1990.

holidays at which they might gather—such as No Ruz and Sizdah Bidar—are shared with other Iranian ethnic and religious groups, partly because these celebrations predate the development of Islam in Iran. In this sense, secular Muslims in Los Angeles are more disenfranchised socially than other ethnic and religious groups that left the homeland for America. In Iran, Jews, Baha'is, Assyrians, and others had developed their own networks and organizations to enable them to survive and even prosper. After leaving Iran, these minority groups adapted such organizations to America. While there are Assyrian, Baha'i, and other Iranian minority centers in Los Angeles (often holding lists of fellow members), there is no equivalent for secular Muslims, whose friendships and associations often extend well beyond the Muslim population.

Whether religious or not, most of those born to the Islamic heritage would probably agree that Iranian Shi'ism has contributed to their psycho-social development and worldview. Most secular Muslims recognize the complex emotional terrain of their countrymen and countrywomen and acknowledge its effects on their daily lives. Even if they were raised in nonreligious families, Islam enveloped them. Family alignments, marriage, and other social arrangements were based on Islamic tenets.

The Iranian atheist, sipping tea, nodded reflectively as she concluded her case for being a Muslim, underscoring her belief that Islam—Muslim claims to the contrary notwithstanding—is unjust to women. But even as she spoke critically, she acknowledged all the good things lost to her in her homeland. She smiled as she described her life as a little girl in Tehran, the streets, the shops, the summer dust, the cacophony of the fruit and vegetable vendors, the scent of their wares. She confessed her love of the Muslim call to prayer each morning on the street where she lived. It transcended dogma. She sighed at the memory of it. Now it was simply the impossible call to come home.

FIGURE 33. Shi'i Muslims
(predominantly Pakistani) striking their
chests in mourning the martyr Imam
Husain. Jafaria Hall, the mosque at
which this photograph was taken, is an
important religious center for Shi'is
from many nations, including a number
of Iranians.

FIGURE 34. Iranian, Iraqi, and other
Shi'i Muslims at a protest rally against
Saddam Hussein and the sufferings of the
Iraqi people. This rally was held on
Ashura, the most important day of
mourning during the month of
Moharram. Westwood, July 1991.

FIGURE 35. Shi'i Muslims from Iran
and other nations join hands in solidarity
to conclude commemorative services on
the anniversary of the death of the
Ayatollah Khomeini. Jafaria Hall.

*Interview*

Pari, a practicing Muslim woman, was interviewed at the Islamic Center of South Bay, Lomita, California.

RON KELLEY:   I'd like you to tell me about the difficulties you've had here in Los Angeles practicing the Islamic faith.

PARI:   As far as the practice is concerned, I don't have any problem praying because you can do it in your own home. But an Islamic woman in a *hejab* looks different from everyone else in this society. To be honest, I haven't had any difficulties, as far as the American people are concerned; they never give me a hard time because they understand, once I explain. But sometimes it looks very strange to them. I have been questioned many times. When I have this scarf on, they ask, "Is it cold outside?" Or, "Why are you wearing this?" They don't know how Muslim women should dress. I don't think it's their fault.

Q:   What about the Persian community here? You said there is some trouble.

PARI:   Well, not really trouble. But they look at me even more strangely than the Americans do. It's because of the political situation, the conflict between the regime in Iran and the people here. If they find out that this *hejab* is part of your sympathy for the regime and the Islamic government, then they don't want to be around you. If I were an old woman and couldn't speak English, they'd say, "OK, she's ignorant and she just wears it traditionally." But when they find out that I chose this dress, it's different.

  The *hejab* is not just a tradition. It is ideological; it says to the West and to other parts of the world, "I am myself—I am a Muslim woman and I dress the way my Book asks me to." I haven't had many problems with Americans, but I remember in Frankfurt, Germany, I was wearing a *hejab*, and two Iranian ladies approached me. I was sitting in a park, feeding my daughter a hamburger. And one of the women started to swear. I said, "Why are you doing that?" She said, "You're part of that regime. Why did you come here? Go back to your own country. Go back to where you belong." I said, "I don't understand your attitude toward me. What have I done to you?" Then she walked away. I have had this experience a few times. Sometimes they really give you ugly looks.

Q: A significant part of the Iranian community in Los Angeles is wealthy. How do you, as people supportive of the Islamic Republic, view these people? Who are they to you?

PARI: You can't stereotype all of them who have a Mercedes and say they stole the money from Iran. There are doctors who have been here for many years, for example, and they're good people. They're not anti–Islamic Republic and not pro-regime. They're just wealthy because they work hard. I have nothing against somebody who has a Mercedes. But there are people who, during the first two or three years of the revolution—when the government wasn't really stable and didn't control the borders—got money out of the country. Millions of dollars, believe me, came to this country, to the banks. And that's why our country is in such a broken state economically now, because all the money—that's part of it—went out of the country.

These people, of course, lost many things back home. They'd like to see the Islamic Republic destroyed—many of them are pro-Shah. The Shah's son is active and wants to go back, and many of them support him. They say they're Muslims. Even the son of the Shah says he's a Muslim and wants to practice Islam back home. But look at the way he lives.

Another group doesn't believe in any system. They just want to have fun. They want all the cabarets, the way of life they used to have. That's what they want. They can't live under a controlling regime like the Islamic Republic. They don't like it.

There are many groups, not all from the same background. But the people who brought money from out of the country, I think they're traitors to spend it in this country. They made an economic disaster for us back home.

Q: What about temptations here in this country? It must be difficult to maintain the Islamic faith where everything is pulling the children away from it.

PARI: Yes. I have had many questions from my daughter. She's eight years old. When we came here she was four. She asks me, "Why are you different from other women?" Before she met the Muslim community—because at first I didn't know the Muslim community here—she always asked me, "Why do you do that and other women don't? Mommy, I like you to be pretty. I like you to put on makeup like American women, like my teacher. Look how she dresses and how nice she looks." I found the best way for her to understand is to take her where she sees other Muslim women. She sees my friends when I come to the Islamic Center. They wear the *hejab*. Then she says, "Oh, mom, is this why you wear the *hejab*? You have to?" I said, "Yes, that's why we wear it." Many times she asks me why some other Muslims don't wear the *hejab*. That's the important question in her mind. She understands the difference between Christianity and Judaism and Islam; the others don't have the *hejab*, but we do. But she doesn't understand why some other Muslim women don't wear it. That's on her mind constantly. So I'm going to take her home to Iran, and she's going to find out more about Islam. That's the best way for a child, to be around the Muslim community. But, yes, I have a difficult time with her. She says, "Mommy, I can't wear a *hejab* when I'm nine. How could I go to school? The children would make fun of me." I say, "No, if you realize that what you're doing is right. The Jews who put the cap on their head are not ashamed of what they do. So we're Muslim, and we should follow our own beliefs." She realizes, but for a child it's very hard.

Q: Does she wear the *hejab*?

PARI: No. When she's nine, then she has to start wearing it. But now she's eight. So she knows. She knows, and she says, "I have one more year to go."

Q: What about for adults? Are there a lot of temptations here in America that pull people away from Islam?

PARI: As far as I'm concerned, since my standards and my values have been set, there is no problem. But for the children, yes. I have this one child, and I know the difficulty. She wants to go ice skating and wear a kind of dress. She wants to go swimming. And you can hardly find a woman's swimming pool here—someplace where only girls are allowed. So these things make it difficult to live in this society. You have to deprive your child of many things.

I'll give you an example. A few days ago she wanted to spend the night at somebody's house, one of her friends. And we had an argument about that. Finally, she realized that we weren't going to allow her to go. The friend's mother is a nice American lady, and her daughter invited my daughter for her birthday party. But this lady is not married. She lives with her boyfriend, and they asked my daughter to come and spend the night. We rarely allow her to go out of the house for the night. But she insisted, "Mommy, since I'm going back to Iran for the summer, please let me do it." I said no. According to our standards, you are not allowed to go and spend the night with unmarried people who are living under the same roof. She said, "Mommy, she's a very nice lady. How can you say that about her? She buys me ice cream. She's so nice to us." I said, "I know. I know all of that. But we have to live by our standards, and they have to live by theirs." That confuses her. She doesn't understand. This lady comes to school and gets involved in everything, every activity. And she's a nice person. That's just an example of how difficult it is.

Q:      Are your plans for your daughter that she will live in Iran?

PARI:   Yes. As a matter of fact, this summer—hopefully, *enshallah* [if God wills it], as we say—we're going back home, and I'm going to try and keep her over there and put her in school. Even if my husband can't make it for a few years, we're going to try to stay there so she can become familiar with the Islamic environment.

Q:      There are a lot of stereotypes here about the Imam Khomeini, Iran, and Iranians. As you've probably heard, the mass media often portray Iranians as terrorists, fanatics, barbarians, crazy, savage, all that. What's your sense of this?

PARI:   It really bothers me. I went back to my country the first year of the revolution, even before its victory. And for seven years I stayed home and was in close contact with everything that was going on—the war, the Imam Khomeini's popularity among his own people, and also his moral standards and views about Islam. When I came here to America, I saw a totally different picture of him. I was shocked. But I didn't expect anything else because of the big difference in values and standards. After the hostage situation, the American view changed. I could see why. I knew that the Shah had destroyed our country, but they didn't care. They always said he was a benevolent leader. When the Imam Khomeini came to power, at first they thought they could buy him. But he could not be bought. He only saw God. His life was dedicated to God, not even to his own people. I remember one day he said, "If I see something wrong, deviating from Islamic values and principles, even if the whole country said it was right and we had to do it, I would say, no, all by myself." So he doesn't care whether people like him or don't like him. He just sees God and that's it. It's very hard for this country to understand his views. He was more beneficial to society—human society as a whole, not only his country—than any other leader in the world. If they realized his views about humanity . . . I know the view here is totally different. But he always warned us. He said, "If today the Prophet Jesus—peace be upon him—rose from his grave, or if he came down from the sky (we believe he never died), he would be surprised at what kind of people his followers are."

Q:     You told me earlier that you did not wear the *hejab* before the Iranian revolution.

PARI:   That's right. I was raised in a traditional Muslim family. I prayed and fasted, but not all the time. I wasn't a liberal or a feminist, but I didn't wear the *hejab*. When I came to the United States as a student, I was about twenty years old, and I started to study about Islam.

Q:     Here? You studied Islam and started wearing the *hejab* here?

PARI:   Yes. Because in our country we didn't have enough information, and I was a young person. I wasn't in the university environment to become familiar with Dr. Shariati's work. [Ali Shariati is a well-known Islamic scholar and intellectual.] I didn't even know of him before I came to this country. So I started to read Dr. Shariati's books here. Meanwhile, the revolution happened, and I found out that as a Muslim woman, if I wanted to maintain my standards, I had to wear the *hejab*—not because my mother did but as a part of my faith. So I started to wear it when I went back home, before the revolution.

Q:     But you began to regain your Islamic faith here, in America?

PARI:   Yes. When I came here I studied, and I got in touch with the Muslim community, which had a great impact on me, especially Dr. Shariati. I owe most of my information and faith to him. He had such a great impact on my life. He changed me. And then the revolution came and Imam Khomeini. I realized I had to wear the *hejab*. I had to accept it. So I changed totally.

FIGURE 36. Iranian Jews gathered for
*tish'a be*-Av (ninth day of the Hebrew month
Av), in remembrance of the destruction
of the First and Second Temples in
Jerusalem by the Babylonians and Romans.
Hillel Council, Beverly Hills, July 1988.

## Jews

The Iranian revolution brought a twenty-five-hundred-year history to a close for the Jews who left their Persian homeland for America. After the Babylonians' destruction of the First Temple in Jerusalem in 586 B.C. and the subsequent Jewish exodus, many Jews traveled to the region encompassed by present-day Iraq and Iran. When the fortunes of competing empires shifted and the Persian king Cyrus the Great took control of Palestine, the Jews were allowed to return to Jerusalem. Most, however, either unable or unwilling to take advantage of this opportunity, remained in their new homelands as traders and craftsmen. One of the earliest mentions of Jewish life in Persia is provided in the biblical Book of Esther, which forms the basis for Purim, one of the most festive holidays in the Jewish calendar.

Like many Middle Eastern Jews, the Jews of Iran are collectively known as *mizrahim* (of the East), some tracing their descent to the large Jewish community expelled from Spain in 1492 that subsequently dispersed and settled throughout Southern Europe, Turkey, and the Arab world. Like all their coreligionists, the Iranian Jews follow the Halacha (codified Jewish law) as well as a common Sephardic religious liturgy, to which they brought minor variants related to Jewish Iranian literary traditions and the melodic influences of Persian music.

In Iran the major Jewish populations are concentrated in urban areas including Tehran, Shiraz, Esfahan, Hamadan, Yazd, Kashan, Kermanshah, Mashad, and other provincial cities. Sizable numbers of Jews also resided in Uremieh, Sanandaj, Bijar, and other towns and villages in Iranian Kurdistan. Engaged in farming or commerce, Iranian Kurdish Jews spoke Neo-Aramaic (like the Assyrian Christians of the region) and maintained traditional Kurdish dress and customs. Over the years, many migrated to the larger cities, especially Tehran, where they adopted an urban Persian lifestyle.

The safety and prosperity of Iranian Jews fluctuated according to the reigning religious faith (from Zoroastrianism to Islam) and politics. With the coming of Islam to Iran, special taxes were instituted on all non-Muslims. Although Jews and other minority religions with sacred texts were given the right to practice their faith, they have sometimes been persecuted or pressured to convert to Islam. Riots against Jews in the capital city of Tehran, for instance, took place as recently as 1922.

The Iranian Jewish section was coauthored by Jonathan Friedlander.

The enthronement of Reza Shah in Iran in 1925 had positive repercussions for Jews and other minorities as the newly self-appointed king undermined the Muslim clergy's secular authority. The tax on non-Muslims was banned, as were dress codes and restrictions on residence, education, and employment for non-Muslims. No longer confined to ghettos, Jews began entering universities in large numbers. During the Iranian oil boom, many expanded their range and power in the business world.

Despite such progress, the opportunity for Jews and other minorities to advance under the Pahlavi dynasty was clearly limited. Jews rarely attained top academic or research posts in the universities. Certain governmental positions were reserved by constitutional decree for Shi'i Muslims. Even in the bazaars, where Jews were a significant presence, Muslim merchants rarely invited their Jewish counterparts to drink tea. After 1948 Jews were increasingly identified with Israel and hence considered politically suspect.

Over twenty-five centuries, the mainstream Iranian culture exerted a significant influence on the Jews. Like Muslims, Iranian Jews made pilgrimages to local (mostly Jewish) shrines and sometimes sacrificed animals on important religious occasions. Like members of other traditional societies, many arranged marriages for their children, and many more played significant roles in their children's choice of spouses. Many Jews adopted the Muslim practice of refusing their unmarried daughters the freedom to date. Jewish first and often last names, moreover, were indistinguishable from those of Muslims in the surrounding community. Other Iranian influences included an emphasis on personal and family status.

One traditional practice of Iranian Jews appears to echo Shi'i rituals of self-flagellation that commemorate historic tragedies. During the Passover meal (Seder), Iranians strike other members of the family with scallions when the Hebrew word *dayenu* is read. At this signal, diners leap up and—in remembrance of Jewish bondage—family members chase each other around the table, playfully whipping whoever falls within reach.

Rabbi Yedidya Shofet, with sixty years of service to Iran's Jews as the chief rabbi of Tehran, is now the dean of Iranian Jewry in Los Angeles. Although his speeches were closely scrutinized by SAVAK, the Shah's secret police, he and other leaders of the minority communities were invited to meet the king twice annually, on the occasion of the Shah's birthday and during the Iranian New Year holiday. Three years before the revolution, the rabbi, sensing troubles ahead for Jews in Iran, advised his coreligionists to leave the country. When the Ayatollah Khomeini took power, the rabbi—like other citizens—had no recourse but to support the new regime.

FIGURE 37    Iranian Jews during Sukkot, a harvest holiday of
thanksgiving commemorating the wandering of the ancient Hebrews
in the Sinai wilderness during their Exodus. The *sukkah*, as depicted
here, is a temporary makeshift structure with a roof of leafy boughs
erected near a home or synagogue to symbolize this sojourn.
Encino, October 1989.

Uncertain about their safety in the looming turmoil of the Iranian revolution, many Jews decided to leave Iran. Those with foresight departed with most of their life's savings intact. Those who emigrated after the revolution were not always as fortunate. Some lost their businesses and assets to unscrupulous Muslim partners and government confiscation. Many immigrants went to Los Angeles and New York; some ended up in Chicago and San Francisco. Others went to Israel. A number of those who stayed in Iran were accused of political and Zionist activities and executed.

Before the 1979 Islamic revolution, the number of Iranian Jews in the Los Angeles area was in the hundreds. By 1990 the community claimed nearly 30,000 people, or more than a third of the pre-revolutionary Jewish population of Iran. The San Fernando Valley and the West Side have the largest concentration of Iranian Jews.

Although Los Angeles has a well-established, multifaceted Jewish community, Iranian Jews have not become part of it in expected ways. They have established only minimal contacts with the social service agencies that are the backbone of the community because most have not required the financial assistance and support needed by other Jewish immigrants, especially the Soviet Jews (though more recent immigrants, less affluent, have sought medical aid). Nor have they affiliated themselves with Jewish-American political groups. Even though many have relatives in Israel, they have only begun to form ties with the large Israeli population in Los Angeles. On many occasions Iranian and Israeli Jews have found themselves competitors, especially in the lucrative clothing industry.

On the whole, the Iranian Jews have kept to themselves, preferring the familiarity of their own social networks and Persian cultural traditions. They celebrate the Persian New Year and have sponsored gala events featuring noted Iranian singers. Like other ethnic and religious minorities, they fear that their children, as they grow up in America, will abandon their Jewish faith and Iranian culture.

These immigrants are largely self-employed. Many have college degrees, and those with graduate or professional credentials are often successful physicians, dentists, lawyers, engineers, and financiers. Most Jews are members of the middle and upper classes.

Much of the visible Iranian Jewish business activity—in retailing and real estate—is centered in the garment district of downtown Los Angeles. Another concentration of economic enterprise is the Pico-Fairfax area. Entrepreneurial efforts range from jewelry stores to major real estate developments. Some Iranian Jews have been successful in these ventures with no knowledge of English.

The Jewish Iranian community's self-reliance and independence carries

FIGURE 38. Passover Seder, a ceremonial meal served on the first and second evenings of the week-long Passover celebration, during which the Exodus of the Israelites from Egypt is recounted in both word and symbol. Family members here are striking each other with scallions, a distinctly Jewish Iranian tradition. Hollywood Hills, 1991.

over into the religious sphere. Lacking, until recently, permanent places of worship, Iranian Jewish congregations have held all-day Yom Kippur services in a hall in the UCLA student union building, weekly Sabbath rites in a local theater, and smaller observances in a West Side Hillel library. During a recent Passover, Iranian Jews met for an official social function at a Scottish Rite Masonic Temple, one floor above a corporate sales meeting. In Iran the members of the Jewish community would have visited friends and relatives during this holiday. But in Los Angeles the distance between homes is so great that they decided on a central meeting place and a communal form of socializing.

The establishment of Iranian synagogues focused the cultural and religious activities of Iranian Jews. Although the Iranian-founded synagogues have not identified themselves along the denominational lines common to American Jewry, the two largest Iranian synagogues, the Nessah Educational and Cultural Center in Santa Monica and the Valley Cultural Center in Reseda, are both nominally rooted in Orthodox Judaism. The newer Santa Monica site includes a school, a synagogue, and an office building. The Reseda complex is a single large building that houses a prayer hall, office, and multipurpose rooms. On the street no outside sign or symbol informs the passerby that the site is Jewish. Other places of worship attended by Iranian Jews include Ohel Moshe and Torat Chaim, both Orthodox synagogues, and the conservative Sephardic Temple Tifereth Israel and Sinai Temple, both located on Wilshire Boulevard on the outskirts of Beverly Hills.

Perhaps even more than synagogues, Iranian Jewish schools are keys to religious and ethnic preservation. In Iran the Islamic government has limited both the number of Jewish schools and what is taught about Judaism in public schools and has further suppressed the teaching and use of Hebrew by insisting that the Old Testament be taught in Persian. Although the situation in Los Angeles is less ominous, Iranian Jews there nonetheless face the problem of providing religious education for their children. Many have chosen private schools to gain their children an edge in the business world. Other Iranian Jewish youngsters are enrolled in Beverly Hills High School and other public schools and, in lesser numbers, in non-Iranian Jewish day schools. A relatively small but growing number of students, however, have enrolled in parochial schools affiliated with synagogues that offer both a secular and a religious education. The challenge for these synagogues and parochial schools is to make religious education relevant and affordable for the young couples who are themselves returning to the faith in increasing numbers or want to nurture their children's unique Jewish Iranian identity.

This task is complicated, according to Rabbi Chaim Seidler-Feller of the Hillel Council at UCLA, because the younger generation, having generally received little or no Jewish education, has developed "a rather cynical attitude toward their elders' religion combined with an old style scientific positivism." This generation gap has widened further because "young Persians raised in Los Angeles no longer speak the same language as their parents, both literally and figuratively."

"In Iran, Jews had no choice but to identify as Jews since there was no possibility of ethnic or religious neutrality," Seidler-Feller asserts. This identity protected them from the actual and potential threats posed by Islamic overseers. Even nonreligious people were active members of a unified community. "Having come to America and confronting modernity with its complex choices," he continues, "the community may not have the wherewithal to withstand the assimilationist pressures."

"In Iran," confirms Yedidya's son Rabbi David Shofet, "no one talked about change in our community. But here in America there is much demand for change, so much demand to be like Americans."

FIGURE 39. A Queen Esther look-alike contest (subsequently won by the girl in the foreground) held during the Purim celebration at the Sinai Temple in Westwood. The holiday celebrates the deliverance of the Jews from a massacre plotted by their archenemy, the Persian prime minister Haman. Esther, King Ahasuerus's Jewish queen, interceded with her husband to allow the Jews to defend themselves. March 1990.

FIGURE 40. Hanukkah dance at the Nessah Educational and Cultural Center in Santa Monica. This winter holiday commemorates the victory of the Maccabees over Antiochus of Syria in 165 B.C. and the rededication of the desecrated Temple of Jerusalem. This victory temporarily stemmed the assimilationist tide of Hellenism in Judea.

*Interview*

A twenty-year-old Jewish woman tells of her escape from Iran to Pakistan in 1986. Her sister aids in the descriptions.

WOMAN: I wanted to leave my country, but we are Jewish, and the government wouldn't let us come out with our parents. So my parents left legally, but I had to come illegally.

WOMAN'S SISTER: The government doesn't let everyone out together; my sister had to stay in Iran so that my parents could get a visa. They think that if they give the whole family a visa, none of them will come back. They want you to come back, right? They don't want you to come to the United States and stay.

WOMAN: So I promised them that I'd stay in Iran, and my parents would leave and come back. There are smugglers who take care of everything. So we talked to one, and he said that I had to take the plane or bus to Zahedan, a small city near the Iran-Pakistan border.

RON KELLEY: When you want to leave Iran like this, how do you find a smuggler?

WOMAN: I don't know what to say, but Jewish people know.

WOMAN'S SISTER: They know among themselves who is good, who is bad. They have had experience. They let each other know.

WOMAN: Yes, they know. Muslim people have their own smugglers. Some wanted to send their boys out of Iran because of the war; they used a different organization. My uncle referred us to a smuggler. We talked to him and decided on a plan, to come out through Zahedan.

Q:       Did anyone warn you of the risks in leaving Iran illegally? The dangers?

WOMAN'S SISTER:    They were told that if the authorities found them, they had to say they were escaping without their parents' permission because they wanted to study. They were not to say anything about their parents. If caught, they would probably be taken to prison for a few days. The rabbi or someone would have to come and promise that they wouldn't try to leave the country again. And they were told that if the police chased them, the smugglers wouldn't stop and the police would start shooting. I remember my dad's saying that when they were in Zahedan, they saw officers shooting at someone who had speeded up. They were so worried.

WOMAN:    One of my old friends was killed. They shot at her and the smuggler.

Q:       What did you pay these smugglers?

WOMAN'S SISTER:    Six hundred thousand tomans. That's a lot. It's about six thousand dollars.

Q:       So right from the start you trusted these smugglers?

WOMAN:    You have to. There's no other way.

Q:       Is all the money paid in advance?

WOMAN:    You have to pay the first time you talk. All of it.

WOMAN'S SISTER:    Can you imagine? Giving your daughter to some stranger! Especially for Iranians—you know how they are. Connected, close.

WOMAN:    I was afraid the first time I saw him. So ugly! So serious! He had to be serious. It was dangerous.

Q:       So how did you prepare to leave? Did you pack your clothes, say good-bye to friends?

WOMAN:    We couldn't say good-bye to anybody. We didn't have permission to let anybody know. I just had a purse. We had no extra clothes, nothing. We were supposed to pretend we were going to see the sights for two or three days. I went with my parents to Zahedan so that if anybody asked, I could say I was there just to buy some folk dresses. The smuggler said

I could not bring anything. He told me to buy one of the dresses the Zahedani wear. So my parents and I went to Zahedan, to the bazaar outside. We walked around till night. The smuggler had said he'd come with a pickup truck. In Zahedan they use that as a taxi. So we waited till it got dark, and a man came and picked us up. He pretended he was a taxi driver. He drove us around the area, because if they find out there was a plan, you go to prison. After about fifteen minutes, we were in the desert. We couldn't see anything. I was so afraid. But I was laughing. We came to a house with a single room, a low ceiling. There was nothing in that room. And the smuggler said, "You have to stay here until my group lets me pass the border."

Q:    You were alone at this point? Was your family still with you?

WOMAN'S SISTER:    My parents had left. But there were three other young people in the house.

Q:    You were going as a group? All relatives?

WOMAN'S SISTER:    Yes. They were all relatives.

WOMAN:    So we stayed there, and the smuggler said, "You have to buy a special outfit for the boys." We were two girls and two boys. We had to look like Zahedani people. So we hid there and slept until morning, when the smuggler told us they still weren't ready. We had no food or drink, nothing. And the water was so bad! The food, so dirty! We were sick just looking at it. We didn't eat anything. And the smuggler asked, "Why didn't you eat?" We couldn't say anything. It was so depressing. It was summer. It was hot. There weren't any trees. They had built this house as a way station in the middle of the desert.

Q:    The smuggler went off and left you there?

WOMAN:    Yes. But another boy from the group of smugglers was with us.

Q:    Were these Jewish people smuggling you?

WOMAN:    No. They were Muslim. Baluchis. We waited there until seven o'clock; we sat on the floor and looked at the walls. The boy told us that when the truck came, we had to be ready. We would have to run. And when we got in the truck, we'd have to lie down in the back.

FIGURE 41. Iranian Jews reading from the Torah scroll containing the Pentateuch, or first five books of Scripture. Hillel Council, Beverly Hills, 1988.

| | |
|---|---|
| WOMAN'S SISTER: | There was nothing on the bottom of the truck. So they lay there on plain metal. |
| WOMAN: | We were lying down, our heads hitting the metal hard because the driver was speeding. He was flying. Up and down. Up and down. |
| WOMAN'S SISTER: | He didn't want to use the main roads because the police could get him. |
| WOMAN: | There were a lot of stones there. |
| WOMAN'S SISTER: | The smugglers had set out stones to mark their way. |
| WOMAN: | When we got to the mountains, the smuggler said we could sit up. The side panels of the truck were very low, and we could have fallen out. He said we had to sit carefully, gripping the side panels a particular way. "If you fall off, we can't come back."<br><br>We drove from seven till midnight on dirt roads. When we got to the mountains, we had to walk for two hours. Then we slept till five in the morning. It was so cold! We had no blankets, no warm clothing, no food, no drink. Nothing. They made a fire with stones. Have you seen that? They hit two stones together to make a fire. Then they brought wood. Then the smuggler said he had to leave to get the others, so he left us; he came back at eight in the morning. We were in the mountains, hiding; we could see the police guards nearby, but they couldn't see us. We couldn't even talk.<br><br>Later, we came out of the mountains and waited for another truck with another driver. We drove till two in the morning, and it was so hot that my jeans stuck to my leg. I was crying because it was so painful. We got to another house and stayed there. It was strange; how did they know where it was in the desert? |
| Q: | Did you have access to water? |
| WOMAN: | Yes, but the water was thick, like jello. |
| Q: | Like jello? |
| WOMAN: | Yes. When you poured the water into your hand, it was like yogurt, but dirty. It was possible to get malaria. We had to get shots in Iran before we came out. I know a woman who got malaria in Pakistan. |

We left the second house and drove till late and came to another house. Because we were sick, sweating, we had to stay there. Then we drove again all the next day and came to a coffee shop. The driver gave some money to another man so he wouldn't report us. The coffee shop was in Pakistan. We stayed there for two hours, but it was still dangerous. There was a hiding place between the stairs and the kitchen. We had to stay there. We couldn't go out. They brought us some rice, but there were signs of mice in it. After we got out of Iran, we were in pain for a month. Our backs hurt; our hands were blue. My back ached so much that I couldn't lie on it. But we were happy.

FIGURE 42. Armenians gather at a
memorial to the Armenian genocide by
the Turks. Montebello, April 1989.

## Armenians

The kingdoms of the ancient Armenians, an Indo-European group, included parts of what is today northern Iran, where Armenians have lived for centuries. Most accounts of the Armenian contributions to Persian history, however, begin in 1604, when the Iranian Safavid king, Shah Abbas, at war with the Ottoman Empire, embarked on a scorched-earth policy to hinder Turkish advancement and forcibly deported thousands of Armenians living in and around the city of Julfah, in Azerbaijan. The Armenians, admired by the Shah as craftsmen, traders, and builders, were relocated across the river from the Iranian capital city of Esfahan and allowed to practice their faith. (Armenians note with great pride that they were the first nation to accept Christianity as a state religion.) Armenians in the self-contained town near Esfahan called New Julfah were granted a degree of self-government and monopolies in a few trades. They developed commercial links to India and prospered despite sporadic religious persecution and economic exploitation under later regimes. Trade between Iran and Russia during the seventeenth and eighteenth centuries, for instance, was conducted mostly by Armenians.

In the late 1700s, many Armenian merchants moved to Tehran, which had become the new capital. Armenian exiles escaping from the post–World War I genocide in Turkey and refugees from the Stalinist-era purges in the Soviet Union have given Tehran the largest concentration of Armenians in the country. Although Armenians rarely held important government or military posts in Iran, they were never confined to ghettos like the Jews. A few Armenians have become celebrities in pan-Iranian culture, including Viguen, the "Persian Elvis Presley," arguably the most successful male singer in Iranian history, and, more recently, Rafi Khatchetorian, a comic and television personality who gained renown in Los Angeles.

Within the Armenian community in Iran, however, tensions sometimes developed between those whose history in Persia went back centuries and newer arrivals, particularly those from the Soviet Union, who were often perceived as too blunt, demanding, and aggressive.

In 1944 the Soviet Union began to allow the repatriation of Armenians from Iran. Many Armenian peasants sold their belongings and made their way to Tehran as the first step in leaving the Islamic country. When the repatriation project was suddenly canceled, however, the peasants found themselves trapped in the capital city. Living in poverty on the outskirts of Tehran, these Armenians were distinctly different in social class and culture from the Armenian doctors, engineers, merchants, and other professionals

In the Middle East, life doesn't stop after six o'clock. Shops are open, cabarets are open, restaurants are open, people are in the streets. They eat, laugh, talk. And when Armenians come here, they feel they're in a cultural vacuum because after six o'clock all the streets are dead. And the newcomer feels cooped up in his home. Nobody comes. Nobody goes. The American next door doesn't come out. He says hello but won't sit with the Armenian and drink coffee or tea on the front lawn. The Armenian thinks that Americans carry their dogs around with them because they are lonely. They have no guests.

Let me give you an example. When I came to America in the 1950s, it was Thanksgiving time. An American friend took me home, and everybody gathered for dinner. Now, in Iran there is a holiday called Thirteenth Out [Sizdah Bidar]. It's like Halloween. Everybody leaves town for the day. They go picnicking out of town. So I asked my friend after two weeks, "How come nobody comes back?" And he said, "What do you mean, nobody comes back?" I said, "Well, they went out of town on Thanksgiving day, and they should come back." He said, "Well, they are back." I said, "Where are they?"

That's what bothers Iranian Armenians. So many come to America. If he is fortunate enough to come to Glendale, Los Angeles, Chicago, or Boston, where there are Armenians, he can come to the clubs and feel better. Alone in the city, he is miserable to the point of suicide. Money troubles don't bother Armenians. We'll work anywhere. We'll earn money. It's the lonely American society that makes Armenians depressed. They say it wasn't always like this in America.

whose families had lived in Tehran for generations. Uneducated and provincial, they were disparaged by some indigenous Armenians of Tehran as "the Texas people." The Tehrani newcomers were quick to adapt to their new economic milieu, however, developing successful trades such as tire recapping, plumbing, and, in more recent times under Islamic restrictions, bootlegging alcohol. The gulf between the newer arrivals and Armenians long established in Tehran has narrowed over the years.

When Iranian minorities began to feel threatened by the Islamic revolution in the late 1970s, thousands of Iran's 150,000 Armenians decided to emigrate. Those who were wealthy, some linked by business and other associations to the Shah's government, often managed to leave quickly. Many came to the United States, and a significant number eventually settled in the conservative, largely Anglo, middle-class city of Glendale, where a small community of Armenians from Iran had established itself immediately after World War II to take advantage of economic and educational opportunities. Like Armenians elsewhere in the United States, these earlier immigrants to Glendale established a strong cultural, economic, and political network that later groups of immigrants, particularly the affluent, quickly joined.

The Armenian Iranians who arrived in America during the late 1970s, like Iranians from other ethnic groups who arrived early in the revolutionary period, often preserved their wealth. With exchange rates favorable, they were able to pay cash for luxurious homes in the most prestigious areas of Glendale. Successive waves of immigration from Iran brought less affluent Armenian Iranians; the most recent refugees have often arrived with nothing.

By 1991 nearly 10,000 of the 26,000 children in the Glendale public schools were of Armenian descent and from Iran. (This figure does not include students in three private Armenian schools in the area.) The estimate of the Armenian Iranian population of Glendale based on such figures is 30,000. The ability of the Armenian Iranians to build a firm economic and social foundation for their lives in the city has apparently attracted other Iranian immigrants to Glendale as well. By 1991 nearly four hundred non-Armenian Iranian children were also enrolled in the Glendale public schools.

This dramatic influx had a noticeable impact on the city of Glendale. Initially Glendale residents resented the soaring prices of homes and the new arrivals' purchase of businesses and business property throughout the city. Armenian professionals and entrepreneurs became deeply involved in contracting, architecture, engineering, and real estate. Armenian Iranian children were often taunted at school and suffered physical as well as verbal attacks during the Iran hostage crisis. Many American adults in the area were also suspicious of the Armenians' practice of Christianity in Iran. Later, less affluent, less sophisticated refugees alienated Glendale residents, whether Iranian or not, in other ways, particularly if the newcomers became welfare recipients.

Tensions between Armenian immigrants and non-Armenians in the city have surfaced in other areas. The city of Glendale has been sued, for instance, by Armenians accusing it of favoritism and discrimination in selecting project contractors. Non-Armenians commonly complain about the lack of Armenian involvement in community affairs, particularly volunteer work. An Iranian-born former mayor, raised in Glendale, is cited as an anomaly. Some critics resent the Armenians' ethnic insularity and the ostentatious wealth of some Armenians from Iran.

Though families inevitably suffered when the male heads of households left for extended visits back to Iran to tend to unresolved business matters, Armenian Iranians have generally experienced less trauma in resettling in America than other Armenians of the diaspora. Unlike the Lebanese Armenians who had been contained in West Beirut ghettos, or Soviet Armenians who knew how to function only in a communist system, Armenian Iranians arriving here were usually both economically solvent and, because of westernization under the Shah, familiar with Western culture and business practices.

The relatively great per capita wealth of the Armenian Iranians represents the biggest difference between the Iranians and other Armenians. This has contributed to the stereotype among other Armenians that the Iranian immigrants are exceptionally conscious of fashion, status, and class. Some non-Iranian Armenians complain that those from Iran are aloof. In the school system, merely being from Iran—rather than from Soviet Armenia or other places—can enhance a student's status. This class consciousness manifests itself at intra-Iranian as well as intra-Armenian levels. Some Armenian Iranians long established in Glendale have complained to the local school board about the Armenian Iranian refugees flooding the city's school system and lowering its lofty standards.

Some differences between Armenian Iranians and other Armenians are rooted in Persian culture. Armenian Iranians—particularly women—borrow from spoken Persian an almost song-like inflection that is not present in the Armenian spoken by other groups. One of the behavioral differences is the Persian tradition of courtesy called *taarof* (ritualized sweet talk). Iranians often feel that other Armenians in the United States are far less hospitable and polite than they are, too blunt in speaking their minds, and rude and antisocial.

FIGURE 43. Services held at St. Mary's
Apostolic Church in Glendale for earth-
quake victims in then–Soviet Armenia.
December 1988.

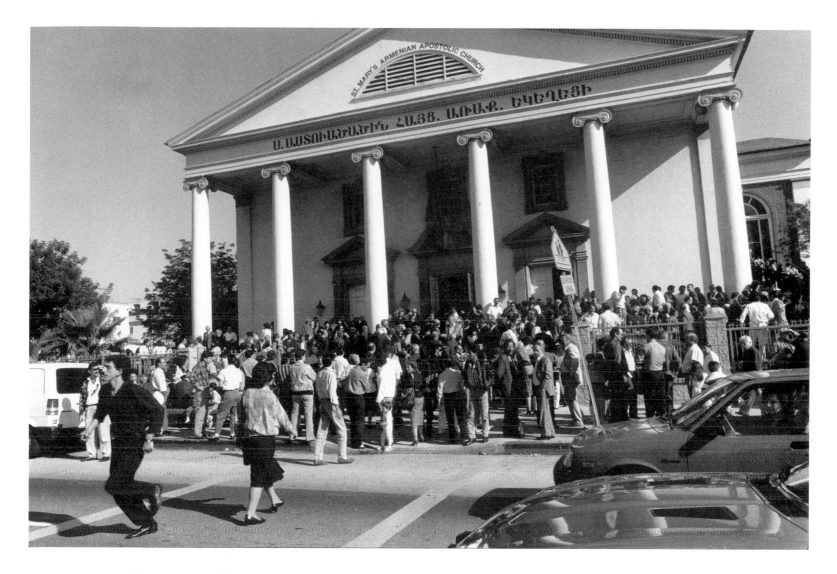

FIGURE 44. Congregation in front of
St. Mary's Apostolic Church in Glendale.
1988.

Many well-to-do Armenians in Los Angeles look back on Iran fondly. They are nostalgic, not for the Islamic environment, but for their own comfortable lives. Like other affluent Iranians, many had servants to take care of their children and homes. With a return to Iran possible since the end of the Iran-Iraq war, many wealthier Armenians have traveled to the homeland to investigate the business and social climate there.

Although small numbers of Armenian Iranians are Protestant or Catholic, the overwhelming majority belong to the Armenian Apostolic Church. The church has its own supreme leader, bishops, and doctrine. The Armenian church is closely tied to the Armenian national identity; both are sources of communal strength in the international population, particularly in a Muslim environment. In the Armenian psyche, the notion of being Armenian and anything other than Christian is a contradiction in terms.

In Glendale, St. Mary's Armenian Apostolic Church is the religious hub of the Armenian Iranian community, particularly on Sunday afternoons. The church, host to a steady stream of weddings, baptisms, and religious ceremonies, has also functioned as an emergency center, for relief efforts following the 1988 earthquake in Soviet Armenia, for example. The church itself symbolizes the transplanted Armenian nation and offers the community a place to chat about common hometowns, mutual concerns, and shared memories. Every Sunday large numbers of men, even the non-religious, gather outside the church in groups while the women lead children inside for Mass.

One of the earliest Armenian associations in Los Angeles, the Iran Armenian Society, was founded in October 1956 by thirty Armenian Iranians who sought social and emotional support from one another in the new country. The society was established to raise money for the Armenian community in Iran as well as to hold dances, picnics, and social programs in Los Angeles. By 1963 all the money raised by the society was put into programs here.

The society functioned out of a rented building in Hollywood until 1980, when it purchased a small two-story structure in Glendale. With eight hundred official members, it sponsors a choir group of seventy-five people, dance classes taught by a Russian Armenian émigré, and basketball and soccer teams. The society has an Armenian language library and holds senior citizens' meetings as well as weekend classes in Armenian language and history attended by five hundred children.

When Americans were held hostage in revolutionary Iran, angry Glendale vandals responded to the Iran Armenian Society sign on their building by scrawling "Go home" and "We're going to burn your place" on the

FIGURE 45. *Opposite, above:* Mass at St. Mary's Apostolic Church in Glendale. 1988.

FIGURE 46. *Opposite:* Baptism at St. Mary's Apostolic Church in Glendale. 1988.

FIGURE 47. Armenian dance class at a church hall in Montebello.

walls. On one occasion, a rock was thrown through a window. The time had come, board members agreed, to change their name to the Armenian Society of Los Angeles and to open their doors to the broader Armenian community.

Homenetman, a pan-Armenian organization, has existed in Los Angeles since the World War I era. Basically a sports and cultural network, Homenetman has twelve branches throughout the western United States. Most of the Glendale chapter's 1,500 formal members are Iranian-born. Nine hundred children are involved in Homenetman activities, half of them as Boy Scouts and Girl Scouts whose Sunday morning flag ceremonies pay homage to the United States, the Homenetman organization, and Armenia. Homenetman both preserves Armenian consciousness and helps children adapt to the American environment. The scouting organizations in particular provide a link between life in Iran, where many children were involved in scouting, and life in the United States.

Unlike the Iranian-oriented Armenian Society of Los Angeles, Homenetman was actively committed to the establishment of a free Armenia, independent of the Soviet Union. This emphasis further distances Armenian Iranian children from the concept of an authentic Iranian homeland.

In recent years, Armenian Iranians have identified with the city of Glendale, establishing a firm socioeconomic base for their community there. Although many adults are concerned about conditions in Iran, the younger generation's last day-to-day links to Iran are Persian pop music and the occasional Persian words that have found their way into the young people's colloquial Armenian. World events, however, have an inevitable impact on all generations. With the breakup of the Soviet Union, hostilities between the newly independent Armenian nation and Muslim Azerbaijan, just north of Iran, have distanced many local Armenians even further from their Iranian homeland.

FIGURE 48. Gathering in memory of the Baha'is executed in Iran in the wake of the Islamic revolution. Baha'i Center, Los Angeles.

## Baha'is

On December 14, 1981, after Islamic officials confiscated the Baha'i ceme-tery, Mahmoud Madjzoob, chairman and one of nine elected members of the National Baha'i Assembly, held an emergency meeting with other Iranian leaders in a home in Tehran. Everyone at the meeting was arrested that night, taken to jail, and never heard from again.

Shokooh Madjzoob, Mahmoud's wife, sitting in the Los Angeles Baha'i Center, recalls how her husband, one of over a hundred Baha'is, many of them the group's leaders, was executed by the Islamic government.

"We weren't even told they killed him," she says. "They didn't even give us the bodies. But after three days they came to my place and confiscated all our property, everything we had. Even my child's toys. My son had had a teddy bear since he was born. And he was hiding it, fearing they would take that too. I still have this teddy bear. Every night he talked to it of what had happened to us. It was winter when they took everything; it was very cold. We didn't have a car. Every night my son had a fever. He said he had pain in his foot. I thought he was complaining . . . Then one day I saw that he couldn't walk. I couldn't go to the doctor because we didn't have a car—they took our car—and I couldn't call because even our telephone was monitored. And no one would help me for fear of being accused. I didn't know what to do in the cold weather with my sick child. Then one of the Baha'is came and helped me. They took X rays, and the doctor told me my son's hand too was becoming paralyzed, because he was in shock.

"The authorities had taken everything we had. They gave us a room and several pots, and they told me, if you need something, call us. And every day they came and asked, why didn't you call us? Where do you get money to eat? Where do you buy your things? They thought I had some other source of money. They wanted to take it.

"But I should say that many of my Muslim friends helped me too at that time. They were not afraid. They helped me a lot. One day I opened the door and saw all kinds of food! Meat, fish . . . You couldn't find such things at that time in Iran. All kinds of food. Some really helped us. But my son was . . . because of his father. And because of the confiscation. Children are attached to things. One day they came to take my son. They said a Baha'i child is not a legal child. He is illegal. That was the night I decided to escape."

More than any other minority group, Baha'is have borne the brunt of Islamic rage since the Iranian revolution. Some were executed. Others were stripped of their jobs. Children were refused access to schools. In addition to executions and assassinations, there were mob actions across the country against those who refused to recant their faith. Baha'i deaths in the revolutionary era eventually numbered over two hundred. Because the regime had confiscated lists of Baha'i members, victims were usually easy to find.

Muslim animosity toward the Baha'is in Iran has deep roots. Jewish and Christian faiths predate Islam and hence are accepted by Muslims as part of the historical lineage of prophets leading to their own—considered the final one—Mohammad. The Baha'i religion, in contrast, was revealed through prophets in the mid 1800s, after the Islamic revelation, and thus the newer faith was condemned as heresy. In the Islamic Republic, Baha'is are considered followers of an illegal, immoral religion. Many Shi'is do not recognize Baha'i marriages and consider the children of such marriages illegitimate. Despite the Baha'i tenet that forbids political activity, in the revolutionary fury against the deposed Shah, Baha'is were widely considered a political, rather than a religious, group. A number of prominent Baha'is, including powerful businessmen and high-ranking appointees of the Shah's overthrown government, became scapegoats.

Many Iranian Muslims are suspicious of Baha'is, considering them a religious front for British and/or Russian imperialism. That the Baha'is had established their religious center in Haifa, Israel, only fuels such suspicions, as does the ability of Baha'is to attract many converts from Western countries. The Baha'is' rejection of all clergy has also been perceived as a direct threat by the Muslim clerical establishment. Baha'is reject all the Islamic charges against them and are eager to explain the history and tenets of their faith.

The Baha'i faith emerged as a messianic movement in 1844, when a young Iranian merchant, Ali Mohammad, challenged Islamic institutions with calls for religious reform and pronounced himself the spiritual *bab* (gate) to prepare followers for a future prophet of God. Originally linked to the tenets of Shi'i Islam, the new faith pulled away as it developed its own creed. Between 1848 and 1852, over three thousand followers of the Bab were executed or assassinated or perished in riots and religious fighting.

In 1863, after the Bab's execution for heresy by Islamic authorities, a second prophet, Baha'u'allah, rose in exile to lead the new religious community. He developed many of the core Baha'i beliefs. Despite a long history of persecution, members of the Baha'i faith today constitute Iran's largest religious minority, with 250,000 members living in both major cities and rural areas.

Baha'is believe in an actively developing religion, shaped by a continual

FIGURE 49. Baha'i picnic in Long Beach.
The banner reflects central Baha'i tenets.
1988.

progression of prophets—religious visionaries from Jesus and Buddha to the most recent, Baha'u'allah, whose teachings Baha'is consider most relevant to the modern world. Like Shi'i Islam, from which it originally developed, the Baha'i faith in Iran has a tradition of martyrdom, from the execution of the Bab and his followers to the many deaths during the Islamic revolution. The theoretical underpinning for this tradition of self-sacrifice is the Baha'i injunction—under penalty of excommunication—that no believer deny the faith, even in the face of death.

Baha'is emphasize the equality of races, sexes, and classes as well as universal education and world peace. They disdain public rituals and religious hierarchy, although they have administrative leaders. They gather on the first day of each of the nineteen Baha'i months for prayer and the reading of sacred texts. Non-Baha'is are not permitted to attend these functions. Alcohol is forbidden to observant members, as is premarital sex. The international Baha'i community blends spiritual and secular affairs and sees its own administrative model as an ideal prototype for world organization.

In Los Angeles, the Baha'i Center is a converted bowling alley at the edge of a predominantly African-American neighborhood. Mayor Tom Bradley's presence as the keynote speaker at the Baha'i Center dedication ceremonies in 1988 suggests the high esteem in which the community has come to be held. As an actively proselytizing faith, the religion continues to explore inroads into the spiritual landscape of America. In Long Beach, for instance, a small group of Persian and American Baha'is picnic regularly at a park, a huge Baha'i banner tied between two trees as a grassroots advertisement.

Weekly Baha'i "firesides" are another function of the faith in Los Angeles. These are meetings held so that interested people can learn about the Baha'i religion and discuss theological questions. Larger gatherings held in the Baha'i Center's main hall range from a Martin Luther King Night to music concerts and a memorial slide show paying homage to Baha'i martyrs killed during the revolutionary upheaval in Iran. All such activities begin with prayers in different languages, from Persian to Samoan, led by members of the diverse Baha'i community.

Iranian Baha'is began arriving in Southern California in substantial numbers in the years preceding the Islamic revolution, after which their influx accelerated. The five to six thousand Iranian Baha'is who currently live in the greater Los Angeles area constitute more than half the total Baha'i community.

To spread the Baha'i faith to all areas of the globe, some American Baha'i leaders encouraged Iranian refugees to settle in countries other than the United States, particularly in the Third World, where few Baha'is live. A

FIGURE 50.   Reception following the
dedication of the new Baha'i Center.
Los Angeles, 1988.

small number of Iranian Baha'is did immigrate to Latin America, remote areas of Canada, and elsewhere, but many of them ultimately made their way to the United States.

Concern that trouble-making agents of the Islamic Republic might infiltrate the Iranian Baha'i community in the United States aroused fear and paranoia. And indeed, Shi'i Muslims' animosity toward Baha'is can be extraordinary. When questioned about Baha'is in Iran, one important Shi'i religious figure in Los Angeles shook his head, saying simply, "Baha'is are animals." During the height of Islamic persecution in Iran, the American Baha'i organization required refugees to document their faith. Often this was impossible, and ultimately a system by which two Baha'is could vouch for a third was instituted. After confirming their identity, Baha'i centers provided refugees and immigrants with financial and cultural support as well as help in dealing with the INS and other bureaucracies. Immediate problems for newcomers usually involved visas, language, and employment.

Not surprisingly, this great influx of the faithful from Iran did not always fit smoothly into the established American Baha'i community. Whereas most American coreligionists tend to be from middle- and working-class backgrounds, many Iranian Baha'is—like most Iranians in America—were from relatively affluent families. Although few would charge the newcomers with racism, they were sometimes accused of slighting others, particularly the African-American members of the broader Baha'i community in Los Angeles. Many Persians seemed to associate African-Americans with a lower standard of living and felt their own identities were rooted elsewhere.

Debates arose whether to discourage the newcomers from maintaining a distinctly Iranian Baha'i subgroup that would, for example, conduct religious gatherings in Persian and thereby exclude others. Many Americans argued that such exclusivity went against the universalist principles of the Baha'i faith. Iranian Baha'is waiting patiently in Los Angeles for conditions in Iran to improve enough for them to return home, however, saw no point in putting their full energies into the local community.

Another difficulty between American Baha'is and the newcomers arose from their different histories and the attendant disagreements about religious responsibilities. When the Iranians first began arriving, many local Baha'is expected these newcomers from the birthplace of the faith to be tempered experts with keen insights into the Baha'i religion. In this regard, the Americans were sometimes sorely disappointed. Most Iranians were Baha'is by birth and did not exhibit the zeal of the American converts. Some Persians were more lax than Americans in observing prohibitions against alcohol and formal marriage regulations. Those from Iran were mostly second-, third-, and fourth-generation Baha'is. They were part of extended Baha'i families, and much of their interest in the Los Angeles Baha'i Center related to the opportunities it afforded for socializing with other Baha'is from Iran—much to the chagrin of non-Iranian Baha'is.

Iranians approach their faith somewhat less zealously and aggressively than American converts. They are more likely to believe that through the long-term grace of God the dreams and goals of Baha'u'allah will eventually be realized. After all, throughout their history in Iran, they usually faced prohibitions—and hence were socialized—against religious proselytizing.

American Baha'is, in contrast, tend to be activists. As recent converts, they are often the only family members to accept the faith. They go to Baha'i meetings, not to socialize with old Baha'i families, but to address specific business in the community. Americans tend to be more concerned with organizing, registering members, fulfilling their creeds to the letter, and seeking to convert others. American Baha'is typically perceive themselves as a dynamically expanding community governed by rules and laws rather than as a passive sacred community governed by God.

In Iran most converts to the Baha'i faith came from Muslim families, though Jews and Zoroastrians also converted in smaller numbers. The animosity toward Baha'is in the Muslim community was often so great that some Shi'i families completely cut off any member who converted to the Baha'i faith or married into it. In contrast, Jews and Zoroastrians who became involved with the Baha'is were more likely to maintain relationships with their families. In Los Angeles, this has translated into a limited relationship between Iranian Baha'is and Iranian Jews. Although the two faiths have no formal and official relationship, a number of Jews have familial and, by extension, business links to the Baha'i community. Tensions sometimes arise when Baha'is attend Jewish functions and vice versa. Relations can be particularly strained by struggles over the religious environment to be provided for the children of mixed marriages.

The tensions and difficulties experienced by Iranian Baha'is entering the U.S. Baha'i community have generally eased as they have become acclimated. Iranian and American Baha'is have increasingly come to focus on their common religious interests. Although the Persians' habit of holding carnivals and social gatherings as fund-raisers for the faith was weakly endorsed in earlier times by many in the American Baha'i community, now such activities are recognized as valuable. Moreover, that four of the nine members of the local Baha'i Center's Assembly are now Persian exemplifies Iranian participation in the broader Baha'i community.

FIGURE 51. Assyrian folk dancers at the Assyrian Community Center in North Hollywood.

## Assyrians

Assyrians trace their ancestral roots, language, and culture to the ancient land of Mesopotamia, between the Tigris and Euphrates rivers, a region now largely in Iraq. Even people who know nothing of Assyrian history may recognize the Assyrian icon, a winged bull with the head of a king—usually sculpted atop huge city walls and temples—as one of today's enduring symbols for ancient civilization.

Assyrians speak a modern form of Syriac, a branch of the ancient Aramaic language. During the time of Christ, Aramaic was the language of major areas of the Middle East, including most of Palestine. When Islam came to the area, many indigenous people were Aramaic-speaking Christians who eventually converted to the new faith and the use of Arabic. Christians who resisted conversion include the ancestors of today's Maronites, Greek Orthodox, Nestorians, and Jacobites. Some Assyrians argue that all such religious groups should claim Assyrian identities, based on common language and ancient histories, but there is little agreement on this matter.

Assyrians have sometimes been known as Nestorians, a term derived from the name of the patriarch of Constantinople who was consecrated in A.D. 428. After a bitter controversy among Christians over the nature of Jesus Christ—in which Nestorius argued that the human and divine natures of Jesus Christ were conjoined but were not a single, unified person—Nestorius was deposed, accused of heresy, and sent into exile. One of the chief theological concerns of the Nestorians, like the earlier Zoroastrians, was the dualism of good and evil. By the Middle Ages, Nestorians were the most widespread Christian church in the region. By the end of the twelfth century, however, with mass conversions to Islam, the faith was in serious decline, and Nestorians were ultimately reduced to small communities in the Iraqi and Persian highlands. Their progeny included peasants from the plains who fled the Mongol invasions of the thirteenth and fourteenth centuries.

In the Middle East today, Assyrians, like Armenians, remain a Christian minority in a predominantly Muslim environment; intermarriage with other Christians in Iran and elsewhere is not uncommon. Unlike Armenians, however, Assyrians are Semites and in modern times are principally associated with the Assyrian (Nestorian) Orthodox Church, the Chaldean Church, and the Syrian Orthodox Church.

Originally members of the Nestorian Church, residing mainly in northern and central Iraq, the Chaldeans became converts to Roman Catholicism in the sixteenth century. The Chaldean Church became one of the

FIGURE 52. Assyrian Boy Scouts and Girl Scouts pledging allegiance to the American and Assyrian flags at the Assyrian Community Center in North Hollywood.

six Uniate branches of the Roman Catholic church in the Middle East, accepting papal supremacy but maintaining local religious customs and traditions.

The Syrian group, sometimes called the Jacobites, took issue with Nestorians over the nature of Jesus Christ, an important theological issue of the time. The Jacobites maintain that the human and divine in the person of Jesus Christ constitute a single, thoroughly unified, nature.

In recent history, along with the Kurds and other minorities, the Assyrians have endured the forcible repression of their language and culture by the region's governments, particularly that of Iraq. In the face of violent struggles with the Kurds over their mutual homeland, other wars, conversions, and Islamic persecution, many generations of Assyrians left their ancestral home. Some made their way to nearby Iranian urban centers; others went to Lebanon or Syria or elsewhere. Small numbers still remain in the central homeland, mainly in the mountainous regions of northern Iraq and northwestern Iran.

An early wave of Assyrian immigration to the United States followed World War I. Assyrians, enlisted by the British as auxiliary troops, also sided with Christian Russia in 1915, so that Muslim Turks and Arabs widely perceived them as traitors in their midst. Although Assyrians had been promised a national homeland, the League of Nations proved unable to fulfill the promise. According to some estimates, up to one-third of the Assyrian population perished in World War I or its aftermath, in massacres paralleling the better-known Armenian genocide.

With the termination of the British Mandate in Iraq in the early 1930s, the Assyrians, who had continued to work with Westerners after the war, were abandoned to the vengeful Muslim Kurds and Arabs, who burned and pillaged Assyrian villages. Many Assyrians remain bitter to this day, holding the British colonizers—with their intrigues, manipulations, and ultimate betrayal—responsible for the tragedies that befell them.

Part of the day-to-day minority experience was the humiliation that could result from being recognized as a Christian in Iraq and Iran, particularly in rural areas. Iranian minorities are sometimes referred to as *najes*, a Persian term used by Shi'i Muslims to describe all non-Muslims as ritually unclean, religiously dirty and polluting. George, a middle-aged member of the Assyrian Community Center in North Hollywood, remembers the insults he faced growing up in the Iranian town of Uremieh: "I took a taxi. I asked the driver how much for the ride. He knew I was a Christian. He said ten tomans, whatever. So I held out the money to him. He said, put it here. When I put it next to him, he blew a puff of air at it. He believed now that it was clean, and he put it into his pocket . . . When I was eighteen years old, we didn't have water in the house. There was a place where everyone went to get it. I went over with a bucket to fill it up. And there were some Muslims around. When I turned the faucet hard, water splashed on them. They took my bucket and smashed it! Then they washed themselves. They believed that the water that jumped on them was *najes*. When they took my bucket, I ran away. The situation for Assyrians in Iran is like the situation of blacks in America before Kennedy."

Of the three million Assyrians scattered about the world today, fewer than forty thousand live in Iran. The figures are uncertain, however, because Assyrian estimates tend to be inflated whereas non-Assyrian governments in the region underestimate the size of the population. Many—predominantly farmers—live in the Uremieh area of Iran along the Iraqi border. Other Iranian cities with Assyrian populations include Hamadan, Kermanshah, Esfahan, and Tehran.

Because of their treatment as second-class citizens under Muslim majority rule, particularly in rural areas and provincial towns, many Assyrians feel less deeply the wistful allegiance to the nation and culture of Iran common among most other Iranian groups here. More typically, their nostalgia for their homeland focuses on ancient Mesopotamia.

According to the Assyrian Community Center in North Hollywood, about half of the five to six thousand Assyrians living in Southern California are from Iran, 45 percent from Iraq, and the rest from Turkey, Syria, Lebanon, and other countries. The Los Angeles community constitutes only a small part of the estimated 140,000 Assyrians living in America. The largest community is in Chicago. The Assyrian American National Federation claims thirty-one branches throughout the United States. Local religious centers in Los Angeles include St. Peter's Chaldean Church and St. Mary's Church of the East, both in the San Fernando Valley.

For eight years after the Iranian revolution, during the Iran-Iraq war, Assyrians in Los Angeles felt divided loyalties; both of the warring nations had Assyrian citizens. For a few Assyrians, the recent Persian Gulf war against Iraq created even more deeply torn allegiances. Some in America had relatives in both the American military in Saudi Arabia and the Iraqi army.

Of all the Iranian minority groups to come to America, Assyrians are among the most eager to assimilate. They have found the process of assimilation easier, in part because of the established Assyrian immigrant base in Los Angeles and in part because their Christian tradition fits more easily into the American religious environment than other faiths. Their comparatively weak allegiance to Iran and their long experience of Islamic

FIGURE 53. Holy Communion at the
Assyrian Chaldean Church in Van Nuys.

FIGURE 54. Easter services held at a cemetery by the Assyrian Church of the East in Los Angeles. April 1989.

discriminatory practices also lessen their dedication to the land of their birth. Although they speak fluent Persian, they usually speak Assyrian at home and English in the outside world. When Assyrian Boy Scouts and Girl Scouts pledge allegiance at the Community Center, they face only Assyrian and American flags.

Although some Assyrians listen to local Iranian media broadcasts and attend pan-Iranian social functions, for many, especially among the younger generation, Persian culture is of little consequence. Few pay attention to Iranian holidays such as No Ruz and Sizdah Bidar. Nothing distinctly Iranian is featured in the Assyrian Community Center; instead, officially sponsored center activities include trips to Las Vegas, bingo nights, scouting events, Assyrian language instruction, Assyrian history and cultural preservation nights, Halloween costume contests, disco dances, and a yearly visit by Santa Claus. The center's monthly magazine, *Shotapouta*, regularly features articles on Assyrian history and the preservation of ethnicity. Although Iranian and Iraqi Assyrians in Chicago have separate organizations, Assyrians in Los Angeles claim that their differences are minor. They point to the Persian and Arabic loan words that each group has incorporated into the Assyrian language.

In Iran, particularly in rural areas, Assyrians and Muslims rarely mingled except for necessary day-to-day commerce. Barriers between cultures and faiths were clear, and it was relatively easy to preserve the distinctive Assyrian culture and heritage in the home or the broader community. In America, however, pressures on children to abandon the Assyrian language and customs are enormous. Recent immigrants point with concern to older relatives who, after decades of living in America, have largely abandoned their Assyrian identity.

Sitting in his office, surrounded by photographs of Assyrian youth activities, Walter Yaeger, president of the Assyrian Community Center in North Hollywood, put the issue of being Assyrian in Los Angeles this way: "We just love being Assyrian, I guess. We hate to see our kids forget the language. We hate to see thousands of years of history go down the drain. For all these years we kept the heritage, the language, the customs, and I don't think they will fade away. I was born in Iran, but what matters to me is being Assyrian. If there was a chance for me to have my own nation, my own country, my own homeland in Iraq, I would go there. I wouldn't go to Iran. I'd go back, you see, to the homeland."

FIGURE 55. California Zoroastrian
Center in Westminster. 1987.

## Zoroastrians

Early in 1986 a small group of homeowners in Westminster, California, became concerned about a new building approaching completion in their quiet neighborhood. The structure, near two Christian churches, looked peculiar to them. They were particularly concerned with what appeared to be four goat-head (actually bull-head) statues set atop pillars above the door.

One night someone threw a rock through a front window. And when a local Christian pastor telephoned the proprietors of the new building to find out if they were, as suspected, devil worshipers, leaders of the new religious community quickly drafted an introductory pamphlet about themselves to be distributed throughout the neighborhood. The Westminster City Council was contacted, the mayor was invited to the building's official opening, and a concentrated effort was made to explain to the local community exactly who the newcomers were.

Farangis Shahrokh, president of the California Zoroastrian Center, laughs about the incident now. The irony is not lost to her that many of the Zoroastrians, no strangers to harassment in their homeland, Islamic Iran, had come to Los Angeles in recent years to escape such absurd misunderstandings about their religion. Wildly ridiculous rumors about them in this land of religious pluralism were not what the Zoroastrians had expected.

Americans ought to know who the Zoroastrians are. The Three Wise Men, the Magi, following the star of Bethlehem in Christian tradition, are generally recognized by biblical scholars to have been Zoroastrians. The religion—founded by the prophet Zoroaster in a Bronze Age culture—is widely acknowledged as the oldest of the revealed creedal religions. Zoroastrianism influenced the development of Judaism, Christianity, and Islam and branches of Sufism, Hinduism, and Buddhism as well as Greek philosophy. Many scholars argue that it has had more influence on religious development than any other faith. Zoroaster is credited as the first to teach the doctrines of individual moral choice, heaven and hell, the future resurrection of the body, the Last Judgment, a coming Messiah, and life everlasting for the reunited soul and body. The early prophet insisted on the innate goodness of material creation under a divine justice. Zoroaster further taught that personal salvation depended on an individual's conscious choice of good thoughts, good words, and good deeds.

The central symbol of Zoroastrianism is fire. Because they generally pray near a fire, Zoroastrians throughout history have been called fire worshipers, by their enemies and by the merely misinformed. Zoroastrians still bristle at the misnomer. They assert that they are no more fire worshipers than Christians are cross worshipers. For them, fire is a sacred symbol of enlightenment, truth, and purity.

At its zenith, centuries before Christ, millions of people followed the Zoroastrian faith from Arabia to China. It was the state religion of three Persian empire dynasties spanning a millennium. King Cyrus the Great, who freed the Jews from the Babylonians, is often cited by Zoroastrians for his religious tolerance and model leadership. Later, Alexander the Great won his crowning victory over a weakened Zoroastrian empire. As Islam spread in the seventh century A.D., most Zoroastrians converted to the new faith. A small minority, however, remained dedicated followers of Zoroaster's teachings in Iran, despite hundreds of years of pressure and sometimes persecution.

In part because of Islamic chauvinism and in part because of the deposed Shah of Iran's ideological embrace of the ancient Persian (Zoroastrian) monarchies, followers of the Zoroastrian faith have not fared well under the Islamic Republic. Although Zoroastrians, unlike the Baha'is, have not been actively persecuted, the current regime has discouraged traditional cross-cultural links to ancient Zoroastrian holidays and festivals—including non-Islamic New Year's celebrations.

Worldwide, the Zoroastrian population numbers about 125,000, including 80,000 in India, 30,000 in Iran, and over 3,000 in the United States, with congregations in New York, San Francisco, Chicago, and Los Angeles. Besides the California Zoroastrian Center, two other Zoroastrian associations in the United States are specifically Iranian—the Persian Zoroastrian Association in San Francisco, and the Iranian Association of New York. Roughly 1,500 Zoroastrians now live in Southern California, two-thirds of them Iranians and most of the others from India.

The first known Zoroastrian in North America settled in San Francisco in 1892, but most have arrived in the last fifteen years. Because of an active commitment to education, Zoroastrian communities worldwide have a high rate of literacy. And like most other Iranian immigrants in the United States, Zoroastrians are usually well-educated professional and business people.

In Iran and India, where elaborate rituals of fire are practiced, it can take up to two years to enthrone a flame in a Zoroastrian temple. In the United States, however, Zoroastrians have made pragmatic adaptations. The fire in the Westminster Center was lit with sandalwood but remains gas-fueled, its intensity adjustible. Furthermore, six agricultural festivals based on a solar calendar are celebrated here on weekends even if they fall in midweek, to accommodate the job and organizational demands of American society.

FIGURE 56. *Mobed* (religious leader)
reciting prayers from the fire chamber in
honor of Zoroaster's birthday. Zoroastrian
Center, 1989.

FIGURE 57. Zoroastrian Parsis at prayer
in the fire chamber of the Zoroastrian
Center after an initiation ceremony.
Westminster, 1989.

Some religious requirements, such as wearing a white cap and taking off one's shoes on entering a fire chamber, remain mandatory. A Zoroastrian in good standing is also expected to pray five times a day facing a light.

The California Zoroastrian Center was founded by Iranis (from Iran), who make up the majority of Zoroastrians in Southern California. A smaller group of about five hundred Zoroastrian Parsis (from India) are scattered throughout the Los Angeles metropolitan area. Their organization—the Zoroastrian Association of California—has no official building but rents halls for religious and social gatherings. Occasionally they rent the Irani Westminster facility, but more often they use temporary spaces in the city of Downey. Non-Zoroastrians are not allowed to witness certain Parsi religious ceremonies. Iranis generally have no such taboo.

Zoroastrians, faced, like all faiths, with increased secularization, have not increased their number in recent times. The Parsis in India, currently numbering 80,000, have lost 30,000 members since 1951, largely because of orthodox injunctions against conversion to their faith. Moreover, a theological rift has developed worldwide, mainly between liberalizing Iranis and orthodox Parsis. Cultural and theological differences between the two groups can be especially heated in the United States. Iranis perceive the Parsis as holding too tightly to antiquated rituals and beliefs; conversely, many Parsis view the Iranis as a corrosive influence on their own unwavering faith.

The roots of the differences go back to A.D. 936, when a group of Zoroastrians fled religious persecution in Islamic Iran. They sailed to India, where a local ruler granted them conditional asylum, requiring them to refrain from proselytizing their faith to the native Hindu populace and to adopt the Gujarati language and the customs of their hosts. The Parsis—as they came to be known—borrowed customs from the Hindus, including painting dots on women's foreheads and wearing the Indian sari. Even today some Parsis variously celebrate New Year's Day according to three different calendars. The most commonly celebrated Parsi New Year, however, is in August, unlike the Irani New Year, which is in March.

Many orthodox Parsis still follow religious beliefs and practices that are foreign—and sometimes startling—to Westerners. Nor do most Iranis here have any use for the ancient Parsi beliefs in sanctified albino bull urine, the notion that one can see "heaven" in the eyes of a dog, and the practice of leaving the deceased in open "Towers of Silence" to be devoured by birds and to decompose.

"Feeding the birds with your own body is a last act of charity," says Maneck Chichgar, who has a doctoral degree in geology and is director of operations for a local consulting firm as well as a Parsi Sunday school teacher. He is troubled at being mistaken for a Hispanic, an Egyptian, or a Greek, for his faith and beliefs are a deep source of pride and the root of his identity.

Farangis Shahrokh does not embrace practices born in an ancient agrarian society thousands of years ago. In their community centers Zoroastrians debate whether the differences between Iranis and Parsis are matters of religious interpretation or merely the habits of different cultures. "A lot of tradition is mixed with Zoroastrianism," she argues. "The Parsis put on a white suit and sit on the floor and pray. Why? In Iran we sit in a chair and pray. These are customs and traditions. Culture has separated us."

Chichgar, who claims he is not orthodox because some other Parsis are stricter than he, sees it otherwise. He contends that the Parsis have become the guardians of the faith, fiercely preserving customs once common to all Zoroastrians. "In Iran," he says, "Zoroastrians have been persecuted, their religious rights limited. A majority of Iranian Zoroastrians don't wear the *kosti* [a belt-like undergarment the orthodox are required to wear]. They don't want to be known as different from Iranians in general. They had to practice our religion quietly in Iran. Iranis smoke cigarettes more readily than we do, for instance. They don't consider that an offence against our religion. We do. In India, because we were free to practice our religion, we could maintain our orthodoxy. We may have adapted our social and cultural life to the outside community, but not our faith. In Iran persecution forced Zoroastrians to change their religion."

"We are progressives," Ms. Shahrokh says of the Irani center. "We follow the message of Zoroaster, but we try to omit as much as possible of the 'tradition' that does not correlate with today's world. We are following his philosophy. His message never says, 'Eat like this. Sleep like this. Clean like this.' Zoroaster says individuals decide for themselves how to be clean, how to be righteous. It's open. That's what we're trying to be."

"Iranian Zoroastrians," charges Chichgar, "to some degree want to change everything, from our ceremonies to our prayers, to liberalize, to shorten them. They say, 'You don't need a fire; you need a light bulb.' That's good enough! They ask, 'Why do you have to have this ceremony that lasts hours when you can have it done in five minutes?' It's contrary to what we Parsis grew up with."

A major question in the contention between the two Zoroastrian communities is whether non-Zoroastrians should be accepted into the faith. In an American culture teeming with religious "salespeople" aggressively seeking converts, Zoroastrians are an anomaly. The idea of actively soliciting converts is repugnant to both Iranis and Parsis.

"We don't compete with other religions," notes Ms. Shahrokh. "Even today many Iranians come here and are shocked to find Christianity marketing itself, collecting millions of dollars to tell the world it is sinful."

Although proselytizing is anathema to both groups, progressive Iranis are willing to accept to the faith those who freely choose to convert on their own initiative. In contrast, orthodox Parsis insist that the religion is exclusively hereditary; that is, one can only be born a Zoroastrian.

Caught within this controversy is Ali Jaferi, the resident scholar of the California Zoroastrian Center. Formerly director general of anthropology for the government of Iran, he is an articulate, devout, and highly educated man who at age sixteen decided to forsake his Islamic heritage and become a Zoroastrian. He has studied and researched the faith for many years, has written a number of books on Zoroastrianism, and has lectured on the faith at educational forums. He is also the editor of the center's periodic newsletter, *The Zoroastrian*.

"Slowly Zoroastrians in America are coming to these new notions," he says. "We will never be a zealous missionary people. We don't 'go after' others. We don't preach. We give you books, explain our religion, and leave. It is up to you to think it over, ponder, and decide for yourself. And if you decide to come, you're welcome."

This kind of talk outrages some orthodox Parsis, who insist that Jaferi, who was not a Zoroastrian by birth, is not now Zoroastrian. Worse, they are incensed by his daring to teach the faith, liberalizing and hence changing it.

As Jaferi and others point out, the argument that no one can become a Zoroastrian except by birth doesn't hold up under logical scrutiny. By that rationale the prophet Zoroaster would have been the only Zoroastrian. Technically, even he was not born one.

"The argument against that," insists Chichgar, "is that we will lose our uniqueness. The daughter of one of my best friends married a black man last month. I tried to talk her out of it because what's going to happen when ten more of these girls marry outside? Or ten boys? We're going to have black Zoroastrians, Chinese Zoroastrians! We're going to have, God knows what! There will be no uniqueness left. That will ring in more change because they'll be influenced by other non-Parsi members of the family who will say, 'My religion says this; why can't you adapt it to Zoroastrianism?'"

Even their continually declining numbers and the threat of religious extinction do not sway some Parsis who insist that the orthodox faith be preserved and that Zoroastrianism is a birthright. "It's a matter of preserving our identity even if we risk extinction," Chichgar says. "But in the back of our minds is another thought, that we will be saved before that happens.

The Great King [the Messiah] will come back, and he himself will convert everyone to Zoroastrianism and bring all past souls to life. It's a traditional view. We left Iran for India to save our religion. We died in Iran for our religion. How could we face our forefathers if we let converts come in?"

Ms. Shahrokh offers a historical interpretation of the conversion controversy. "In the past," she says, "according to Islamic beliefs, any Muslim who accepted another religion was subject to execution. Any convert from Islam could be executed. That is why in Iran we could not accept anyone into our religion. In India, it's another story. When the Zoroastrians went there, the governor of Gujarat gave them sanctuary. But he had conditions: You can have your religion only if you don't convert people. Women should wear the Indian costume. Even today the Parsis respect their promises to him. And the Parsi philosophy is that their religion was Aryan, so it should be kept only for Aryans."

The Zoroastrian immigrant experience in Los Angeles has developed from the story of two peoples with the same historic, religious, and racial roots who in the face of Islamic persecution divided and followed different roads to religious survival. Reunited centuries later in Los Angeles, they find themselves seriously clashing on both cultural and theological issues.

As a London contributor to the California Zoroastrian Center's newsletter suggested, "It is important for the community to understand that the survival of Zoroastrianism depends upon making some changes in our socio-religious practices before it is too late." In another issue of the newsletter a local writer wondered, "Will there remain a continuing Zoroastrian community in North America, or are we the last practicing generation here?"

FIGURE 58. Man in traditional Kurdish dress at a Kurdish picnic in Temescal Canyon Park. Pacific Palisades, 1988.

## Kurds

My friend's American girlfriend asked him, "Where are you from?" He says, "I'm from Kurdistan." She says, "Where's that?" He says, "It's in the Middle East." She says, "Where is the Middle East?" He says, "Well, I'm from Iraq. Kurdistan is divided between Iran, Iraq, and Turkey." She says, "Where is Iran, Iraq, and Turkey?" He gets confused and says, "It's a kind of Mexican food." She says, "Oh, I see."

The American people consider themselves the leaders of the world, but how can you be the leader of the world if the American people are not up-to-date on the issues? How can you appeal your cause to them if they don't know anything about the situation?

—Shad Sooran, *an Iranian Kurd, Los Angeles*

In 1979 a photograph of a line of blindfolded men about to be executed by agents of the new Khomeini regime in the Iranian province of Kurdistan was smuggled to Europe and published in the French magazine *Paris Match*. It was widely reproduced in other major European and American magazines as a symbol of the brutal excesses of the Islamic Republic and became a rallying point for groups opposing the revolutionary regime.

Monir Nahid, the mother of two of the victims in the photograph, is a political refugee in Los Angeles. Soon after the death of her sons, she delivered an impassioned speech before thousands of people at a rally at Tehran University. Tipped off that the authorities were coming to arrest her, she escaped from Iran the next day.

Hours before her sons were shot, she was allowed to speak briefly with them in their cells. What, she asked, was the crime of which they were accused? The youngest son told her that the well-known mullah Khalkhali (whom the Western media later called the Hanging Judge or Judge Blood) had explained to them that they deserved to be executed for any one of the following reasons: They were students, they were Sunni Muslims, and they were Kurds.

Few Americans had ever heard of the Kurds until March 1988, when the world press reported Iraqi poison gas attacks on the Kurdish village of Halabja. Five thousand men, women, and children dropped dead in their tracks, and suddenly the Kurdish people were the focus of a whole new round of international debate about modern warfare and its potential for new horrors. In 1991 the Kurds in Iraq again made the international news as victims of an even larger-scale tragedy, Saddam Hussein's brutal response to their rebellion after the Desert Storm military operation.

FIGURE 59. Kurdish demonstration against Iraqi gas attacks on the Kurdish town of Halabja. Westwood, March 1988.

Despite press coverage of the Halabja and post–Desert Storm atrocities, few Americans know much about the Kurds or the "Kurdish Question," as scholars and the Kurds themselves call it. The recent Kurdish exodus from Iraq to Turkey and Iran was merely the most sensational and best-documented incident in a history of punitive actions against Kurdish nationalism. Kurds in the United States bemoan the failure of even progressive American groups to take up their cause. "It is not that these groups have intentionally ignored the Kurds," suggested Shad Shapole, a Kurd living in Santa Monica. "It's just that they, like everyone else, know so little about the Kurds and our confounding predicament."

The Kurds in America have little chance of drawing widespread attention to their dilemma. After all, they estimate their own numbers at well under a thousand in Southern California and at only a few thousand in the United States as a whole. A tiny minority here, they also lack the economic power to lobby their cause effectively.

The Kurdish story is long and tortuous. Their most recent problems arose in the aftermath of Western colonialism. Nation-state boundaries established in the Middle East after World War I suited colonial interests in controlling the region. Kurdistan—a predominantly mountainous area the size of France that has been the Kurdish homeland for over three thousand years—was divided among four surrounding nations—Iran, Iraq, Syria, and Turkey.

Estimates vary on the number of Kurds living in these four countries as well as in the former Soviet Union. The high-end estimates of close to seventeen million make them the fourth largest population in the Middle East. Because there is no legitimate census, the number is hotly disputed, with scholars and Kurdish activists pitted against the governments that control parts of Kurdistan, whose best interests are served by severely underestimating the Kurdish population.

Most Kurds live in villages and rural areas. Illiteracy in some regions is 80 percent; for women it can be even higher. The Kurds are ethnically, racially, culturally, and linguistically distinct from surrounding—predominantly Arab—peoples, but even among Kurds themselves dialects, customs, and a few religious practices differ.

There are parallels between the current plight of the Kurds in the Middle East and the American Indian's struggle for cultural (and literal) survival against systematic governmental persecution over the past 150 years (Kurds in the Middle East, like American Indians, are stereotyped as warlike and physically intimidating). Kurds have faced persecution, repression, purges, displacement, and pogroms from four different governments determined, to varying degrees, to subjugate and effectively erase them as a distinct people. The Kurds in each country, isolated from one another, transplanted, displaced, and forcibly assimilated into the dominant culture around them, have been unable to develop the self-awareness that could foment a united rebellion.

The Kurds note another important political difference between their situation and that of American Indians: at least the American Indians are free now to address the injustices of the past against them and to reclaim their ethnic heritage and identity. To this day, the Kurds do not have such opportunities in any of the countries that control most of their homeland. In each of these nations the very idea of Kurdish identity is perceived as a threat to the state.

In Turkey, for instance, it has been illegal to speak or print books in the Kurdish language since 1925. The history of the Kurdish people has been officially obliterated. Kurds are recognized by the Turkish government as "Mountain Turks," who live in the "wild East." Kurdish national clothing, including the distinctive headdress, baggy pants, and cloth belt, is banned. From time to time in this century, Kurds who have publicly dared to raise the issue of their cultural and ethnic identity have been imprisoned or, in extreme cases, executed. In Syria, the government, following an ideology of pan-Arab nationalism, has refused to recognize its Kurdish citizens' rights as a minority.

In Iran, when the Soviets and British intervened against Axis activities during World War II, the Kurds managed to set up an independent, autonomous Kurdish state. The centralized government of the Shah quickly crushed it, however, when foreign troops pulled out of the country after the war. Over the years, the Pahlavi regime imprisoned hundreds of Kurdish nationalists and mounted ongoing efforts to make the Iranian Kurdish regions more homogeneously "Iranian." With the Iranian revolution against the Shah in 1979, armed Kurdish liberation movements fought against, and were ultimately subdued by, the new Islamic Republic.

The Kurds' situation in Iraq is somewhat different from that in Iran because Iraq's Kurdish population constitutes 30 percent of the country's population and because the government has been unstable for decades. For forty years Mostafa Barzani led armed guerrillas against the Iraqi government in a fight for the autonomy of Iraqi Kurdistan. At one point in the mid-1970s, over a hundred thousand Pesh Mergas, "those who face death," could be counted on to fight the Iraqi regime.

The Kurdish struggle for self-determination has been ruthlessly exploited by both Middle Eastern governments and the so-called superpowers. The Soviet Union granted Barzani political asylum for a short while in 1957, but as new Iraqi regimes warmed to the Soviet influence, support for the Kurds vanished. The CIA took its turn supporting the Kurdish resistance in 1963 (and, later, in the 1970s) to hinder the pro-Soviet Iraqi regimes. Likewise, at times when it was politically expedient the Shah of Iran offered economic and military assistance to the Kurds of Iraq to keep the Iraqi government occupied militarily. But in 1975, at the peak of a large Iraqi-Kurdish guerrilla war, the Shah—with CIA sanction—struck a deal with the Iraqi regime of Saddam Hussein and suddenly withdrew his support of the rebellion. With no logistical backing, the Kurdish movement collapsed, sending thousands of Pesh Mergas into exile. Some have lived in refugee camps in Iran for over a decade. Many of the Iraqi Kurds in Southern California, particularly in San Diego, are here as a consequence of this surprise truce between Iran and Iraq. (Some Iranian Kurds in the United States are also political refugees. One middle-aged man lost his university teaching position after Iran's revolution, made his way to Los Angeles, and since 1984 has been seeking official political asylum here. Suffering through a second kidney failure, unemployed, he has found it necessary to store his belongings and live with Kurdish acquaintances, hoping for a day when his prospects brighten.)

Geographically central to the Middle East, Kurdistan has represented a valuable strategic area; hence, competing governments have long struggled to maintain the status quo and prevent the reconstitution of an autonomous Kurdistan. The United States, for example, by arrangement with the Turkish government, has maintained sensitive military bases and listening posts along the former Soviet border in Turkish Kurdistan. In Iraq, most Kurds consider the Kirkuk region, one of the richest oil sources in the world, part of Kurdistan.

Angered at being manipulated and exploited, Kurds are also embittered by the dominant nations' refusal to permit them an ethnic identity. Born and raised in Iran, Shad Shapole admits with deep chagrin that he actually discovered his Kurdish identity here in America.

"It was here as a student that I finally found access to some books on Kurdish history," he says. "I read whatever I could. When I went back to Iran, I was a different person. I left as an Iranian; I returned as a Kurd."

"If a Kurd names his child Hama," explains Goran, another Iranian Kurd living in Los Angeles, "six months later he goes to the registration office for a birth certificate. The Iranian representative—a bookkeeper for the region—says, 'What's your child's name?' The Kurd says, 'Hama.' 'Ah, wait a minute,' says the Iranian. 'What is the closest name to that in Persian? Your son from now on will be called Mohammad.'"

The Kurdish resistance has its own factionalism. The Patriotic Union of Kurdistan, the Kurdish Democratic party, and Komaleh (the Kurdish

Communist party) are among the groups with opposing views, all struggling for Kurdish autonomy. Further divisions stem from the cultural influences exerted on the Kurds in each nation-state claiming part of Kurdistan, as it banned or suppressed the Kurdish language and Kurdish cultural expression. Because the Kurds are a tribal culture, tensions have sometimes existed between Kurds in the same valley.

"In Los Angeles," says Shapole, "if we have Kurds from Syria, Turkey, Iran, and Iraq get together, we have no choice but to speak English. Each dialect is distinct. We cannot communicate in Kurdish. Historically, there has been no Kurdish free press, no publication of ideas."

"When it comes to the Kurdish language," says Shad Sooran, another Iranian Kurd in Los Angeles, "there are so many Arabic words that have entered the language of the Iraqis, so many Persian words in the Kurdish of Iran, so many Turkish words for the Kurds of Turkey. It makes it difficult to communicate. In this way the governments hope to separate Kurds from each other and, to some extent, they have been successful. Divide and conquer. That's the policy."

Most of the Kurds now living in Southern California emigrated from Iran and Iraq, with the majority of the Iranian Kurds living in the Los Angeles area, and most of the Kurdish Iraqis in San Diego. In Los Angeles, the Kurds' occupations vary from business entrepreneur to truck driver to university student. The Kurds tend to be highly politicized, particularly with respect to Kurdish autonomy. The overwhelming majority are male. A number of Kurds have married local Hispanic women, finding traditional Latino culture and family values somewhat similar to those of their own homeland. (Exceptions to some of these generalizations include a community of Jewish Kurds in Los Angeles, many from the Sanandaj region of Iranian Kurdistan. Although they share the Kurdish language and many customs, their identity, especially for the younger generation, tends to be Jewish before Kurd. Few associate themselves with the pan-Kurdish struggle for autonomy and independence. A 1989 music concert by Nasir Razzazi, a Jewish Kurd living in Europe, attracted a large audience and gave local Muslim Kurds their first inkling that several hundred Jewish Kurds were also in the Los Angeles area.)

The Kurdish community tries to perpetuate its cultural heritage with occasional picnics and social gatherings as well as political meetings. A recent gathering of the Komaleh political party at a local university featured Kurdish music and dance. The event attracted 250 people, of whom many were not Kurdish. (The Kurdish cause has been a popular rallying symbol for liberal and leftist members of the Iranian intelligentsia.) A Kurdish cultural association is developing in San Diego, but the small number of potential supporters in Southern California makes it difficult to maintain an effective organization. In recent years, UCLA became one of only two or three universities in the country to offer Kurdish language classes.

At a Sunday picnic in West Los Angeles, eighty Kurds gathered to eat, sing, and dance and to celebrate their cultural heritage in this new, ethnically corroding—albeit more tolerant—environment. The picnickers delighted in pointing out that Kurdish women have always had more freedom than traditional Shi'i Iranian and Iraqi women. There are no Kurdish injunctions against women dancing. Their traditional clothing, moreover, is not dark and demure like traditional Shi'i dress but rather bright and colorful.

"Fifty years ago in my hometown, Kermanshah," said one Iranian Kurd at the picnic, "Kurds could not speak Persian. All the communication was in Kurdish, the native language. Now, eighty percent of the people can't speak their own language very well. The same thing is going on in Turkey and Iraq. The hope of the governments is that in one or two hundred years there will be no such thing as a Kurdish language or culture. There won't be a Kurdish cause. That is the final objective: we would be like the California condor, on the verge of extinction."

PART III

FAMILY, GENDER, AND SOCIAL RELATIONS

FIGURE 60. *Khosh amadan* welcoming,
the traditional Iranian exchange of
pleasant greetings. Zoroastrian Center,
Westminster, 1986.

FIGURE 61. Guests arriving at an anniversary celebration for the local newspaper, *Iran News*, held at the Beverly Hilton Hotel. 1988.

*Interview*

Homa Mahmoudi is a Clinical Psychologist at Cedar-Sinai Hospital. She is also the founder and president of the Transcultural Communications Center in Los Angeles.

RON KELLEY:    What is the attitude in the local Iranian community toward psychiatrists and psychologists?

MAHMOUDI:    In Iran, psychiatry was used only in severe cases—schizophrenia, severe depressions. However, we find—at least I find—in this community that after I give talks to groups of women or students, I get a lot of those people coming to therapy to deal with issues that are really very similar to those that other Americans are trying to deal with—making decisions about marriage, difficulties in relationships. But still there is a stigma attached to therapy in the Persian community. I see young women that come from Beverly Hills High School whose mothers say, "Could you see them in your house, because if anyone ever sees them around Cedar-Sinai, they're doomed and they'll never be married in the community." They say, "I will talk to you on the telephone, but I don't want you to know who I am." So I have to be very careful. I always tell them that if I see them at a wedding or sit with them at a funeral, if I don't say hello it's not because I don't recognize them. It's because I don't want them to have to explain to their family why they know me. I have a lot of incognito patients. I just know them by their first name or a pseudonym or something.

Q:    Could you give me some background on that? From what I know of the Persian community, there's a great sense of pride, of shame. What are the reasons an Iranian would be so reluctant to solicit your help?

MAHMOUDI:    Shame and guilt have been ways of controlling society. Iranian society is very clannish; there's an extended family and an extended society. All

Iranian women overdress; if they're going down to the grocery store to buy a can of tomato paste, they will dress up or not go at all. God forbid that someone see you in your jeans and sweatshirt, you know? "Oh, did you see her?!" It's that kind of control that they always have over you—you must always put your best foot forward. It has to do with denial too, denial that there are any problems. And it really causes a lot of tension now in Los Angeles. Especially in the young families. I see a lot of married couples. They say, "Well, everyone else looks so wonderful and happy. I am the only person that has these problems and it's miserable!" The couples go to weddings and they see that "they're so much in love and they get along so well, but my husband and I are having problems. We can't agree on finances, and this and that. And we are the only ones!" Because people do not share the difficulties they experience, there is a lot of personal tension and problems. One of the main areas that the younger groups like college students are having such a hard time understanding, focusing on, is which way of living is right. If this is right—but causes so much tension that it makes me feel superficial and dishonest—then how can I deal with it?

Q:     What are some of the most common personal problems you run into here?

MAHMOUDI:     The most difficult one is depression. Isolation, depression, a sense of uprootedness. Feeling like a tiny fish in a big ocean and having been a big fish in a little pond. That kind of thing. Men feel disconnected, not successful. They fear old age and all that. The second thing is that marriages are in great trouble in Los Angeles. The tension in marriages is tremendous. There is such a vast difference in the way their parents lived in Iran and the way they live here. They have no role models. Women don't know what they're doing. Men don't know what they're doing.

Q:     Are we speaking of younger couples or older ones?

MAHMOUDI:     Both. Many of these people in Iran lived in a men's culture or a women's culture. Here they have to get along together, and it's very tough. In Iran, women focused more on the family or they had extended women's groups, and the men had more of the external—Rotary Clubs, this club, that club, the business community. Here they have to get along and make decisions together, and it has caused a lot of problems.

FIGURE 62. Anniversary celebration for
*Iran News*, 1988.

FIGURE 63.  A party for *Rahezendigee*
magazine held at the Ramada Inn in
Beverly Hills. 1988.

Q:    Could you talk about the issue of status? From what I've seen in the Persian community here, there is a lot of concern with class, quality, fine taste. As you say, dressing up to go outside. I see men dressed in suits on their day off. Could you explain this? I know that many Iranians here have lost some of the status they had in Iran . . .

MAHMOUDI:    There are several layers. Marvin Zonis wrote a book in the 1960s saying that in Iran there were a thousand upper-class families, the name families, and they ran the country. These people were the upper class; it was a feudal system. Before the land reform they really owned all the villages. These people emulated European ways of living. You go to a ski resort at Mammoth Mountain or Lake Tahoe, and the men in suits and ties are the Iranian men. You see that. If they're going to wear ski clothes, they have to be designer ski clothes. It's the whole thing about taking care of the external and putting your best foot forward. Culturally, in old Iran, we had two homes, side by side. We called them the external house and the internal house. The internal house had the kitchen and the women and the kids and all of that. The external house, with fancy furniture, paintings, carpets, and all that, was for men. The women guests would come to the women's side, but mostly the entertainment was done in the men's area. Guests! The importance of guests in the Iranian community is unbelievable! If you don't have anything to feed your own children, you feed your guests the best! It really is important. That's where people judge you. Because Iranian society and the Iranian community ran on connections, importance, and status rather than on your education or expertise, the external—"how you walked in"—became important. The superficial.

Q:    Are Iranian women more inclined to see you than men?

MAHMOUDI:    Usually, women come first, but I also see, for instance, two Iranian physicians who are men, and they don't want their wives to know. Iranian men are reluctant to come, but I believe that if the marriage is to work in the Iranian community, both of them have to be here. But usually the woman initiates it. "My husband this and that, and I want to get a divorce!" But you have to understand that the Iranian woman doesn't come to the therapist to get a divorce. She comes as she would to her daddy or someone to say, "Go beat up on him! Tell him to behave." It's that kind of thing. "I feel helpless. Would you try and put some sense in his head?" And so I always tell the man, "Your wife has come. She has some problems. I would like you to come in. If she tells me that she loves you, I want you to be here to hear it. And if she has problems, let's solve them together." I've never had anyone refuse to come in. Never. Whether it's a seventy-year-old man or . . . I've always had the husbands cooperate.

Q:     I've heard that many Iranians have difficulty with intimacy, talking about things with friends or even spouses—that there are deep barriers in the culture against revealing to anyone your innermost thoughts and feelings. I wonder if you could talk about that, particularly in light of your professional role.

MAHMOUDI:     Iranian culture is a very secretive culture. And it's a very individually isolated culture. Among Iranians intimacy does not necessarily go along the same lines as in Western culture. We have the nuclear family that is intimate. But in the Iranian culture you have a very close friend that you talk to intimately. Not your wife. And your wife has a friend too. It's along sexual lines—men to men and women to women. And it's not as if you can let your hair down completely with some other person. I might know all about this person's sexual problem, but I don't know how much money he makes. His banker might know all that, but nothing about how he is getting along with . . . It's very compartmentalized. The unconditional trust and openness we might have here is very seldom found in Iranian society. You find conditional relationships. By that, I mean it's like having several different consultants on different issues. Families—parents and children, husbands and wives, brothers and sisters—keep a lot of secrets from one another. There is a word *haya* that means "shyness." When you talk to a girl and she blushes, she feels something but is not able to respond with that feeling. They say that you are not to break that code even in marriage. That kind of intimacy and openness destroys a relationship, because it is just too close.

Q:     What happens to Iranians who come here and find the so-called freedoms here? Sexual freedoms, economic freedoms. This issue of control changes here.

MAHMOUDI:     There's a definite double standard. Yes, men need sex and it's OK for them to have American girlfriends, Mexican girlfriends, or whoever, because, oh yes, men have to have sex. But God forbid that an Iranian girl has a boyfriend and is seen outside! You can, you know, keep it private. Many Iranian women do have relationships. And they also—as a therapist, I am telling you—have had sexual experiences. You know, they had a boyfriend and they went to Europe together for a while. The mother thought the girl was staying with an uncle, but she was traveling with the boyfriend. They become sexually intimate, and now these women are terrified. They have to be a virgin on the night of their marriage, and they're not. How are they going to tell their boyfriends? Do they tell them right up front? Do they tell him before marriage? Now that they've lost their virginity, how do they repair themselves? It becomes a big issue.

Q:     So a woman's identity is entirely linked to marriage . . .

MAHMOUDI:     Regardless of what you do, ultimately they see you as part of where you go, what happens to you, how much money you make, how much money you lose. Those are all outside factors. The family, the clan, the grandchildren, the grandparents are what is important. The focus is not on your career. Money comes and goes, but it's the name—the reputation, the marriage, the status—that is important. The focus is on maintaining this.

Q:     What about interracial marriages, interfaith marriages, marriages to Americans?

MAHMOUDI:     It seems that the Muslim community is more integrated than Iranian minority groups. There seem to be more cross-cultural marriages in the Muslim community. More Iranian men have married American women. It's because the Muslims are not formed as a community. Until recently, when the Iranian Cultural Center opened, a young Muslim who went to USC didn't have a place to meet like that of the Baha'is or a nineteen-day feast to go to, and he didn't have the Jewish synagogue, all the weddings and cousins and all that. With the revolution, there has been a cultural regression here. Iranians here have lost their homeland. I get a lot of young people who say, "My mother forces me to study Persian. When we were in Iran, we spoke English in the house because we were visiting Los Angeles all the time." People here are trying to hold on to their cultural heritage, listening to Persian music, doing things that even my grandmother didn't do. In Iran, everyone was trying to become very westernized, going to Europe, to America for education. And when they came back, they would speak English, and then, suddenly, now, they are becoming super-Iranians!

Q:     And this is peculiar to Los Angeles; it's not the same, say, in Washington, D.C.?

FIGURE 64. Pro-Shah demonstration on
the anniversary of the establishment of
the Islamic Republic of Iran. Westwood,
February 1987.

MAHMOUDI: This is peculiar to Los Angeles. Because the materials are available. If you go to a Persian wedding here . . . Go to Westwood. It's like walking in a bazaar in Tehran. It's available. If I want to have a dinner party, I can have a real traditional Iranian party because the necessary materials are available.

Q: I understand that it's very difficult for Iranian individuals to say they love someone. Husband to wife, lover to lover . . .

MAHMOUDI: Romantic love is a bonus in a relationship rather than a given. I go out with someone because I'm attracted to him, I love him. In Iran, the parents get together, they decide how much money there is, what kind of family he has, whether there are any black sheep in the family. Is there dirt? Then they make arrangements and these two go out together. Usually, nowadays, if some feeling develops, then they get married.

    The other thing that I have to deal with in therapy is the issue of control and the maintenance of control. If I tell you that I love you every morning, you're going to become obnoxious, bold, too secure in this relationship. Then you're going to have an affair. As long as I can have you suspicious of my love, I have you hooked. This ritual gamesmanship is played with sex, money, time, moodiness—one day hot, one day cold. It's done through coyness, through withdrawal. And Iranian women really believe it has value. I tell them, "This man is dying for a little love; why don't you tell him that you love him?" And she says, "If I tell him that I love him, he's going to become so secure in this relationship that he'll become attracted to other people." A lot of women overspend every month, consciously, to make him run harder and faster to make more money.

Q: What happens then to the Iranians who come here and get romantically involved with Americans or somebody else?

MAHMOUDI: It doesn't work because they can't figure out what the other person is doing. Let's talk about cultural differences. In Iranian society, if I have a cold, I expect my mother to be there with soup and my cousins to call every five minutes. Neighbors come by, and they all smoke cigarettes and sit there and talk and have tea while I'm sick in bed. When Americans get sick, they take two aspirins, pull the curtains, go to bed, and don't want to hear a thing. Now you have a husband and wife. The poor American wife gets sick, and the mother-in-law or sister-in-law is sitting there. "Oh, you're sick! Can we get you some more soup?" The wife interprets this as their not wanting her to get sick. She thinks they are after her to get up and make tea and work. When an Iranian husband gets sick, his American wife says, "Honey, here's a glass of orange juice, here's two aspirin, I'm going to make sure that nobody knows about it so you don't get bothered by them." She closes the curtains and goes shopping. He thinks she's cold and uncaring, unloving. He thinks, "I have shown her that when she was sick, I had all my relatives here taking care of her. She doesn't care about me."

Q: What do Iranians think about America?

MAHMOUDI: They see American society and culture as sick. They see the loss of family—that old people are alone and lonely and have no respect. Children don't respect their parents. Parents don't care about their children. It's the whole control issue. You know, "If these kids who were in gangs had better parents, they wouldn't be in gangs." They see all the illnesses of society rooted in the lack of family structure, lack of control, lack of depth in the culture. And that's very important to them. They are concerned to see their children associating with Americans. I went to get my hair done, and the woman said, with such pride, that they have been here for ten years and her daughter does not have one American friend! It's as though she was a straight A student! She wasn't contaminated by this ugly culture.

Q: What about tenets of faith—Islamic, Baha'i, Jewish, or whatever— versus psychoanalysis, a scientific analysis of mind? Are there tensions in the Persian community there? Do you get religious people into therapy?

MAHMOUDI: I have a Khomeini woman that comes to see me. I love her. She comes to my house, actually. I always enjoy that. I say, "Can I get you a cup of tea?" And she says, "You know I don't drink your tea." I'm dirty! [Mahmoudi is a Baha'i, considered unclean by strict Shi'i Muslims.] She sits there, and she's had three daughters that have had problems. And I've helped with each one of them. She takes a hundred-dollar bill and puts it on my table. I don't know her name. She calls and says, "You know who I am," and she comes, keeps the time, and after an hour, goes out. She has total faith in me, yet she doesn't want to touch my house or have my cup of tea! I love her.

Q: Could you tell me something about your center, the Transcultural Communications Center?

MAHMOUDI:       What we have done through the years is to try to train people to transcend the culture they are living in, and be able to incorporate. When I see a patient who says, "I don't know whether I'm American or Iranian," I always respond, "You are both of those things and many more." I feel that whenever you put yourself into any form of dichotomous situation, you lose out. You put yourself into tension. "It's not whether you're American or Iranian. Part of you is American, part of you is Iranian, part of you likes art, part likes the cinema." That kind of thing. I would point out to Americans who came to Iran to work for Bell Helicopter that they didn't have to become like Iranians and start *taarof*ing and doing all those Iranian things. They were Americans.

Q:              Do you get many patients suffering this kind of identity crisis?

MAHMOUDI:       Yes. "Who am I?" And especially, "When you get married, what does that mean? If I marry an American, what does that mean? What does it mean to have children? Where do they belong? Where do they go? Who are they?"

FIGURE 65. Woman at home.

# IRANIAN WOMEN AND GENDER RELATIONS IN LOS ANGELES

*Nayereh Tohidi*

Immigration is a major life change, and the process of adapting to a new society can be extremely stressful, especially when the new environment is drastically different from the old. There is evidence that the impact of migration on women and their roles differs from the impact of the same process on men (Espin 1987; Salgado de Snyder 1987). The migration literature is not conclusive, however, about whether the overall effect is positive or negative. Despite all the trauma and stress associated with migration, some people perceive it as emancipatory, especially for women coming from environments where adherence to traditional gender roles is of primary importance. As Park said, "When the traditional organization of society breaks down as a result of contact and collision . . . the effect is, so to speak, to emancipate the individual man. Energies that were formerly controlled by custom and tradition are released" (Furio 1979, 18).

My own observations of Iranians in Los Angeles over the past eight years, as well as survey research I carried out in 1990,[1] reveal that Iranian women immigrants in Los Angeles are a homogeneous group, despite ethnic diversity. Most of them come from Tehran and represent an urban cosmopolitan subculture. And most are educated members of the upper-middle and middle classes who oppose the present regime in Iran and its repressive policies against women.

Migration has had both costs and benefits for women. Positive experiences include the sense of freedom, new opportunities and options, increased access to education and gainful employment, and a move toward egalitarian conjugal roles in many Iranian families. On the negative side is grief over the loss of the homeland, loved ones, and the social and emotional support of the kinship network. Many also feel marginal and, at least initially, experience a decline in their own socioeconomic status or that of their husbands. Moreover, conflicts between parents and their children and between women and men have heightened tension and led to an increasing divorce rate.

Migration involves culture shock. Immigrants' experiences of migration and the process of adaptation are influenced by a number of variables (Dane 1980; Melville 1978; Taft 1977; Salgado de Snyder 1987; Espin 1987; and Shirley 1981). Personal characteristics, such as age, language proficiency, educational level, and job skills, influence the migrants' ability to adapt. Immigrants are also affected by attitudinal factors, such as their own perceptions of the decision to emigrate, their sense of responsibility for those left behind, and their perceptions of the conditions in both home and host countries. Economic factors also play a role, especially the immigrants' ability to find a job, their financial resources, and their losses or gains in social status or class. Another set of influential conditions includes the attitudes of the citizens of the host country toward the migrant group and the degree of similarity between the two cultures. Finally, some personal factors, such as ego strength, decision-making skills, resolution of feelings of loss, and the ability to tolerate ambiguity (including ambiguity about gender roles), also influence the intensity of the culture shock experienced by the immigrants and their ability to adapt.

All these factors vary substantially for men and women, with the result that the processes of acculturation and adaptation differ for them as well.

## ACCULTURATION AND CHANGES IN GENDER ROLES

All immigrants experience acculturation, a process involving changes in values, beliefs, attitudes, and behaviors. The inevitable collision of home and host cultures ensures that some acculturation will take place. This does not mean that all values, customs, and behaviors originating in the home culture will disappear. In fact, the healthiest experiences of acculturation result in biculturalism or multiculturalism. Not every individual immigrant, however, manages to attain a bicultural balance. Many never cease feeling alienated in the new society, while others experience complete assimilation.

As part of the process of acculturation, all immigrants develop a "new identity" that integrates elements from the host and home cultures (Garza-Guerrero 1974). A psychologist who experienced the challenging and often painful process of migration first hand writes:

> Immigrants in accepting a new identity (or a new version of the old one) at the price of instant identification and intense work must leave behind not only old countries but also unlived futures, and not only enemies to be disavowed but also friends to be left behind—maybe to perish. What right, then, does the immigrant have to usurp a new identity? (Erickson 1974, 77)

FIGURE 66. Portrait.

For Iranian women, the process of developing a new identity is perhaps the most psychologically challenging and delicate aspect of immigration.

Studies of immigrant women from various societies indicate that when acculturation and adaptation are taking place, women's sex-role attitudes, gender identity, and gender roles may change more dramatically than men's (see, for example, Tharp, Meadow, Lennhoff, and Satterfield 1968; Torres-Matrullo 1980; Espin 1987; and Salgado de Snyder 1987).

Iranian women and girls are entering North American society at a time when the role of women is changing, both here and in their homeland. During the peak of the Iranian influx into the United States, the progressive forces of revolution, on the one hand, and the subsequent character of the Islamic government, on the other, fostered a transformation in the role of women. The Islamization of the last decade, however, has enforced a uniform identity for Iranian women, based on traditional and restricted roles. The difference between appropriate behavior for women in Iran and in the United States is much greater than that for men in the two societies. The differing demands on men and women can either facilitate acculturation or create confusion and conflicts for women.

My survey indicates that changes in traditional conceptions of womanhood, manhood, and marriage—from an autocratic male-dominated model to a more egalitarian one—are taking place faster among Iranian women than among Iranian men. Studies of Latina immigrants reveal similar patterns. Even though the pace of acculturation tended to be slower for Latinas in other respects, the women exhibited more egalitarian attitudes toward gender roles than men (Vazquez-Nuttall, Romero-Garcia, and DeLeon 1987; Espin 1987).

In studies of the acculturation of Iranians in the United States, Ghaffarian (1989) found the same patterns, that is, that Iranian male immigrants were more acculturated than females and that despite their lower level of overall acculturation, Iranian women migrants had more egalitarian views of marital roles than Iranian men. Such a discrepancy would naturally lead to new conflicts between the sexes.

This is not to say that changes in sexual attitudes and family roles are the result of migration and acculturation into American society. Actually, the cultural collision between modernism and traditionalism, between liberalism and conservatism, and between male chauvinism and feminism had begun in Iran long before the major waves of Iranian immigration to the United States. By the turn of the century, growing urbanization and the introduction of new industries, new modes of production, and new ideas had wrought major changes and raised questions concerning the proper role and place of women in the new society, and their access both to

FIGURE 67.    Young Muslim woman at
home preparing for religious services.
Torrance, 1990.

education and to work outside the home. Long-standing cultural and religious traditions, such as the segregation of women's space from men's and veiling requirements, were called into question. During the 1978–79 revolution, special emphasis was placed on discovering the authentic (*aseel*) identity of Iranian women, especially in comparison to "West-struck" or "Westoxicated" (*gharb zadeh*) women. All these issues have remained unresolved since the Constitutional Movement in Iran during the first decade of the twentieth century.

WOMEN AND THE FAMILY IN IRAN

During the years preceding the 1978–79 revolution, the "woman question" became part of the Iranian intelligentsia's debate about national identity, development, modernization, and cultural and moral integrity. Those participating in the discussion included Iranian nationalists, Islamists, Marxists, and those influenced by the West.

Islam undergirds the patriarchy in Iran, just as Judeo-Christian ethics justify the same system in the United States. The family, with its patrilineal and patriarchal structure, is the basic social unit. Male and female roles are organized in a hierarchy based on sex, age, and experience. A traditional Iranian woman's place is in the home. Because her role and activities are limited to familial and domestic spheres, she has no identity outside the family. She is identified only by her connections to her male kin—she has status only as the daughter, sister, wife, and mother of male family members. As a wife, her status is determined by her fertility, especially her ability to give birth to sons. The wife is always under her husband's tutelage or, in his absence, that of her eldest son. Her honor (*namus*) requires that she never be left unprotected by her father, husband, or other male kin (Nassehi-Behnam 1985, 558).

An old Persian expression illustrates the traditional conception of women in Iran: "Woman is a sweetheart when a girl and a mother when married." Such a view reduces women to their sexual and reproductive capacities.

The gender-based discrimination and double standards that pervade Iranian social life restrict women's movements, the physical spaces they may enter, their work and economic autonomy, their access to education, their personal power and authority, their sexual behavior, and their ability to express themselves artistically. From childhood, the members of each sex are socialized to prescribed roles. Boys are taught to command, to protect, and to make a good living for themselves and their families. Girls learn to be chaste and beautiful and to find a good husband. The resentment

FIGURE 68. Winner of a Persian beauty
contest held at a West Los Angeles nightclub. At the same time, religious Shi'i
Muslims were holding Moharram
commemorations. West Los Angeles,
September 1990.

adolescent girls feel at the discrimination and constraints they endure is reflected in a poem by Mahvash Qadiri, a woman poet living in Iran, translated here from the Persian:

### I Was Born a Girl

I was born a girl
So that I'd be given a doll and broom
To sew the hem of men's shirts with gold lace
And to sweep the dust from the home.
My brother is playing in the street.
He takes off with his bicycle,
And I remain in the corner of the house.

I was born a girl,
In the chapter of questions and search
My questions are left unanswered and
My search is futile.

My brother, in the winding streets,
By playing with the dirt and the pebbles,
Is experiencing life.
My experience does not pass beyond these walls.
I do not know the streets.

I was born a girl
So that in the dawn of puberty
My frightful eyes,
Like the eyes of a restless deer,
Would give away my secret.
My brother didn't come home tonight,
He is considered a man now.

I was born a girl
So that I'd be the loser in the aftermath of each war
When they make peace,
I'd be the sacrifice.

In war
The Mongol soldiers and Timur's attendants
Will make my painful cries echo against the blue dome of the sky
And in peace time
The Amir and his servants will.

After each war
My sisters put on the ugly dress of the prostitutes
And in the tranquility of each peace
They circle around the wine at the lustful feasts of their masters.

Yes,
I
was born a girl.

## WOMEN AND MODERNIZATION IN IRAN

From the 1920s to the 1970s, Iran was transformed from a semifeudal Asiatic society to a modern centralized capitalist state. The process of modernization was neither uniform nor all-encompassing, with social and political changes lagging far behind economic transitions. The deformations of capitalist development, uneven and restricted industrialization, the continuing despotic monarchy, and the lack of secular democratic political and legal systems reinforced the precapitalistic modes of production and patrimonial social relations (Tohidi 1991).

Emancipatory changes for women during the Shah's regime affected only a small number of women from the upper and upper-middle classes. Modernization under the Shah was imposed from the top down, and there was little popular participation in the nation's development process. In many ways, the modernization of Iran during the Shah's regime merely meant emulating as many of the outward features of Western societies as possible. The adoption by the upper classes of Western trappings and consumption patterns resulted in the bizarre contrasts noted by Bill and Leiden (1984, 2–3): "Discotheques and mosques, modern luxury hotels and squalid mud huts, nuclear energy programs and the fuel of animal droppings, F-16s and old rifles and daggers, palaces and tents, computerized libraries and omnipresent illiteracy." The exploitative and uneven character of the development process caused widespread resentment. Men and women began to perceive and reject modernization as imperialism in disguise.

Iranian women's adoption of elements of Western culture did not necessarily emancipate them, nor did it automatically make gender relations more egalitarian. Given the extent to which Western culture itself is male dominated, one could scarcely expect the westernization of Iranian society to emancipate women or to overcome the crippling effects of patriarchal family structures.

Both the Shah and Khomeini were grand patriarchs of the Iranian nation. The authoritarian political structure headed by these patriarchial

SARSHAR:
Men blame the distress in the Iranian family and divorce on women. They say we're liberated here, and they're not happy about that. They think that maybe women will find out more about their rights here than in Iran. We are not as naive as we were in Iran.

I wrote an article that didn't please the community. It argued that women were stronger than men here, more reasonable and practical. Before the revolution, the men in Iran were working, and they were the king of the house, as we say in Iran. Here they were shocked. Here they were immobile, doing nothing. The first ones to go out and look for a job, the ones who tried to keep the family together, were the women, even if they were second-class citizens in Iran. But here they were stronger than men in facing the situation. And after a while, if the man was not getting himself together, there were problems between them.

The number of divorces and separations is multiplying. So men are blaming the women: "Oh, you're liberated! Oh, you want to be like American women. You don't think about the family anymore. You want your rights. You say that if we get divorced, half of the property is yours; half of the money is yours. You're not ashamed of yourself." A lot of men seem to feel that Iranian women have lost their integrity. But I don't think they're right.

figures and the authority of husband and father in the traditional family are highly complementary. Any transition toward egalitarian relations within the family must be preceded by the democratization and secularization of the state and its political structures.

## THE IMPACT OF MIGRATION

The impact of migration on Iranian women in Los Angeles depends on the reasons for their migration and the conditions under which it took place. My 1990 research identified a number of reasons for women's migration. Educational opportunities were cited most frequently, followed by the disturbing situation in Iran, the desire for more freedom and opportunities, the lack of other options, political persecution, economic reasons, and interest in American society.

Some women left Iran (with or without their husbands) to provide their children with better education and broader opportunities. They found the Islamization of the educational system and the political indoctrination of their children unacceptable. Other women accompanied their adolescent sons into exile to ensure that the youths would not be drafted during the Iran-Iraq war. Still others came to the United States alone, leaving their husbands and other family members behind because of economic considerations or to increase the likelihood of their getting a U.S. visa. These motivations are reflected in the immigrants' sense of marginality, their development of a new identity, and other aspects of acculturation.

## INDIVIDUAL AND POLITICAL FREEDOM

In comparison with women living in Iran, migrant and refugee women have gained considerable personal and political freedom. Their basic human rights are no longer violated by such institutions of control as the mandatory veil, strict dress code, and sexual apartheid. Many middle-class and professional women who found these repressive measures intolerable appreciate their new freedom. The sense of relief is even more profound for those women who escaped persecution and imprisonment in Iran.

Women who migrated alone may feel free of familial control, of constant surveillance by the kinship network. They may feel free to experiment with new patterns of behavior and to search for a more autonomous personal identity. The opportunity to become self-reliant and to develop a personal identity is often considered the most positive consequence of migration for women. Many Iranian women who immigrated alone, however, feel shame and guilt for developing an American-influenced identity.

RON KELLEY:
And the community criticized you for this article, particularly the men?

SARSHAR:
Oh, yes. I was even insulted. You can ask my colleague here how many people called and said, "What is this she is saying on the radio?"

Q:
Complaints from the men?

SARSHAR:
Women were happy, and they said, "Yes, this is our story! You should tell more!" But the men were not. Even my [male] colleague was unhappy! [*laughter*] He said, "How dare you!" I was also talking about sexual relations, saying that Iranian men don't think about a woman as a person. They consider her an object. I even mentioned two or three times the word "rape," that they are raping their women every night or every week. And they said, "Oh, your views are American. This is Western civilization." They didn't like it. But women are more aware of their situation here.

Q:
Isn't it true that marriage in Iran is historically a procreative and economic relationship? Isn't it true that a Persian man and wife are not necessarily friends?

SARSHAR:
Yes.

Q:
That is to say, you don't share everything with your wife or husband.

Other Iranian immigrants or family members back home may criticize them for not conforming to traditional roles. Although they may have left their families behind, the success or failure of individual family members reflects on the family as a whole. A woman's misbehavior, especially sexual misbehavior, brings shame not only on her, but on all members of her family (Barakat 1985).

Iranian women who successfully adapt to American society are often rejected by the home culture. Iranian immigrants in Los Angeles, especially the women, have a reputation for conspicuous consumption among other Iranian immigrants in this country and in Europe, as well as back home. They are stereotyped as *taghooti*, a term rooted in idolatry that in this context implies decadence, narcissism, immorality, and hedonism. The Iranian community in Los Angeles is known in Iran as the source of contraband music videos—vulgar and commercial, these represent the worst elements of westernization.

Because of love-hate sentiments toward the West in general and Americans in particular, immigrants in Los Angeles, particularly the females, must prove that such stereotypes do not apply to them. To be westernized or Americanized has strong negative connotations, politically, culturally, and sexually.

Even before the revolution, westernized members of the urban upper-middle and middle classes were regarded as a fifth column, promoting imperialism, family disintegration, moral degeneration, and cultural erosion. In the campaign against westernization waged by the Iranian intelligentsia, particularly the Islamists, westernized women were held to epitomize all social ills (Najmabadi 1989; Tohidi 1993). The clergy cleverly pointed to a few highly visible upper-middle- and middle-class women preoccupied with Western fads and fashions in condemning all unveiled, nontraditional, and progressive women as "Westoxicated." In the Islamic clergy's political discourse, modern women were stereotyped as frivolous and westernized and condemned as *fitna*, the erotic agents of social and moral disorder (Mernissi 1975). The clergy demanded a return to the veiled Islamic model of womanhood. During the Islamic revolution, the Iranian women's rights movement, which opposed the discriminatory and retrogressive policies of the new government, was crushed as an accomplice to imperialism.

With such a political history, Iranian immigrant women have had to search for a new identity acceptable to their ethnic community and appropriate to the realities of their host country. To avoid becoming marginal members of both societies, these women are trying to find their way along a painful and tangled route between tradition and modernity. The quest for

You don't tell your wife how much money you have. You don't tell your wife what you are doing in your business. Your wife is supposed to run your house, to give you services, to cook, to clean, to take care of the children, and to shut down.

personal as well as national and cultural identity has become a major concern of educated and politically conscious Iranian women, immigrant or otherwise. A very difficult challenge for a migrant woman is to balance her individuality and personal aspirations with a positive ethnic identity.[2]

Migration studies show that "light-skinned, young, and educated migrants usually encounter a more favorable reception in the United States than dark-skinned, older, and uneducated newcomers" (Espin 1987, 493). Even though the majority of Iranian women immigrants in Los Angeles possess these helpful attributes, hostile political relations between Iran and the United States have kept them from being accepted. The American bias against Arabs and other Middle Easterners was compounded by the "hostage crisis," making Iranians one of the least liked minority groups in American society.

Nevertheless, Iranian women migrants perceive less ethnic and racial discrimination against them in American society than do Latinas, for example. They are less worried about having an Iranian surname than Latinas are about having a Spanish surname (Blair 1991). No significant differences were found in the perceived prejudice against Iranians in Los Angeles based on gender.

The marginality of Iranian immigrants and the other difficulties they encounter in the United States are not without rewards for women. Women can wield power from their position as mediators between the two cultures. But the positive potential of marginality can be realized only by women of the right age, class, and educational status, with the right reasons for migrating. For others the cost of being marginal to both societies is overwhelming. Isolation from one's family, especially if the separation from parents and loved ones is premature and traumatic, exacerbates the sense of belonging nowhere.

## SOCIOECONOMIC IMPACT OF MIGRATION

According to the 1980 Census, the rate of participation in the labor force among Iranians in the United States, excluding students, was 55 percent, lower than the figure for natives, 73.3 percent, or other recent immigrants, 64.4 percent (Bozorgmehr and Sabagh 1988). Though no precise data are available on the employment patterns of female Iranian immigrants, it is generally accepted that the lower rate of Iranian women's participation in the labor force depresses the employment rate of Iranian immigrants as a whole. Census figures fail to reflect women's participation in the informal labor market and in paid housework. Compared with natives and other recent immigrants, Iranian immigrants have a considerably higher rate of self-employment (Bozorgmehr and Sabagh 1988). Women actively participate in family businesses and entrepreneurial activities and occasionally own or manage them.

A high level of educational attainment and an upper-middle- or middle-class background prior to migration seem to be common characteristics among male and female Iranian immigrants in the United States. In my study, which is not necessarily applicable to the whole population of Iranians in Los Angeles, 37 percent of the women and 39 percent of the men had a college education prior to migrating. In the United States 74 percent of the women and 76 percent of the men enrolled in college-level academic or vocational programs. Forty percent of the women and 58 percent of the men were proficient in English.

Migration has provided diverse employment opportunities for Iranian professional women with proficiency in English, job skills, and work experience. A number of these women now work in service and technical fields, including computer programming, nursing, medical technology, and engineering. In addition, they are well represented among financial, insurance, and real estate workers; in sales and clerical services; and in government offices, private companies, and banks. Like male Iranian immigrants, many of the highly educated professional women, at least initially, experience a decline in their economic status and career satisfaction. In my sample, 35 percent of the women reported that their economic status had declined after immigration, and 28 percent that it had risen. More than a third of both women (35 percent) and men (44 percent) agreed that Iranian women immigrants have enjoyed greater opportunities than Iranian men.

Many of the less educated immigrant women, or those lacking proficiency in English, previous work experience, or marketable job skills, have generated income by mobilizing their ethnic resources, personal abilities, and cooking, sewing, and knitting skills. Although Iranian clothing and jewelry businesses are largely controlled by men, women participate by dressmaking, doing piecework, running boutiques, and working in sales. Among married women, those who are either unemployable or who find family responsibilities or attitudes in conflict with outside employment may become involved in home-based enterprises. Many operate catering, baking, or pastry-distribution businesses, often supplying Iranian food stores. Others provide services for women, such as hair removal, hairdressing, manicures, and facials. An additional advantage of such home-based economic activities, as far as the women are concerned, is that they

FIGURE 69.  Rodeo Drive. Beverly
Hills, 1987.

FIGURE 70    Iranian Student Group
dance at UCLA. 1987.

are usually paid in cash and can avoid paying taxes on their incomes. But because these enterprises offer little prestige and have the clear disadvantage of jeopardizing family privacy as clients and outsiders invade the household domain, they are generally a last resort for the economic survival of the family.

## IMPLICATIONS OF WOMEN'S EMPLOYMENT FOR GENDER RELATIONS

Women's employment outside the home conflicts with the cult of domesticity and the traditional ideal of femininity among the Iranian urban upper class. During the Shah's modernization of Iran, a growing number of women secured work for pay as the labor market expanded, the working and middle classes grew, and the nation's economy and industries were transformed. Women never participated in the labor force at a high rate, however. During the 1970s, the peak years of modernization, women made up only 12 percent of the labor force. Many women who worked outside the home did so out of economic necessity rather than out of a desire for self-actualization or career status.

Though the number of educated, career-oriented, and professional middle-class women was small, these women were visible and vocal. Their impact on the family, male-female relations, and gender attitudes manifested itself in the prominence of women's issues and sexual politics during the 1978–79 revolution. The present tension in many Iranian immigrant families over women's economic role may be seen, therefore, as a carry-over from recent transitions in Iranian society. Factors related to immigration, however, have exacerbated the tensions between Iranian women and men. Men who reluctantly approved of women's employment accepted it only as a source of pin money or luxuries, or as a supplement to their own income. Other men have welcomed their wives' access to paid work.

With their husbands' reluctant approval—or ready support—many Iranian women immigrants are playing an unprecedented role in the economic survival of their families. Most immigrants were from the upper-middle and middle classes in Iran, their social and economic position supported by the husbands' positions as army officers, high-ranking government employees, factory managers, businessmen, or professionals. Many were able to transfer their wealth and standard of living to the United States. Those who lost their property in Iran often faced unemployment and depression in the years after emigrating, because of a combination of pride, unrealistic expectations, and a lack of skills for available jobs. To help the families survive, the wives found work, even if they had to use their homemaking skills in low-paying, low-skilled jobs. Though the women may have gradually gained power and a better self-perception from their work, the men's loss of economic and social status in public and their role reversal in private have dealt severe blows to masculine ego and pride.

Socioeconomic realities, coupled with women's faster acculturation to new gender norms, affect the male-dominated power hierarchy in the family. A lessening of male dominance and control in both public and private spheres may lead to a "crisis of masculinity," which affects not only the position and psychological state of the "head of the family" but also the whole family unit (O'Keely and Carney 1986, 145).

Men in cultures that define masculinity as the capacity to earn a salary perceive unemployment and underemployment as threats to their manhood. For such men, who expect to be the family's sole or primary provider, a woman who earns a salary, especially if that salary is the family's primary income, is considered either unfeminine or castrating. If men's privileges become accessible to women, then men may seem ineffectual and effeminate (Mernissi 1975, 104). In her analysis of male-female dynamics in the modern Muslim society of Morocco, Mernissi refers to the pervasive belief that "there is no power but in men. There are no men without money."

A middle-aged Iranian man, complaining about the negative impact of immigration, described the crisis of gender roles: "You know, one of the most demeaning effects of this damn migration is that many men have to become the wives of their wives." For their part, some working women suffer from guilt for not spending enough time with their children and not meeting their "feminine" responsibilities adequately.

Further confusion and anxiety stem from the children's own experiencing of role reversals. When they fail to show respect for adults, especially the elderly, and begin to question their parents' authority, children jeopardize the traditional power and authority of the father in the family.

ROLE CONFLICTS AND FAMILY DISINTEGRATION

The increasing tension in both marital and intergenerational relations stems from confusion and ambiguity about the proper role for each family member in the new social context. A sense of urgency about family disintegration, the rising divorce rate, clashes within families, and the degeneracy of youth is voiced frequently among immigrant Iranians, as well as in the Iranian media in Los Angeles.

FIGURE 71. Couple on the street in
Westwood.

FIGURE 72. Iranian Student Group
dance at UCLA. 1987.

*Intergenerational Conflicts*   Immigrant parents tend to be distressed by the rapid pace of their children's acculturation, brought about by the media, American schools, and American peers. Whereas parental authority in the traditional Iranian family is based on the parents' passing on to their children their own knowledge of life, children in immigrant families cannot readily apply their parents' knowledge to their own new lives. Instead, roles become somewhat reversed. The children are the ones passing on important information to their parents, correcting their English, and helping them in their daily interactions with Americans.

Such role reversals threaten traditional relations in the family and create tension. The children's development of an identity culturally different from that of their parents intensifies intergenerational conflicts. The gap is especially wide in families whose children grow up in American society.

One particular area of conflict concerns children's rights to privacy and personal boundaries. For example, reading mail addressed to an adolescent son or daughter is considered part of an Iranian parent's responsibility rather than an invasion of privacy. Iranian parents often resist their children's wishes to become financially independent or to move into their own apartments once they turn eighteen. While the children complain about their parents' interference in their lives, the parents complain about their children's lack of respect.

Adolescent girls and young women, especially those who immigrated with their families, must decide how to "become American" without losing their own cultural heritage, if they decide to "become American" at all. Role models of successful and respected bicultural Iranian American women are scarce, and for young women the negative cultural and political connotations of being westernized or Americanized are particularly problematic. Given the myth prevalent among Iranians that American women are sexually loose, being Americanized may be equated with sexual promiscuity. Conflicts between female adolescents and their parents frequently focus on appropriate sexual behavior. Hanassab's 1991 study of dating and sexual attitudes among younger Iranian immigrants shows that the women are torn between two norms: behavior acceptable to their American peers, on the one hand, and their parents' expectations and their own obligations to their native culture, on the other. Some young women rebel against parental pressure by turning their back on Iranian culture and customs—changing their Iranian names to American ones (Blair 1991), for example, or refusing to speak Persian at home.

*Gender Role Conflicts*   Commentators who cite cultural collision, economic pressures, and sexual freedom as the causes of familial instability among Iranian immigrants also blame women for the current crisis because of their failure to fulfill their proper role. Women who have become "Americanized" are criticized for their loss of originality (*esalat*) and Iranian "female virtues," including obedience (*etaat*), chastity (*nejabat*), patience (*saburi*), and self-denial (*fadakari*). Americanization, which is equated with individualism and selfishness, undermines the commitment to family and the endurance needed to withstand the hardships of immigration.

In response, some immigrant women, particularly feminists, criticize Iranian men for failing to adjust their attitudes and expectations in the face of new realities. Women criticize their resistance to egalitarian relationships and their conscious or unconscious adherence to traditional values and patriarchal norms.

Some men actually cling to traditional norms for gender relations as a reaction to the perceived threat of women's new independence. A similar reaction is also seen among parents who perceive their children's faster pace of acculturation and parent-child role reversals as intolerable challenges to parental power and authority. When adult immigrants are uncertain and confused about what is right and wrong, many hold on to the "old ways," which they idealize in defending against a loss of identity. This refusal to accept change may intensify both intergenerational and gender-role conflicts in the immigrant families (Espin 1987, 493).

*Ethnic Variations* Such defensive loyalties to the traditional gender norms of the home culture seem to be less common among Muslim immigrant families than among the religious and ethnic minorities. In my survey, for example, Jewish and Armenian Iranians exhibited more conservative attitudes toward sexual norms and gender roles than their Muslim counterparts,[3] perhaps in part because Iranian Jews and Armenians tended to migrate to the United States as families and kinship groups rather than as isolated individuals. Therefore, from the beginning of the acculturation process, ethnic pressure and the surveillance of the kinship network have reinforced conformity to traditional norms. The very presence of the kinship network may protect young women so that they need not develop self-reliance and autonomy.

Muslim Iranians tend to be more secularized than other Iranian ethnic groups. Perhaps they developed an antipathy to Islam and Islamic tradition out of their own political and cultural opposition to the Islamic theocratic government in Iran and found that it was reinforced in the United States by the pervasively negative image of Muslims in the media and public opinion. For most Muslims Iranians in Los Angeles, male and female alike, language and national culture, rather than religion, seem to constitute the primary components of identity (Ansari 1990).

FIGURE 73. Couple at an Andy and
Khuros concert at the Hollywood
Palace. 1988.

FIGURE 74. Guests arriving for a Persian
New Year's concert at the Bonaventure
Hotel. March 1986.

## DIVORCE

In adapting to a new society and new expectations, many Iranian couples manage to maintain their marriages and hold families together. An increasing number, however, are experiencing family instability, separation, and divorce. In part the rising divorce rate among Iranian immigrants is a carryover from the situation in post-revolutionary Iran. Until the 1960s, Iran's divorce rate, 16.5 percent, was one of the highest among Muslim countries, for men could divorce their wives with few legal restrictions and financial obligations. Socioeconomic changes and legal reforms from 1967 to 1976 included the Family Protection Law of 1967, which restricted both polygamy and men's unilateral rights to divorce and child custody. During this period, the divorce rate dropped to around 10 percent, and it decreased even further during the first years of revolutionary upheaval to a low of 6.8 percent. In 1980 the divorce rate reached its lowest point and the marriage rate its highest (Aghajanian 1986). But in 1981 the divorce rate started to climb; by 1988 it had reached 13.1 percent in urban areas, with the rate in Tehran higher, at 17.8 percent, than that of any other city in Iran.

From 1979 to 1988, trends in divorce rates among Iranian immigrants seemed to parallel trends among urban Iranians inside Iran. Immigration may have exacerbated familial tensions, or it may merely have facilitated some impending separations.

Five factors directly or indirectly contribute to the rising divorce rate among Iranian immigrants:

1.  *Economic pressures*, including the downward economic mobility experienced by many immigrants, at least during the years just after immigration; the underemployment of many male and female immigrants; drastic shifts into unaccustomed and usually less desirable jobs; and exhausting work schedules, especially for self-employed immigrants;

2.  *Changes in women's roles*, including women's greater access to education, vocational training, and paid work; their expanding financial and other contributions to the family; and the impact of changes in self-concept on the traditional division of labor and power hierarchy at home;

3.  *Demographic factors*, including the unbalanced age and sex distribution of immigrants (half of them are between twenty and thirty-five years old, the age range with the highest rate of both marriage and divorce; and there are nearly two males for every

female in this age group); high levels of education; and geographic distance from members of the extended family (the resulting limits on the family's intervention during crises can be beneficial as well as harmful);

4. *Effects of "cultural collision,"* including confusion about values, personal and cultural identity, and gender roles; pressure for instant changes in language, behaviors, and beliefs; introduction to different family dynamics and structures and egalitarian ideals; fierce competition for jobs and money; and daily exposure to a host society that questions old conceptions of marriage, masculinity, and femininity and fosters materialism, individualism, and disregard for the family; and

5. *Social, political, and legal factors,* including the high divorce rate in America; the ease with which divorces can be obtained and the extent to which American society tolerates them; the lack of obvious stigma attached to divorced women; the existence of a legal system and family code that protect women's rights; women immigrants' exposure to and growing sophistication about women's rights and options; more respect for individual freedom and civil rights; less glorification of women's self-denial for the good of their families, coupled with greater emphasis on realizing individual aspirations; and more respect for democracy and democratic relations, at both social and familial levels.

According to my survey findings, 66 percent of divorces among Iranian immigrants are initiated by the women. While this pattern also holds in Iran, there are some important differences. The male-biased family code in Iran, including men's unilateral right to divorce in all but the most extreme circumstances and the father's automatic right to the custody of his female children over the age of seven and his male children over the age of two, usually works as a strong check on a wife's desire to free herself from an abusive husband or an otherwise miserable marriage. The economic dependency of most women on their husbands, their fear of losing their children, the stigma attached to divorce, especially for women, and the lack of legal, social, and familial support make divorce a terrifying nightmare for most women in Iran. Instead, they "endure while burning inside" (*misuzand va misazand*).

FIGURE 75. Rodeo Drive. Beverly
Hills, 1991.

FIGURE 76. Couple at a Faramarz Asef
rock-and-roll concert at the Hollywood
Palace. 1990.

Although Iranian men desiring a divorce are also under considerable sociocultural, moral, familial, and economic pressure, their options and legal protections are greater. The only economic protection for a divorced woman is her bride price (*mahr*). To avoid ceding this money to his wife, a husband may try to portray her as the initiator of the divorce or may refuse to go through the legal procedures unless his wife forfeits her right to *mahr*.[4] Thus, women in Iran who file for divorce generally do so out of desperation or as a result of their husbands' manipulation. Immigrant Iranian women, however, may see divorce as a way to improve their lives when they see no hope and, specifically, no love in their marriages.

Close to half the women responding to my survey cited lack of love as a reason for obtaining a divorce. Over one-third cited incompatibility, another third violence and other forms of mistreatment, and close to a third felt they had married too young. Drug addiction or alcoholism and economic and financial problems were each listed by 14 percent of the sample. Among divorced Iranian men incompatibility was the reason for divorce most commonly cited, followed by economic and financial problems. Only one in ten men cited lack of love as a reason.

In contrast, reasons for divorce in Iran are reported to be excessive age differences, drug addiction, moral corruption, wife abuse, interference by in-laws in marital relations, and polygyny.[5]

Child custody is a major issue in the divorce of any couple with children. Of the divorced mothers in my sample, 75 percent were granted custody of their children. Following the divorce, however, some Muslim fathers, refusing to accept the child custody laws of the United States, have resorted to kidnapping their children and taking them back to their homeland. According to one report, twenty-one Iranian children in Europe and thirty-three in the United States have been kidnapped and taken to Iran by their fathers or their fathers' associates. Despite the fairly small number of cases, this practice has drawn international media attention. Because of immigrant women's organized actions, the supportive efforts of women's groups, and diplomatic intervention by some of the countries involved, certain legal protections have recently been established to prevent such actions. The Iranian government has cooperated with the efforts of the French and British governments to return kidnapped children to their non-Iranian mothers in England and France (Hendesi, 1990–1991).

Immigrant women find it easier than their counterparts in Iran both to obtain divorces and to cope with their lives as divorced women. One reason is the relative ease with which divorced Iranian women can remarry in the United States. Economic, legal, and social factors, as well as demographics, favor Iranian immigrant women in the "marriage market."

Although the factors affecting the divorce rate among Iranian immigrants also affect single male and female immigrants who expect to be married, single immigrants feel other pressures either to marry or remain single.

Families constantly pressure unmarried immigrants to marry—especially women, particularly those whose parents still live in Iran. No telephone call or letter from Mom or Dad concludes without some encouragement to marry.

They are also pressured by their own feelings of loneliness. Over half of the men and women who responded to my survey complained of such feelings and of the lack of opportunities to meet a potential partner. The unbalanced sex ratio among Iranians, the absence of the kinship network to help in matchmaking, the residential sprawl of Los Angeles in general, and the lack of a concentrated Iranian neighborhood to facilitate contacts between people have all made it difficult for single Iranians to find potential marriage partners, especially Iranian partners. Some immigrants are overcoming such difficulties by placing ads for potential spouses in various Persian media.

Some single Iranian immigrants, however, have grown ambivalent about marriage. Male immigrants are pushed and pulled by economic insecurity, lowered self-confidence, anxiety about women's changing roles and expectations, and easier access to sex and casual sexual relations, particularly with non-Iranians. Women immigrants feel similarly ambivalent because of a growing sense of independence, frustration with Iranian men's hesitance to adopt egalitarian gender norms, a greater acceptance of women who choose to remain single, and the news of rising divorce rates.

The majority of Iranian immigrants bend to family pressure and follow the culture's customs and rituals regarding dowry, bride price, spouse selection, and marriage. Regardless of the financial burden involved, the groom's family is expected to provide a lavish wedding feast; the groom is expected to ensure the future economic security of his bride through the bride price; and the bride is expected to bring a dowry of furniture and household goods

Although some Iranian immigrants base their decisions about marriage on individual preference and love, the choice of a spouse is generally still supervised, if not actually made, by the family. Among the most important criteria for selecting a spouse are the social reputation and class of his or her family. By marrying into a "good family," both men and women can enhance their own prestige and their chances for socioeconomic mobility, and they can establish ties with an influential kinship network that can be relied on for assistance in the immigration context.

FIGURE 77. Couple sitting in a Santa
Monica park. 1987.

FIGURE 78. Iranian Student Group
dance at UCLA. 1987.

Young men and women are also concerned with other criteria for selecting a spouse. In my study, the majority of both the men and women indicated that character was the most important criterion. Given the fulfillment of this qualification, women then selected husbands on the basis of education, family background, occupation and income, chastity, and physical appearance, in that order. For men, the order was different, starting with chastity, followed by physical appearance, education, family background, and occupation.

As these responses indicate, there is still a considerable emphasis on the virginity of the bride. This is especially true among Jewish Iranians. Although sex outside of marriage is sanctioned for single Iranian men, especially if their partners are non-Iranians, single Iranian women are expected to remain chaste. Shame and dishonor are the costs of sexual relations outside of marriage with Iranian men, and sex with non-Iranians represents betrayal.

When a young single woman meets a potential marriage partner, therefore, she usually avoids any sexual intimacy with him in order to present herself as a non-Americanized (pure) woman who is worthy of marriage. She may act differently with non-Iranian men or even Iranian men who are not eligible for marriage. This is a frustrating game, however, with no established rules of play, and many young Iranian women are trapped in a confusing place between their own needs and desires and the sexual norms supposedly governing their behavior.

Being caught between two cultures causes confusion for young Iranians of either gender, as the following excerpt from an interview suggests:

> *Woman:* If I have no sex with him during our friendship, I may disappoint him by being too old-fashioned and lose him to another woman who is willing to have sex with him. But if I get that close to him, he may look down on me, lose his respect for me, and eventually find me not suitable for marriage. During marriage, if I disregard the customary women's expectations of men regarding things like the bride price, a large wedding party, and expensive jewelry, he might think, how come am I selling myself so cheap; there must be something wrong with me. His family will say, oh, she must have lost her virginity—that is why her demands are so low.

> *Man:* I do not know how to treat an Iranian girl anymore. If I let her have the same share of power and say in decision making, acknowledge her independence, both financially and emotionally (for example, let her pay the bills occasionally and so forth), she may look down on me as a weak and incompetent man to rely on. But if I play the game the way my father's generation did, she may see me as an old-fashioned male chauvinist. Iranian

women have become confused and confusing. On one hand, they want independence and autonomy. On the other hand, they desire to be provided for, pampered, and protected by men. I find it much easier to go out with American women. I know what they want and what I am expected to do. They do not play all these confusing and frustrating games.

Confusion about expectations is compounded by the ample evidence that many sexual norms no longer function. Some sexual relationships end up in marriage, and some marriages might not have failed if the partners had had sexual relations before the wedding. Cohabitation by unmarried couples, though not approved wholeheartedly, is possible for some non-conforming Iranians.

As much as members of the new generation of immigrants may wish to free themselves from the tutelage of the family, the kinship network is an important source of socioeconomic protection. For example, family ties and privileges can sometimes prevail over an individual immigrant's lack of experience or ability in opening up jobs, obtaining financial backing, and subsequently achieving success in business.

Such traditional functions of marriage are present to an even greater extent and on a grander scale in Iran. Marriages can influence the composition of social classes, the social mobility of a kinship network, and the political power hierarchy within a community. Several of the prophet Mohammad's own marriages were contracted for political reasons. In contemporary Iran, both Reza Shah and his son, Mohammad Reza Shah, married daughters of tribal chieftains (Khavanin) to forge alliances with them and to secure their allegiance (Afshar 1989). Although the number of family-arranged marriages has been declining, marriage is still an important transaction between two lineages and the whole community as well as between two individuals.

A new version of the arranged marriage is currently linking Iranian men in the United States with Iranian women in Iran. Through their kinship networks, many Iranian Muslim men are seeking to overcome the shortage of Iranian women in Los Angeles by mail ordering brides from the homeland. For a man who can afford to go to Iran, politically and financially, the exchange of photographs is followed by a short visit to meet the nominated bride in person and to get married. The next step is to help his new wife immigrate to the United States. Because of the repression of women in Iran and the economic obstacles preventing marriage to Iranian men, many young women are quite willing to leave the country. An Iranian man in America who has a green card and a decent income will find the marriage market in Iran very receptive.

FIGURE 79. Halloween concert at the
Hollywood Palace. 1988.

FIGURE 80. Halloween party at a
nightclub in West Hollywood.

In the years before and immediately after the 1979 revolution, Iranians were one of the most politically active ethnic groups in the United States. Since students made up the main body of Iranian residents during this period, grassroots activism took place largely at colleges and universities. Female Iranian students participated in political activities at a rate that was proportional to—if not greater than—their representation in the Iranian population in the United States as a whole.

For example, the World Confederation of Iranian Students, one of the largest and most organized, active, and militant student organizations in the United States, had recruited female students into its Los Angeles chapters (Matin-asgari 1991). Local branches of the confederation, Iranian Students Association (ISA), played a significant role in politicizing several campus environments, including the University of Southern California, the University of California, Los Angeles, and the California State University, Los Angeles. Female members of each ISA chapter participated in the international campaign against the Shah, demonstrations, sit-ins, study groups, publications, political debates, and a variety of cultural activities and student services. It was mainly through the ISA that young Iranian women were politicized. At ISA readings and discussion groups, they were exposed to progressive politics in general and to the idea of women's oppression in particular. They experienced, sometimes for the first time, nontraditional, nonsegregated relations with Iranian men. Some credited the Shah's modernization with allowing women opportunities for higher education abroad. Many women, however, both secular and religious, inside and outside Iran, perceived the superficiality of emancipation under the Shah.

Since the mid-1980s, political activism has declined among the Iranian immigrants. Women have remained relatively active and visible among supporters of the Mojahedin, an Islamic group opposing the present government in Iran. Though isolated and declining in membership, this group has maintained a persistent political presence in the Iranian communities. Political activism among right-wing, pro-monarchy women in Los Angeles appears to be limited to participation in one or two demonstrations a year against the Islamic government. Some Iranian women, accepting their residency in the United States as long-term or permanent, have become involved in U.S. domestic politics. A woman sits on the fifteen-member board of directors of the Iranian Republican party. She also serves as the only female on the party's thirty-member board of advisors.

With the decrease in conventional political activities among the immigrant Iranians, a different social and political activism has emerged. Informally, for the most part, women have taken the initiative in organizing people around cultural, ethnic, social, familial, and gender issues. Formal organizations of Iranians, whether their purposes are related to culture or business, tend to be hierarchically structured, composed of professionals, and organized and managed by males. Immigrant women have organized less formal, less hierarchical, and voluntary cultural activities and social services. The main purposes of these activities include consciousness raising, social networking, maintaining ethnicity and a sense of community, and emotional and moral support.

Iranian immigrant women are expected, even more than women in Iran, to transmit group values and preserve the cultural heritage. Instead of seeing this duty as a burden, some women, especially Jewish Iranians, have taken it up as an honor and privilege. By organizing cultural activities, women activists not only elevate their own position and increase their influence but also help safeguard the cultural integrity, ethnic identity, and mental health of the Iranian immigrants. Such activities include cultural celebrations, religious ceremonies, tours, picnics, and monthly or weekly social gatherings held in homes (*dowreh*) or public places. Women have also been instrumental in establishing schools and classes to teach children the Persian language and Iranian arts and history.

In recent years social and cultural activities pertaining to gender politics have expanded. Former members of Iranian leftist organizations make up the core and leading activists of present-day Iranian women's groups. Disappointed by the failure of political organizations inside and outside Iran to address women's issues, disillusioned with the groups' inability to defend the revolution against the Islamic theocracy, and frustrated with the inequities of men's and women's power in the groups, many political activists have become involved in the women's movement, organizing or joining independent women's groups.

Women refugees, exiles, or immigrants with such political backgrounds have been able to exchange ideas with women of other nationalities in America. In independent women's groups, which do not restrict them to clerical, hostess, and child-care roles, women are making decisions and gaining further political experience and ideological sophistication. The increasing economic independence of Iranian immigrant women, the present tension in male-female relations, and Iranian men's resistance to sharing labor and power in the family help explain the growing influence of feminist ideas among Iranian immigrants.

Feminist activities in the Iranian community include consciousness-raising meetings, study groups, publications, radio programs, and public lectures and conferences on familial concerns. A number of Iranian feminists have also joined multinational, multicultural coalitions concerned with women's issues and antiwar activities. In various ways Iranian feminists contribute to the political enlightenment and cultural dynamism of the immigrant community in Los Angeles as a whole. Among the more active organizations of Iranian immigrant women in Los Angeles are the Association of Iranian Nurses, Association of Iranian Families Solidarity, Association of Iranian Jewish Women, Independent Association of Iranian Women, and Cultural Association of Iranian Women. The publisher Women's Press and two periodicals, *Zan* and *Forugh*, help disseminate women's concerns in print.

While women throughout the Iranian community are involved in preserving their cultural heritage, and relatively few women from any sector are active in politics, the role of women in teaching religious tenets and practices varies according to the ethnic group and its religion. "Religion is in the hands of women," said an Iranian Jewish woman, paraphrasing her rabbi; "it is women's duty to teach, preserve, and safeguard our religion." Jewish Iranian women seem to be doing just that, though they adhere to the practices of the faith with varying strictness.

Among Muslim Iranian immigrant women the obligation to preserve the Islamic religion as such is felt less strongly. In my survey, 20 percent of the female Muslim respondents and 30 percent of the males indicated that they believed in no religion. Only 13 percent of the women and 10 percent of the men practiced daily prayer, and 10 percent of the women and 15 percent of the men fasted on holy days.

Nevertheless, many Iranian women immigrants seem to practice Islam in their own way, even though they may not strictly follow Islamic laws. Most of their religious practices have a cultural as well as spiritual value, helping them assert a group identity. Separation from the security and comfort of the native culture might have deepened their need for and admiration of the spiritual and moral values of Islam. Religious values may help them resist the extreme materialism in the host country and assuage the psychological discomfort of acculturation and cultural collision. For dependent women isolated by their lack of English language proficiency and job skills, religious practices and gatherings provide a comfortingly familiar refuge. Younger Iranian women, uncertain and confused about proper behavior, moral values, and ethnic identity, may attend religious gatherings to seek answers in Islamic spiritual and moral guidelines. This confusion and search for meaning may also account for the growing popularity of mysticism and pantheism among some immigrants and the small steadfast clientele of Iranian women psychics and palm readers.

Often, religious gatherings take place at the homes of some of the wealthier Iranian families. Gatherings held during the holy months of Moharram and Ramadan, when religious restrictions are most likely to be observed, attract the largest congregations, with women, modestly covered, segregated from the men.

The more religious women attend the regular meetings on Thursday nights that commence the Friday holy day. In these weekly meetings of twenty to thirty people, the Quran is recited, beginners receive instruction, and people engage in ceremonial prayer. At gatherings of only women, a well-respected woman with good recitation skills and exceptional religious knowledge—usually the host herself—leads or facilitates the meetings.

Even secular Iranian women participate in a religious meeting called *sufreh*, held exclusively for and by women. The original purpose of *sufreh* was to thank God for a wish fulfilled by laying a charitable table for the poor and hungry. Each of the several different kinds of *sufreh* is dedicated to and named after a female or male figure from an Islamic legend, such as Hazrat e' Fatima or Hazrat e' Abolfazl. A *khanum* leads the ceremony and receives an honorarium for her service. She is not necessarily expected to have formal Islamic training, but she must be well respected for her religious dedication and knowledge of the Quran and religious rituals. She must be witty and have a good voice. The other women sit quietly around a long, white, and tastefully set tablecloth laid on the floor. The *khanum* starts the ceremony with a moral lecture on social issues or family concerns, followed by the recitation and interpretation of Quranic verses and elegies. Hymns and fervent prayers are usually accompanied by weeping. Afterward, the ceremonial dining starts. Women take some of the meal home to share with their family, for *sufreh* food is considered sacred.

*Sufreh* has come to serve contradictory purposes: immigrant women find in it a solemn occasion for spiritual elation, emotional and psychological cleansing, and the reaffirmation of their loyalty to God; but affluent women use it to display their wealth, generosity, and homemaking skills. Although many women hold *sufreh* in the name of charity and religious belief, one of its original charitable purposes, feeding the poor, is no longer part of the ritual. The diversity of foods may vary as well as the generosity and expense involved, but *sufreh* tends to be a chic form of religiosity.

Whereas secular Iranian women immigrants rarely observe other Islamic practices, *sufreh* attracts a diverse group, from cabaret singers and dancers to veiled and strict Islamic housewives. *Sufreh*'s popularity might be due to its flexibility. It involves only a personal wish and a private solemn "contract" between a woman and God.

Although Iranian women immigrants find economic independence more feasible than women in Iran—because of expanded opportunities for higher education, vocational training, and employment, many of them, especially highly educated professionals, have seen their socioeconomic status decline in the United States, particularly when their husbands or male kin are also underemployed.

Other challenges and difficulties facing Iranian women immigrants include the pressure to adapt quickly to a new environment, a different language, and alien cultural norms; a constant sense of loss of the home country; and grief and worry over those left behind. Acculturated women may feel the stress of reconciling motherhood, marriage, and career and of struggling to balance competing identities. They must fight against becoming marginal by simultaneously reclaiming a positive ethnic identity and nourishing their newly discovered personal identity and aspirations. Those who lack the language skills, educational background, or job skills for acculturation may end up more isolated and more dependent on their husbands than they were in Iran.

The decline in the socioeconomic status of many Iranian immigrant men coupled with women's increasing economic independence and expanded contribution to the family's financial well-being has affected the traditional hierarchy of the family. Women's faster acceptance of American gender norms and sexual attitudes has further altered conjugal roles and male-female dynamics. Men perceive the changes for immigrant women as threats to Iranian patriarchy and as the cause of marital tension and conflicts and a rising divorce rate.

Intergenerational conflicts, intensified by the acculturation of children and adolescents, have further jeopardized the power of the father and the authority of the parents. Tension and confusion over proper gender roles, parental roles, and children's roles are among the major immigration-related issues for Iranians in Los Angeles.

Iranian women immigrants, overall, show great resilience, flexibility, and creativity in acculturating and adapting. Perhaps because of recent political history and revolutionary changes in Iran, efforts to push women back into traditional gender roles seem only to have encouraged them to discover their capabilities, strengths, and identities.

The present tension between Iranian women and men is perhaps the inevitable outcome of the collision of cultures and the resulting changes in familial, economic, and cultural roles. There are hopeful signs that Iranian women will continue to play a crucial role in the Iranian community's successful acculturation and adaptation to American society by asserting their own identity even as they retain a healthy sense of their ethnic identity, cultural integrity, and socioeconomic productivity.

NOTES

1.  This article draws on a survey of a sample of 134 Iranian immigrants in Los Angeles, 83 females and 51 males, and on interviews with a smaller sample of women and men. The survey questionnaire consists of a demographic section and five scales measuring acculturation, national/ethnic identity, perceived prejudice, acculturative stress items, and attitudes toward gender roles. To measure the respondents' attitudes toward gender roles, a Persian adaptation of the Spence-Helmreich scale (1978) has been employed. This scale consists of twenty-five declarative statements about proper roles and behavioral patterns for women and men. For each statement there are four response alternatives: agree strongly, agree mildly, disagree mildly, and disagree strongly.

2.  See N. Tohidi, "Identity Politics and the Woman Question in Iran: Retrospect and Prospects," in *Identity Politics and Feminism: Cross-National Perspectives*, ed. V. Mogadam (Oxford University Press: forthcoming).

3.  The number of other Iranian ethnic or religious groups in the research sample was too small to allow any meaningful comparisons.

4.  For further information on divorce patterns in Iran, see Aghajanian 1986.

5.  These reasons were cited by researchers in a 1984 roundtable on the issue of divorce in Tehran, Iran, reported in *Zan e' Ruz*, 4 and 18 of Esfand, 1363 (February 1984).

REFERENCES

Afshar, H. 1989. "Women and Reproduction in Iran." In *Women, Nation, State*, edited by N. Yuval-Davis and F. Anthias. London: Macmillan.

Aghajanian, A. 1986. "Some Notes on Divorce in Iran." *Journal of Marriage and the Family* 48 (November): 749–755.

Ansari, M. 1990. "Nasli Dowwm Iranian dar Amrica: Bohrane Howwiyat meli va mazhabi" (The second generation of Iranians in America: National and religious identity crisis). *Iran Times*, March 23, 9–12.

Barakat, H. 1985. "The Arab Family and the Challenge of Social Transformation." In *Women and the Family in the Middle East*, edited by E. W. Fernea. Austin: University of Texas Press.

Bill, J., and C. Leiden. 1984. *Politics in the Middle East*. New York: Little, Brown.

Blair, B. A. 1991. "Personal Name Change among Iranian Immigrants in the U.S.A." In *Iranian Refugees and Exiles since Khomeini*, edited by A. Fathi. Costa Mesa, Calif.: Mazda Publishers.

Bozorgmehr, M., and G. Sabagh. 1988. "High Status Immigrants: A Statistical Profile of Iranians in the United States." *Iranian Studies* 21:5–36.

Dallalfar, A. 1989. "Iranian Immigrant Women in Los Angeles: The Reconstruction of Work, Ethnicity, and Community." Ph.D. diss., University of California, Los Angeles.

Dane, N. 1980. "Social Environment and Psychological Stress in Latin American Immigrant Women." Ph.D. diss., California School of Professional Psychology, Berkeley.

Erikson, E. H. 1974. *Dimensions of a New Identity*. New York: Norton.

Espin, O. 1987. "Psychological Impact of Migration on Latinas." *Psychology of Women Quarterly* 11:489–503.

Fischer, M. J. 1978. "On Changing the Concept and Position of Persian Women." In *Women in the Muslim World*, edited by L. Beck and N. Keddie. Cambridge: Harvard University Press.

Furio, Colomba Marie. 1979. "Immigrant Women and Industry: A Case Study, the Italian Immigrant Women and the Garment Industry, 1880–1950." Ph.D. diss., New York University.

Garza-Guerrero, C. 1974. "Culture Shock: Its Mourning and the Vicissitudes of Identity." *Journal of the American Psychoanalytic Association* 22:408–429.

Ghaffarian, S. 1989. "The Acculturation of Iranian Immigrants in the United States and the Implications for Mental Health." Ph.D. diss., California School of Professional Psychology, Los Angeles.

Hanassab, S. 1991. "Acculturation and Young Iranian Women: Attitudes toward Sex Roles and Intimate Relationships." *The Journal of Multicultural Counseling and Development* 19:11–21.

Hendesi, M. 1990–1991. "Mohajerat va Zendegiye Zanashooei" (Immigration and married life). *Nimeye Digar* 12–13:74–83.

Matin-asgari, A. 1991. "The Iranian Student Movement Abroad." In *Iranian Refugees and Exiles since Khomeini*, edited by A. Fathi. Costa Mesa, Calif.: Mazda Publishers.

Melville, M. B. 1978. "Mexican Women Adapt to Migration." *International Migration Review* 12:225–235.

Mernissi, F. 1975. *Beyond the Veil: Male-Female Dynamics in a Modern Muslim Society*. Cambridge, Mass.: Schenkman Publishing.

Najambadi, A. 1989. "Power, Morality, and the New Muslim Womanhood." Paper presented at a workshop on Women and the State in Afghanistan, Iran, and Pakistan, Massachusetts Institute of Technology, Center for International Studies.

Nassehi-Behnam, V. 1985. "Change and the Iranian Family." *Current Anthropology* 26, no. 5 (December): 557–562.

O'Keely, C., and L. Carney. 1986. *Women and Men in Society: Cross-Cultural Perspectives on Gender Stratification*. Belmont, Calif.: Wadsworth Publishing.

Salgado de Snyder, V. N. 1987. "Factors Associated with Acculturative Stress and Depressive Symptomatology among Married Mexican Immigrant Women." *Psychology of Women Quarterly* 11:475–488.

Shirley, B. 1981. "A Study of Ego Strength: The Case of the Latina Immigrant Woman in the United States." Ph.D. diss., Boston University.

Szapocznik, J., and W. Kurtines. 1980. "Acculturation, Biculturalism, and Adjustment among Cuban Americans." In *Acculturation: Theory, Modes, and Some New Findings*, edited by A. Padilla. Boulder, Colo.: Westview Press.

Taft, R. 1977. "Coping with Unfamiliar Cultures." In *Studies in Cross-Cultural Psychology*, edited by N. Warren. New York: Academic Press.

Tharp, R. G., A. Meadow, S. G. Lennhoff, and D. Satterfield. 1968. "Changes in Marriage Roles Accompanying the Acculturation of the Mexican-American Wife." *Journal of Marriage and the Family* 30:404–412.

Tohidi, N. 1991. "Gender and Islamic Fundamentalism: Feminist Politics in Iran." *Third World Women and the Politics of Feminism*, edited by C. Mohanty, A. Russo, and L. Torres. Bloomington: Indiana University Press.

———. 1993. "Gender, Modernization, and Identity Politics in Iran." In *Gender and National Identity: The Woman Question in Algeria, Iran, Afghanistan, and Palestine*, edited by V. Moghadam. London: Zed Books.

Torres-Matrullo, C. 1980. "Acculturation, Sex-Role Values and Mental Health among Mainland Puerto Ricans." In *Acculturation: Theory, Models, and Some New Findings*, edited by A. Padilla. Boulder, Colo.: Westview Press.

Vazquez-Nuttall, E. V., L. Romero-Garcia, and B. DeLeon. 1987. "Sex Roles and Perceptions of Femininity and Masculinity of Hispanic Women: A Review of the Literature," *Psychology of Women Quarterly* 11:409–425.

# Interview

Fariba Khaledan, aged twenty-five, arrived in the United States when she was nine. At the time of the interview she worked as an organizer with the United Farm Workers (UFW).

KHALEDAN:     It was very difficult when we first came to the United States. I didn't know what it was going to be like. I didn't have any expectations. I was very sad to be leaving my close family, like my aunt—my father's sister—who lived with us in Iran. The first few months in the United States were the most difficult because I didn't know the language. And I came from what I consider a very warm culture to one where most people are very individualistic and concerned only with their own lives. People just didn't seem as caring—at least not immediately. I was homesick at first, and I missed my family. But after a while, as a child, I adjusted.

  I have a very good memory, so I do remember most of the time when I lived in Iran. People there are very caring—they do things for you. Friendships are not just, "Well, I'll give you a call." You know. "Call me and we'll do lunch." Iranians aren't like that; they're deeper and more loyal. They're more authentic. The relationships in this country tend to be more superficial. Of course, that changes from city to city. In a small town in the United States, people are usually nicer and kinder than they are in L.A. In a larger city people trust others less. But, overall, that feeling of community is very much alive in the Iranian culture. People are much more social. They talk to each other, you know? And that makes them much more sensitive to other people's needs and feelings about things. They go out of their way for others, and they don't even feel they're going out of their way. They're pleased to do something.

RON KELLEY:     Are you conscious of an Iranian side in you, and an American side?

KHALEDAN: Well, not exactly. In the Iranian culture you sacrifice a lot—sacrifice, sacrifice, sacrifice. For your family; they're important. You sacrifice to the point where you're not real to yourself, which I don't believe in. You know you have to do what you believe in, or you're not going to develop as a human being. In American culture, it's good that you can pursue your beliefs and ideals. In Iran it would be a lot more difficult for a woman my age to live alone or to do something like what I did—to move to Los Angeles to work for the UFW. It would be hard to break away from your family.

Q: What's it like growing up in this country, where the prevailing value system says to do one thing while your own Persian family wants you to do another?

KHALEDAN: When I was growing up, especially when I was fifteen or sixteen, I thought all the time: What values should I choose? Which are right, and which are wrong? Because I had been exposed to both sets of values, I had a third choice: to have both. When I was growing up I thought it was difficult, but now I can get along with both Americans and Iranians very easily. Because I'm a combination of both sets of values.

Q: What about *taarof* [the Iranian ritual of courtesy]?

KHALEDAN: You play it by ear. You definitely do *taarof* for Iranians, and not just because it's obligatory. It's a nice thing to do. It feels good to be of service to people. And when it's genuinely felt, then it's a good thing. But when I was growing up, my mom would say, "Even if you're dying of hunger, when you go to someone's house and they offer you something, you say, 'No thank you.' They have to offer again and again, and then you say, 'OK.' You accept." I never liked that. I'm an honest person. I'm very direct. I say, "Yes! I'm hungry. Please! Yes. I'd like something." Most Iranians won't eat anything until they're asked. But if I want to, I go ahead and eat. I mean, that's why it's there. That's the way I am. Americans don't know the concept of *taarof*—that when someone comes over to visit, you offer something. Some Americans are the worst hosts! You go into their houses and they don't care. They sit there watching TV and don't even look up at you. Some people can be like that. I don't like it. But I play it by ear. I'm sensitive to what people want, what they like, and I don't overplay it. Sometimes *taarof* is very much overplayed.

Q: When you were in high school, especially during the hostage crisis, what was your experience?

KHALEDAN: I had problems. One particular person would say, "Go home, Iranian ———!" as I walked down the hall. I don't even like to think about it. Or "Nuke Iran." Things like that. But I had it a lot easier than most Iranians because I speak English with only a slight accent. What about the people who had been here for only a year or two? They had so many problems. They couldn't even speak well, and then they were asked where they were from. "From Iran." "Oh, my God!" And the way the whole hostage thing was . . . It was like Iran had its grip on America. I didn't like the taking of hostages; they were people. But at the same time, it brought America to its knees . . . People finally knew where Iran was! [*laughter*] They knew. When you told them you were from Iran, you know . . . "Oh. You're from Iran."

Q: What tensions exist between immigrant children who are raised here and their parents, who have firmer Persian values?

KHALEDAN: When I was going to high school, I always watched the popular girls— there's a hierarchy in the high schools, from the popular people to the jocks to the burnouts—who went out and had boyfriends and things like that. They'd go to parties and get drunk, and that was the thing to do. I never liked that, but at the same time, if I . . . For example, if anyone liked me, he couldn't ask me to go out. I couldn't go out with him. So being in this environment with Iranian values is difficult. It's in opposition to the values in this country. To keep those Iranian values, you have to isolate yourself. You don't go out. You go home.

FIGURE 81.   Young woman playfully wearing No Ruz (New Year) *haft seen* (seven *s*'s) grass on her head. The Persian New Year tradition of *haft seen* is an assemblage of seven specific items beginning with the Persian letter for the sound "s" placed on a decorated table at home in late March. Two weeks after the New Year, families traditionally leave town to picnic in the country and toss away their containers of grass (one of the seven *s*'s). This particular Sizdah Bidar (thirteenth outside) gathering attracted thirty thousand Iranians for a family picnic at a park in Irvine. April 1991.

# CAUGHT BETWEEN TWO CULTURES: YOUNG IRANIAN WOMEN IN LOS ANGELES

*Shideh Hanassab*

Young Iranian immigrants in Los Angeles are caught between two cultures. They live in the traditional culture of their parents at home, but their social environment exposes them to a very different culture. Bombarded with Western standards and values by peers, schools, and the mass media, their world is neither modern nor traditional, but both. The conflict of cultures can cause pain and can divide young people from their parents. The parents cannot fully understand their children, nor the children their parents. Stress and conflict inevitably arise between the generations.

One of the areas of sharpest contrast between Western and traditional Iranian values is the association of young Iranians with members of the opposite sex. In Los Angeles this contrast is greater for young Iranian women than for men, who in Iran had more individual freedom, self-determination, and contact with the Western world than women. Immigration to the United States, however, has given young Iranian women an unfamiliar personal freedom.

In Iran, marriages usually take place within the kinship network or through a system of arranged marriages known as *khastegari*. In very traditional Iranian families, neither the boy nor the girl is consulted about whom to marry; their parents make all the arrangements. In some cases, the boy does not even know who the bride is until after the wedding ceremony when the bride unveils her face. Even in modern Iran, eligible mates are introduced to each other by family and friends, and the courtship takes place under parental supervision. In the period between engagement and marriage, the couple becomes acquainted. Dating as it is commonly practiced in the West is largely unknown in Iran, where marriage is still the only culturally acceptable path to a sexual relationship. Strong traditions make the issue of dating and intimate relationships a sensitive one—especially for women. Iranian parents condemn the relaxed sexual code of many young Americans; their children, ambivalent about Western values, blame the parents for being repressive or for not understanding.

SARSHAR:
Most Iranians living here want to be
American citizens. Actually, a lot of
them are, but they don't tell you. This
is a matter of prestige. They think that
if they are American citizens, it shows
they don't like Iran, which is not true.
I'm an American citizen myself; I tell
everybody. I didn't want to have my
picture with a chador on my Iranian
passport. And I want to be free to
travel. If I didn't want to be free, I
would have stayed in Iran. I became an
American citizen a couple of years ago.
Before that, I had problems getting
visas. I couldn't go to the countries I
wanted to visit. Three years ago, when
I was still an Iranian citizen, I had an
invitation to go to Russia for a
women's conference. I went to the
Russian consulate, and they didn't want
to give me a visa. So I decided that I
would apply for American citizenship. I
want to travel, and I don't want
anything to prevent me from doing
that. I don't think that I have lost my
attachment to my country by becoming
an American citizen. My citizenship
just makes things easier for me—I have
more freedom. Nothing more than
that. For me no politics are involved.
Being an American doesn't make me an
enemy of Iran or of another country.
No.

RON KELLEY:
Are Iranians here losing their
"Iranianness?" Are they losing their
heritage?

In American society, sexuality is generally accepted as a strong pervasive force. American schools are as much a place for young men and women to socialize as they are institutions of learning. Most Iranian parents are disturbed by their children's interest in the opposite sex and consider it improper. In Iranian culture, sexual attraction is not a matter for public display. In the West, however, sex is everywhere. Television, advertisements, stories, magazines, and the life they see around them inundate young people with examples of boy-girl attraction. The popular girl is the "sexy" one who dates the most; she is the envy of her friends.

There is a gender-based double standard for sexual morality among Iranians, as there is in many other cultures. Traditional Iranian culture distinguishes between a "good" woman, who will be protected as a virgin until marriage and then as a wife and mother, and the "bad" woman, who is available for a man's enjoyment. Although Iranians are extremely protective of their young women, they give much more freedom to their young men. Iranian parents willing to let their sons date freely do not grant the same latitude to their daughters. A young man is expected, and in some cases encouraged, to have sexual experiences before marriage. The myth that males have uncontrollable sexual needs that must be satisfied is still reinforced in most families.

In Los Angeles, Iranian families must struggle to provide their unmarried daughters the same sexual protection they would get automatically in Iran. Exposed to the more permissive attitudes of their American friends' parents and to peer group pressures, young Iranian women often wish to do what their American friends and even their own brothers do—go to dances, date, and associate freely with their friends. As one sixteen-year-old Iranian woman said, "We want to be the same as others." American college students, in particular, face social choices and opportunities that are virtually unknown in Iran. Iranian parents, however, often reluctant even to allow their daughters to go out with friends, are particularly hesitant to allow them to mix socially with the opposite sex or to date.

Many young Iranian women feel pulled in opposite directions by parents who do not let them go out on dates and American friends who encourage them to do so. The parents' usual answer, "We come from a different cultural background and our customs do not allow such behavior," only adds to the confusion. One eighteen-year-old Iranian woman described such feelings this way: "It is like that game tug-of-war. One side is pulling this way and the other side is pulling that way. At the end, you're torn apart." Another young female said, "Many Iranian girls have a hard time drawing a line. They have to pick and choose all the time, especially if the

Well, Iranians are not losing their Iranianness. They are not losing their culture. Actually, they are getting back to their culture. When we were in Iran, to be Western oriented was chic. We used to buy all our furniture from Italy. All the decorations in our house were Western, and the houses built in the last ten years actually looked Western. But now that we're here, we are nostalgic about what we lost. So whenever you go into Iranian houses, you see some touch of Iranian culture. We like to buy from Iranian painters; we are likely to have Persian rugs in our home. And we get together for Iranian nights—music and poetry recitals. In this sense, no, we are not losing our culture. But our children are more inclined toward Western civilization, Western music. They like it here more than in Iran because Iranian culture is, as you know, limited. Young people are not free; they are under the control of their parents. Here they see their American friends at schools and universities, and they want to be independent too. They want to be free. They don't want parental control. So, yes, from that point of view, they are losing Iranian culture. Iranian parents don't like it.

Q:

What do most Iranians here think of this country and of Los Angeles in particular?

SARSHAR:

Well, there are mixed feelings. We love the climate and the weather. We love the easiness of living. Everything is so easy to get, and you can find anything you want, buy anything you want. You are not resented by your neighbors.

parents pressure them. They either have to lie to their parents or hurt themselves and not have the friends they'd like to have."

Iranian youngsters who accept Western culture generally view dating as a socially acceptable way to gain popularity among their peers. They feel dissatisfied when they are judged by the standards of their parents' homeland—standards that are not part of their day-to-day realities here despite their parents' efforts to instill in them a sense of the strength and advantages of traditional Iranian ways.

Young women who accept their parents' values often feel left out in their social environment. One nineteen-year-old Iranian woman remarked, "Sometimes my American friends ask me, 'What is the matter with you? Are you a lesbian or something?' I tell them this is my choice. I don't want to be public property. I want to share myself with one particular and special person. They can't understand it. They say, 'Your parents are crazy. Why is your culture this way?' But I tell them that it is me. I like to be this way." Another young woman explained that she would tell her American friends, "I come from a background where these things are foreign, and I want to keep it that way. . . . I don't care what other people think. I should live my life the way I want to. They should want me for what I am." It is hard for her American friends to understand her explanation because they are not as close to their parents as Iranian children are. "Deep down, we are really close," the young woman added. Another young interviewee indicated, "Once, an American guy wanted to go out with me. I brought up so many different excuses (no time, another boyfriend, and so forth), but finally I said, 'Listen, my parents don't want me to!' He was shocked. He just shook his head. Americans, especially guys, are stunned. They can't believe that another country could be so different from theirs. They just sit there and shake their heads with their mouths hanging open!" One young woman said that many American youngsters think she is "a slave without any brain. A fanatic."

These traditional young Iranian women have accepted their parents' belief that American-style male-female relationships are inappropriate for young Iranians. One of them said, "Sometimes I think, why? I don't see any reason to go out now. If I go out with someone, it will get me nowhere. First, I would fall behind in my studies. My parents probably wouldn't like that. I have seen people who date have so many problems. A friend of mine was an A student. She dropped to C's and D's." Another insisted, "I am completely against having boyfriends. I can tell you very easily I have never had a boyfriend, and I don't want one. This issue goes back to where you come from and how you have been raised and whether you can keep

This is one of the good points about living in Los Angeles, in the United States. If you're in Europe, they don't like foreigners. They look at you strangely, especially in England and France. Iranians are not happy with the French and English people. Actually, there is anti-Iranian feeling among American people, but it's not personal. If you talk to Americans, one person to another, you see that they don't like the Iranian government or the Iranian people, but they do not resent you. At least, I haven't seen any resentment. Nor have my children or relatives.

Q:

Even during the hostage crisis?

SARSHAR:

I didn't experience it. I was on a radio talk show, KABC 790, Michael Jackson's program, for an hour, and we had calls coming in with questions about Iran. And only two of about twenty callers said, "What are you doing here? Just go on back to your country. We don't want you over here." Most of them were just curious. They had questions to ask. How are the Iranians doing here? What are they? We don't know about them. Are you pro-Shah? Are you pro-Khomeini? And I said, no, we are not pro-Khomeini. If we were pro-Khomeini, what would we be doing here? Some people were upset about rich people buying properties in Beverly Hills, and they said we have monopolized the financial schedule—I don't know what you call it—in Beverly Hills and elsewhere. But we feel safe here.

your traditional principles or not." According to still another, a sixteen-year-old, "Many of my friends have boyfriends, and they tell me that they have so many problems. They feel heartbroken, cheated . . . It's like . . . Forget it. I'll wait until I'm older and more serious and have more reasons to go out. I think dating has more disadvantages than advantages. In having fun you might get hurt." These young women felt secure in their convictions. They mentioned divorce, loose family ties, and unwanted pregnancies among Americans in reaffirming their own traditional attitudes and behaviors. They communicated freely with their parents and clearly had internalized their fathers' and mothers' values. One twenty-year-old said of her relationship to her parents, "We talk about problems openly all the time. I can tell them everything, not because I have to, but because I like to share it with them."

There are, of course, many Iranian women in Los Angeles who date and have boyfriends, feeling that it is normal and important and essential for the success of later relationships. One twenty-year-old explained, "Having a boyfriend is not a big deal for me. I've had boyfriends, but I probably put more limitations on my relationships than American women." A twenty-six-year-old said, "Whenever I have had a relationship, even when I was younger, I thought it should have some substance. I had to really love the person. I never thought it was for having fun. If I just wanted to have fun, I could have it with my regular friends. For me, it's deeper than that. But Americans just go out to have fun and spend time together." Another young woman who had a non-Iranian boyfriend stated, "I believe it's normal to have intimate relationships. It's bad not to ever have a relationship and end up getting married to one person."

Some young Iranians complained that their parents were too concerned about the Iranian community's reaction to young women dating. As one young woman described her situation: "My parents are constantly conscious of my reputation in this society and feel I should be very careful. I don't like it. I think we should live for ourselves, not for other people." Another young woman living in Los Angeles for eight years noted, "My parents are open-minded and try to understand my social needs. But at the same time they're concerned about my sensitive position as a young woman in this Iranian community. They always remind me that I'm part of a community with a different background, and I should be sensitive to both my own reputation and my family's."

Many young Iranian women feel that their parents are overprotective when it comes to dating. One young woman who lived with her father said, "My father is very open-minded and highly educated. I can discuss

We have only one big problem: our children. We feel that we're losing them to sexual liberation, drugs, and homosexuality. We didn't consider these things when we were in Iran. These problems worry us a lot. Maybe it's our fault. Maybe we should have been more aware, done more research about the country we were going to. But we didn't have time. We fled Iran. We knew the United States was the land of opportunity, and it would be a safe haven for us. And now, after ten years, we find that something isn't going right: our children and their future.

everything openly with him. But issues related to dating worry him too much. He's afraid I might get hurt." According to another woman, "My parents are concerned too much about what might happen to me. They always tell me that they trust me but not the social environment here." One eighteen-year-old said, "I wish my parents were not so concerned. I'm old enough to know what is right and wrong by now. I myself put restrictions and limitations on a relationship so it won't go too far." Another young woman stated, "I can't openly tell my parents that I'm going out with a guy just as a friend because they start to get protective and say, 'No. You are going to get serious.'"

On the issue of marriage the trend among Iranians in Los Angeles is toward freedom of choice. Few families here expect to arrange the marriage of their children without consulting them. Most parents, however, do not feel that they should leave the matter entirely up to the children. One eighteen-year-old woman said, "Our parents act and behave as though we are their possessions. They say, 'We have to OK the person you go out with first.' But it shouldn't be this way. This is my life, and I think I should be the one who chooses the person I marry!" Many parents claim that they will allow their children to make marriage decisions themselves. Often, however, they influence—and even manipulate—their children's decision by making sure the children know their likes and dislikes. One liberal young woman said, "My parents are different in many ways from other parents. For example, my mom says, 'If you love the guy and if you see some future in it, then why not? Go out with him.' I guess they've taught me what's right and wrong and now they can leave it up to me, to my judgment. But there are some things I won't allow myself to do. For example, I wouldn't have sex just for fun. That's too sacred for me. I have to love the person and see some potential for the future of the relationship to do that." Young Iranian females may be shifting toward individual choice, but they make their choices under restraint, and the parents can still intervene. The community and parents have set criteria for a suitable mate, and children are expected to choose someone who meets those criteria—in nationality, class, and religion. For instance, one sixteen-year-old explained, "Iranian parents don't like us to go with guys and to date because we may fall in love with someone who has a different religion, and we can't marry him because of that. So most girls go out with the right person, of the right religion, and at the right age, and they look for a husband at the same time. It's more serious for us than for Americans." Another indicated, "My parents are afraid that if I go out with a guy, I may like him and he might not be Jewish, and I might do something I might regret in the future." Another indicated, "My parents think the person I go out with must be older—out of college—and have a job and must have the same religion." By setting standards for the young men their daughters may date, parents help maintain their ethnicity and religion in the new country. Parents are especially afraid of losing their traditions if their children intermarry.

Many children feel heavy parental pressure to make a traditional marriage, and some are dissatisfied with the role their parents play in this decision, finding it hard to believe that romantic love will grow *after* marriage. Others try to accommodate their parents' values and wishes. As one eighteen-year-old noted, "I try to compromise and understand their points and also help them accept what I think is right." Another young woman remarked, "You learn to compromise; you have to adjust!" Some women indicate the need to work out new compromises that let them both adapt to American life and retain traditional Iranian values. Many Iranians in Los Angeles have resigned themselves to a prolonged or even permanent stay and increasingly feel the need to adjust to mainstream American culture, with its different norms and social expectations. They will probably, gradually, develop lives that differ from those in both the host culture and their own original culture.

Iranians in the United States must decide how to adapt fully to American life and how much to retain of their own cultural traditions. The gap that exists in any society between parents and children is much greater for Iranian families in Los Angeles. As a result, both parents and their children suffer.

All young adults must ultimately establish themselves. Iranians raised in the confusion of Western urban life find the task more difficult. Assimilation to the larger culture carries overtones of disloyalty and the threat of abandonment; the reaffirmation of Iranian cultural identity, however, still leaves them prey to continuing pressure to assimilate.

SUGGESTED READINGS

Bozorgmehr, M., and G. Sabagh. "High Status Immigrants: A Statistical Profile of Iranians in the United States." *Iranian Studies* 21 (1988): 5–36.

Ghaffarian, S. "The Acculturation of Iranians in the United States." *The Journal of Social Psychology* 127 (1987): 565–571.

Hanassab, S. "Acculturation and Young Iranian Women: Attitudes toward Sex Roles and Intimate Relationships." *The Journal of Multicultural Counseling and Development* 19 (1991): 11–21.

Hanassab, S. "Change of Premarital and Sexual Attitudes of Young Iranian Women: From Iran to Los Angeles" (manuscript).

Hanassab, S., and R. Tidwell. "Cross-cultural Perspective on Dating Relationships of Young Iranian Women: A Pilot Study." *Counseling Psychology Quarterly* 2 (1989): 113–121.

Touba, J. R. "Marriage and the Family in Iran." In *The Family in Asia*, edited by M. S. Das and P. D. Bardis. New Delhi: Vikas Publishing House, 1978.

PART IV

WEALTH AND ECONOMICS

FIGURE 82.  Businessman in downtown
Los Angeles.

*Interview*

Sia Kalhor is a partner in Four Corners Properties, developers of the L.A. Fashion Gallery.

KALHOR: I work with a Canadian company, managing properties here. We have a lot of Iranian tenants—businessmen, merchants. I deal with people from different backgrounds, different religions. We have one hundred and fourteen tenants right now downtown. We own these four corners here, the building across the street, and the building on the corner of Eighth and Santee. We own the site on the corner of Los Angeles and Olympic—the big one, across from California Mart. We have seventeen properties—buildings—and some land.

We're building a thirty-five million dollar project here—it's the biggest shopping center in downtown L.A., called L.A. Fashion Gallery. It's four stories, two hundred thousand square feet of retail and wholesale all under one roof. With the demand here for stores and retail spaces, we are putting everything under one roof, and it's very successful right now. We are excited about it. A lot of Iranians are coming in here too, let me tell you. So far we have leased the first two floors of this building and at least fifty percent of the tenants are Iranians. They're in business, professional people who really have something to say about the economy in downtown L.A.

The role of Iranians in the economy of L.A. is underestimated. We really play a big part in its prosperity and what has happened here lately. You listen to the economic news, and you hear that retail prices have increased, the cost of living has gone up, or inflation is coming. Lately they have been saying, for example, that wholesale prices have increased. That's a scary thing for any economy, any government. But it has nothing to do with Los Angeles. You cannot compare Los Angeles with any other city in America. I've been in the downtown district eleven years, doing what I'm doing. That's why I understand what's

FIGURE 83. Businessmen in the
garment district, downtown Los Angeles.
1989.

FIGURE 84. Persian rug merchant inspecting carpets brought by a prospective seller in the La Cienega district of West Hollywood.

trade. I saw she was working very hard and making only a little money. We had five to ten thousand dollars in savings, and we decided to start our own place and see what happened. We started the business with the help of some Iranian people—some importers who used to bring fabric from the Orient.

Q: You had some economic support.

KALHOR: Yes. They gave us credit. We got the fabric on a sixty-day basis. We made the dresses, put them on hangers, and started selling them. We paid our debts as we made money. Fortunately, the idea was good and we knew where we were going.

Q: I've heard that most of the Iranians now living here were affluent in Iran. Some lost their money, but a lot of developers had money to begin with.

KALHOR: Oh, yes. Iranians are divided into two groups here—I can tell you from my tenants and my experiences with them. Some really need the business; their life and their families—putting bread on the table—depend on it. They have, say, between fifty and two hundred thousand dollars cash. They don't want to work for anybody. They come here, they put all their money in the business, and they really fight and hang on and work. That's one group. In the other are people who have, say, half a million dollars sitting in the bank, different CD accounts—they brought money with them. The majority of Iranian people who live here in L.A. are in this group. They all live in Beverly Hills. They just don't want to sit at home. So they come in here and they play. They buy twenty thousand dollars worth of merchandise, they put up a store, they get a lease, and they sit in their store. At lunch time they go to an Iranian restaurant and sit together, talking. They don't care if today they didn't make the rent or tomorrow they won't sell. Some of them make money, too, just by being in the atmosphere. But I feel that some of them don't care. Some Jewish Iranians don't open on Saturdays, even though Saturday is the biggest day for retail here.

Q: The majority of people down here in the garment district are Persians?

KALHOR: Let me tell you, if Iranians leave this place, you might as well close downtown. The wheels will stop.

Q:     Do you have any idea how many Iranians down here are as successful as you are?

KALHOR:     I am very fortunate to be where I am. It's not all because of my talent. I've been lucky. A lot of Iranians struggle, but they hang in there. They're like the Koreans in this. We are all fighters. We come from a very strong race—nobody wants to give up. They hang on. That's what makes this place successful.

Q:     Were there any troubles with the city?

KALHOR:     They are thrilled to have us here. They're giving a lot of parking tickets. [*laughter*] The city is making a lot of money from this. There's a lot of crime around here. We try to tell them about all the homeless people moving here. They steal from stores and there are no police downtown. They'd rather spend their time in Beverly Hills, on the quiet streets. Here it's rough. But the city should be thrilled with us. Just the money they make from the parking tickets! Unbelievable.

Q:     There are Koreans here, Iranians, Israelis, Americans, and so forth, but is it true that the real estate development is predominantly Iranian?

KALHOR:     Yes. Some Iranians have gotten together, and when they're together, they are very powerful. They have the money to buy, so they're buying land here. They think it's going to happen here and they're right.

Q:     Do you have any idea how many people we're talking about who are developers or tenants? How many developers? How many tenants? Any idea?

KALHOR:     There are a few partnerships that buy properties in this district. Maybe five. But easily fifty percent of the tenants are Iranians. I have about fifty to sixty Iranian tenants myself. And they have Iranian employees. Maybe there are two thousand all together.

Q:     Are there any individuals here who are well known? I know on Rodeo Drive there's . . .

KALHOR:     Mahboubi. Yes, there are some people who know each other. You're talking to one of them, actually! [*laughter*] We know people. If I go on the street, they know who Sia is. They come to me; they want to know what's happening. We have things to say about their business.

Q:     Have you run into any resentment in the American community here for being successful?

KALHOR:   Yes. We had to fight it most of the time. But when we established ourselves, they knew we were there and couldn't hurt us anymore, and they went away. But in the beginning . . . Developing in a big city! Now we have people doing things for us. [*laughter*] But in the beginning, it was hard. They wanted to know, "What are you doing here?" But I think some of them appreciate our guts and our hard work. They like us. Some of them understand that we have things to say about this city.

Q:     Do you have plans beyond the L.A. Fashion Gallery?

KALHOR:   Yes. We just bought a ten-million-dollar parcel one block down; you go one block down and you'll see it. Wall Street and Eighth Street. We want to build a whole complex. It's two and a half acres, the biggest piece of land in downtown L.A.

Q:     Do you have any sense of the value of what this company owns?

KALHOR:   Of course. I know how much we put in the bank every month. Assets? We have about fifty million dollars in assets here. Not what we borrow. What we can cash out now.

Q:     OK, so after the L.A. Fashion Gallery, then you go on to the next phase, and then . . .

KALHOR:   Essentially, we are in our other phase. You can go see it over on the corner of Santee and Los Angeles and Olympic. We just put in the concrete. We're doing another one, a block away from here. You can see there's construction on the corner. All the way to Los Angeles Street. You can see my name and number there too.

FIGURE 85. Perfume billboard in Westwood.

# Interview

Sam Amir-Ebrahami is a financial consultant with Merrill Lynch. He is also the secretary of the Iranian Rotary Club and a member of the Iranian Entrepreneur Coalition.

RON KELLEY:    Why haven't Iranians here in Los Angeles asserted themselves politically? Why haven't they used their economic power for their own political agenda? A lot of minorities are vocal and visible in this country, and I've heard complaints in the Iranian community that Iranians are invisible to the mass media, that the mass media haven't paid much attention to them.

EBRAHAMI:    I'll tell you exactly why they have been invisible. It's because of the negative attitude that the Western media have had toward us during the past ten years, since the uprising in Iran. There are people who are, unfortunately, ashamed of being called Iranian. I've seen it. There's nothing to be ashamed of. People should be proud of what they are. I am an Iranian from day one till the last day I live in this world. But the mass media, the media that were so wonderful to us Iranians before the revolution, all of a sudden turned against us.

Q:    Is it true that, at least in some areas of the Iranian business community, Iranians consider it a disadvantage to be recognized by the American buying public as Iranians? Because of the stereotypes.

EBRAHAMI:    Yes, some people think that way. But I don't, because I live among Americans. I work with them, as you can see right now. And I enjoy working with them and haven't had any problems.

Q:    What do you think the future economic impact of Iranians in Los Angeles will be?

EBRAHAMI: It's going to be massive; it's going to move the economy, especially in Los Angeles and California. Day by day Iranians are getting more involved in every sector of business. Everything—from import and export (I deal with people who are involved in large businesses and I've seen how involved they are getting) to banking. They are doing everything they can.

Q: But are they only now becoming able and recognizing how to use their capital?

EBRAHAMI: Exactly. A lot of people were destroyed completely during the past ten years because they didn't know how to invest in this country.

Q: They got out of Iran with money and lost it here?

EBRAHAMI: Yes. Because they were unfamiliar with this system, the tax regulations and other things. Investments were badly timed, in real estate or the stock market. They lost a lot of money. They were educated people who all of a sudden went into businesses they had never touched, never had any expertise in, and they lost everything. I was one of them. My parents and I went into the restaurant business, catering, in London. That was a business we never had done. There were heavy pressures on us.

Q: Can you list a few of the businesses that Iranians often get into?

EBRAHAMI: In engineering they are perfect. There are very good doctors. The ones who are businessmen are fantastic, but they don't have to be educated. I realized that education has nothing to do with business. Sometimes you only know some ways of making money and that's it. And they bloom; it's fantastic. Sometimes you have all the knowledge in the world, and you can't make as much money as a person with no education. I don't know how I can explain it.

Q: A lot of Iranians are getting into real estate as well?

EBRAHAMI: A lot of people are in real estate. They used to be in the stock market. A lot of people lost money in the stock market—commodities, especially—because they didn't know anything about it and they just were trying to follow their friends. They thought mutual funds were safe, but they didn't know much about them. Education is important. And timing.

Q:     Did they have Iranian financial counselors for this? Or did they go to Americans?

EBRAHAMI:     There were some Iranians who started investment businesses here. They weren't successful. They destroyed a lot of people. They went into other businesses and to American institutions. But because they didn't know about the securities they invested in, they lost a lot of money.

Q:     So what would the differences be, in your experience, between Iranian and American clients? I'm talking about their ways of doing business.

EBRAHAMI:     There are lots of differences. But to me, as a professional, there's no difference. When I pick up the telephone, I don't know who is on the line. It can be an American. It can be a Chinese American. It can be anybody. This is Los Angeles. We are talking about a cosmopolitan town. But being an Iranian, having gone through the same sort of sentimental problems and all the trouble they have, I know how the guy on the line feels. I know what he's gone through. I know how much he values his dollars. And I know his principal is important. I don't like to lose that for him. I try to explain things.

Q:     Are Iranians any more conservative as investors than others?

EBRAHAMI:     Very much so. They've gone through bad experiences in this town. What I'm trying to do is to build back up the reputation this business had in the Iranian community. I want to gain it back by doing proper, honest, and good business for them. You have to come to terms with all the things going on in the market, in the world of finance. And if you lie and things go wrong, it can destroy your image in the Iranian community. It's a very close society. Once you do bad business, you're dead. Once you do good business, you're on top of the world. Believe me, I'm not kidding. I have to watch what I do and how far I go.

Q:     So for Iranians, in particular, you're less willing to gamble or take risks?

EBRAHAMI:     No. There are gamblers among them. Really big gamblers. They lose a lot of money. I can't mention the numbers, but there are people who want to gamble. That's their choice. I am here to take and place orders. To suggest things. But if they want to take risks, it's their money.

Q:     What can you tell me about the change in Westwood over the last ten years in the Iranian business community?

EBRAHAMI: I've lived here since 1983. I've seen the growth of businesses all along Westwood Boulevard. Two days ago I was at home in that area, and two different calls came in Persian, and they were both wrong numbers. People called me and said, "I want to speak to Mr. Hassan," and I said, "Hassan doesn't live here." That was in Persian, and for ten minutes I thought I was in Tehran, you know? Two phone calls came, both in Persian! I couldn't believe it.

Q: I've heard from Iranians and others that under the Shah's regime there was a lot of corruption and bribery, at least in some parts of the business community.

EBRAHAMI: Definitely.

Q: A lot of people here were caught in all that; then they moved here. Would that experience in Iran affect their attitudes toward business here?

EBRAHAMI: Toward corruption?

Q: Well, cause them to be apprehensive, fear being exploited, based on the past.

EBRAHAMI: Yes. A lot of people had been corrupted in the old days. The system went corrupt. Not one person. Not the Shah himself. It was a system that all Iranians were involved in. We caused what happened to Iran. We went out; we shouted for Khomeini. We wanted him. I don't mean "I," but we all did that, as a society. The system was corrupt; otherwise people wouldn't have gone on to something new and different. That is my opinion. If there wasn't something wrong, why should people do that?

Q: So that experience may have been brought here psychologically?

EBRAHAMI: Yes. They've become so conservative that they don't want to mix with each other. They don't want to talk about each other's money, how much they have, what they do. Sometimes they don't want to say what sort of business they do. They've closed all the doors. They just don't want to talk to anybody.

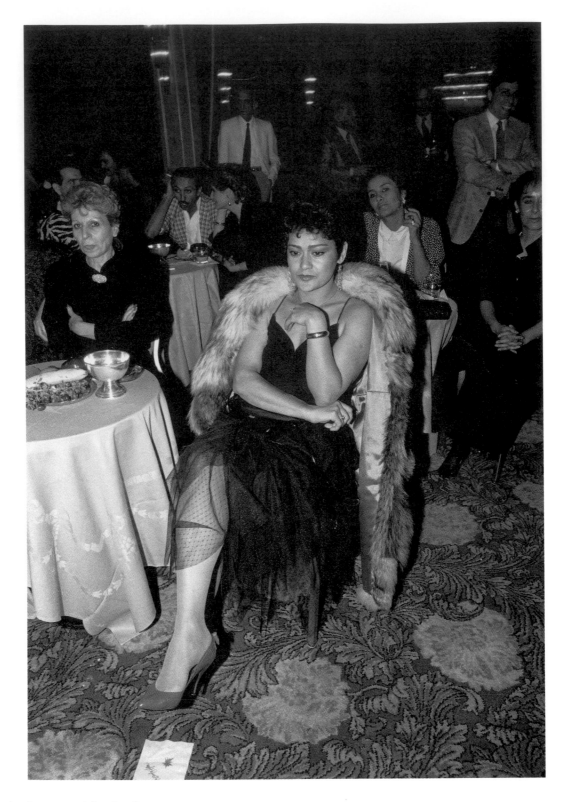

FIGURE 86.  Anniversary celebration for
*Iran News* at Beverly Hilton Hotel. Beverly Hills, 1988.

# WEALTH AND ILLUSIONS OF WEALTH
# IN THE LOS ANGELES IRANIAN COMMUNITY

*Ron Kelley*

Iranians in Los Angeles, once made scapegoats for the 1979–80 "hostage crisis," have seen the broad stereotypes about them as a community gradually change during the past ten years. Perhaps the most prevalent stereotype now is that they are wealthy. A December 1988 *Forbes* magazine article on L.A.'s Iranians exemplifies this view. According to the glowing piece, the estimated Persian population of 400,000 people represents the "top 1 percent" of Iranian society, who, with the fall of the Shah, brought their substantial fortunes to plant in the California economy.

For some critics—particularly in the Iranian intelligentsia, in leftist circles, and among supporters of the Islamic Republic—this idea of widespread affluence has a corollary: that in the Los Angeles Iranian community are many who profiteered under the Shah. The critics argue that others besides the Shah share the blame for the collapse of Iran and that now many of the guilty are here, flaunting their riches in their new homeland. The Iranian journalist Helene Kafi, in a June 1988 article in the French version of *Rolling Stone*, makes a particularly pointed attack upon the Persian wealthy of Southern California, highlighting drug use and decadent lifestyles. Kafi's perceptions of the community were supported in May 1992 by the arrest in Beverly Hills of the late Shah's brother, Mahmoud Reza Pahlavi, for possession of $20,000 worth of opium.

Some Iranians argue that portraying the local Persian community as mostly affluent is unfair to those who are barely surviving. Not everyone in the diverse Iranian community of Los Angeles is wealthy—or even economically secure. Those whose immigration status precludes legal work have an extraordinarily difficult time here, as do many young Iranians, who, unable to count on any economic support from families back home in Iran or Europe, must live with friends in cramped apartments. Many political refugees, both left- and right-wing, especially the later arrivals from Iran, are struggling financially. Others lost their homes and their livelihoods in the revolution and in Los Angeles had to rebuild their lives

247

................

*Interview with Homa Sarshar,*
*Journalist, Part 3*

................

SARSHAR:
What's shocking to us is that most
Americans cannot even differentiate
between Iranians and Arabs. We hate
that! [*laughter*] There are a few
Americans who think we are like
Khomeini's people: Iranians are
terrorists. We don't like this either.
People who have experience with
Iranians—either they sell a house to
Iranians or do business with them—say
Iranians are not honest. They like to
bargain, which American people don't
like. They also try to buy things as
cheaply as possible and they do not
engage in honest competition. If an
Iranian wants to buy a business,
another Iranian might go to the owner
and say, "I will pay you a thousand,
five thousand, ten thousand dollars
more, but don't tell him." I see that
Americans don't like that. But most
property owners like to rent their
apartments or houses to Iranians
because they know that they pay their
rent on time. They are very good
tenants. This is related to our culture,
to put on a good face, to make a good
appearance. We won't admit that we
don't have money. So we try hard. If
we are tenants, we pay the rent on
time. American schools and universities
too are happy with our children. They
say our kids are bright and learn easily.
They try hard as students.

from nothing. Doctors, lawyers, and government ministers opened gas
stations or fast food shops. Other previously well-to-do immigrants drove
tow trucks or taxis.

Persians are quick to tell of compatriots who arrived in the United States
virtually destitute, feeling that the success of these immigrants testifies to
their indomitable entrepreneurial spirit. No doubt this is true in some
sense, but Iranian immigrants "starting from scratch" differ from other
immigrant groups who not only started with very little but also had no
economic reservoirs or financially solvent friends and relatives to help
them acquire the capital necessary to initiate income-producing projects or
new careers. The affluent Persian-speaking community's support of Iranian
business ventures is no hindrance, either.

Although Persians here take particular pride in not burdening the welfare
agencies of this country, there are occasional reports of homeless Iranians in
America. The journalist Homa Sarshar recalls her shock at discovering a
young homeless Iranian who roamed Westwood living off local charity.
Another Iranian who volunteered to distribute free food at an L.A. rescue
mission was likewise stunned to run across a Persian who lived on the
dangerous streets of downtown. As a public service, the weekly magazine
*Javanan* offers free space on its Angel of Hope page for anonymous requests
for help from readers. Benefactors then contact the magazine, which acts as
an intermediary. In a recent issue, the requests for assistance were largely
from women seeking, for example, a sewing machine, a TV set, and a
ticket back to Iran. Another requested employment, and a refugee family
sought furniture.

Unlike other immigrant groups who came to America following the
dream of a better life, most Iranians in Los Angeles—whatever their
economic situation here—lived the good life in Iran. In a country with a
high rate of illiteracy and widespread poverty, labor for the affluent Iranians—even for the self-described middle class—was dirt cheap. Hence,
most of the Iranians now living in Los Angeles had servants in Iran to care
for their children and do menial household tasks.

Sue Kelly, of the Catholic Refugee Resettlement Program downtown,
notes that her group, one of a number of such organizations, still aids up to
seven hundred new Iranian refugees each year. (In 1989, for example, over
five thousand refugees from Iran came legally to the United States.) Although it is expensive just to get to America, most of these recent arrivals
abandoned or were stripped of their wealth in Iran. The Catholic center
deals with people from twenty-two different language groups from all over
the world. Within this service population, Iranian refugees have been
known for their indignant complaints about the charitable offerings for

RON KELLEY:
How did the Iranians here who have money get it into the United States after the collapse of the Shah? What was the process? Some managed to get money here and some did not. What's the difference?

SARSHAR:
The difference is that the people who could get money out of Iran were smarter; they bought money on the black market. They bought dollars from a private party who was like a broker and managed to get them out. There were also people who paid bribes. I can say the difference between the ones who didn't get money out and the ones who did was that those who did were smarter. And they had the courage to do something illegal.

Q:
It was risky to get most of the money out?

SARSHAR:
Oh, yes. I was here and my husband went back to Iran. Every day a box came for me from the postal service or the airport. He would call me at night and say, "Take care of this box. Something is inside." And I knew it was money. There was also some clothing and pistachios in the boxes, and newspapers. He said, "Read the newspaper carefully. There are some good articles in it." And I knew there was money! [laughter] There were cashier's checks, or just cash. In dollars. Or German marks. That's how we got our money out—part of it. The rest he bought on the black market. He didn't hesitate to lose a little money to get most of it out.

them here, which are far more spartan than those in Germany, for example. Unlike other immigrant groups who have experienced harsh economic conditions in their homelands, recent Persian refugees usually take dramatic steps downward on the economic ladder in coming to America. They are often outraged with the modest apartments and secondhand furniture provided for them. Caseworkers are forced to remind the newcomers periodically that their important family backgrounds carry no weight in American society.

The severe shock of their new condition in America can result in personal tragedy. One Iranian client of the Catholic center, formerly a respected and influential community leader in his homeland, was forced to take a job as a gas station attendant in Los Angeles in order to survive. He ultimately committed suicide rather than endure what he saw as further degradation. A prominent jeweler from Iran was humiliated to learn that his younger brother had invested his money in a trash collection business. A prominent doctor from a small city in Iran, forced to carry bedpans here as a hospital orderly, had a nervous breakdown and returned to Iran.

One immigrant woman, whose deceased father had been rich and powerful under the Shah, refused to admit that she could no longer live like a princess. Even when her economic support from Iran dried up, she continued to dress the part, wearing opulent rings and garish eye shadow, even for a trip to the grocery store. No one ever saw her without makeup. Too proud to reveal her predicament to Iranian friends, she and her small son went on welfare and, facing homelessness, stalled for time by suing the motel where she lived for the right to remain. She never told an old friend from Iran, recently rediscovered in Los Angeles, of her troubles. He, in turn, visited her at the motel, parking his white Rolls Royce beneath her second-story window, continually checking to make sure it was safe in the alley because he couldn't afford the insurance on it. In another case, a young Iranian who worked as a clerk in a San Fernando Valley department store was saving to buy a used BMW because he thought it would significantly enhance his chances of finding a Persian girlfriend. Across town at a local college, an impoverished Iranian student's ostentatious display of expensive clothing conveyed a false image of affluence that proved to be harmful in securing financial aid. This need to maintain at least the illusion of prosperity is deeply ingrained in the Los Angeles Iranian community and itself contributes to the stereotype that all Iranians here are wealthy.

"We must slap our cheeks to keep them red." The Iranian community mentions this old Persian folk wisdom about maintaining dignity fairly often to explain their tight hold on illusions to protect their self-image: Iranians are expected to have a rosy complexion, even if it means inflicting

SARSHAR:
No, this was after the revolution.
Before the revolution there was no
problem. He said, "If I bribe
somebody, for example, ten thousand
dollars to get a hundred thousand out, I
will do that, because if I don't do that,
we will have nothing at all."

pain on themselves. Most Iranians, at all costs, maintain a facade of success and happiness. Thus they are extraordinarily secretive, and reluctant to expose personal or familial vulnerabilities for fear that these will be exploited and their status and good reputation subverted. It is a cultural imperative: you must impress others—for the sake of your family's reputation, your own prosperity, and even your love life.

Thus, both the wealthy L.A. Persians and those who attempt to maintain the illusion of wealth contribute to the stereotype of affluent Iranians. According to the manager of the Hollywood Palace, a popular venue for Persian music concerts, Iranians are well known among bartenders as extravagant tippers and are notorious among security guards for attempting to bribe their way into sold-out performances. For the casual observer, a trip to Rodeo Drive in Beverly Hills confirms Iranians' interest in gaudy glamour: expensive cars, flashy clothes, and gold necklaces. Pillars of the Rodeo Drive community include the Mahboubi family—owners of the prestigious Rodeo Collection shopping mall, and Bijan—the purveyor of fragrances, elegance, and high chic. The kinds of Iranians who frequent Rodeo Drive may well be the most visible Persians in America, and they exist in significant numbers, but as other Iranians are quick to point out, they do not represent—especially in their excesses—all Iranians in Los Angeles.

The economic worth of Iranians in Los Angeles is disputed within the community itself. There is no way to quantify Persian assets, wages, economic power, and the range of wealth and poverty within the community, especially given the secretiveness of exiles and immigrants. Immigrant groups have sound reasons for overestimating or underestimating assets and earnings. Many Iranians, for example, continue to hold economic interests in Iran and Europe, manipulating their accounts and transferring them shrewdly for business and tax purposes here. Others, who lost everything they owned in the revolution, usually prefer that no one know the gravity of their current situation.

Even if there are no trustworthy statistics, Iranians have a sense of their overall economic situation in Los Angeles. Most agree that as a group they are economically "comfortable." The presence of large numbers of doctors, engineers, and other highly educated professionals who fled Iran for America is well known, as is the decision of many students in such fields, studying at American universities before and during the revolution, to stay here. The extraordinary economic power base for Iranians in Los Angeles is widely affirmed. Clearly, not every Iranian is part of it, and a few bitterly accuse some of the wealthiest Iranians of hiring, not their own people, but Americans.

Iranian success stories in L.A. abound. Masoud Hakim and his partner, for example, invested in a single department store and built it into a chain of Adray's department stores, a $90 million sales enterprise. An official at the Iranian-owned First Credit Bank on Sunset Boulevard, with assets of $75 million, notes the involvement of the Iranian business community in real estate, shopkeeping, and importing. He estimates that more than a hundred local Iranian real estate developers are involved in construction projects in the Los Angeles area costing up to $100 million apiece. Sohrab Rostamian, president of the Ketab Corporation of Van Nuys (a firm that publishes yearly editions of a nine-hundred-page business directory called the *Iranian Yellow Pages*), suggests that of the approximately 250,000 Iranians he estimates to be in Southern California, 20 percent have assets of $1 million or more and 5 percent may be worth $5 million or more. Mohammad Shadadi, a member of the Iranian Refugee Relief Organization's Board of Directors, conjectures that 1 percent of the Iranians in Los Angeles may be worth over $100 million each. Sam Amir-Ebrahami, secretary of the Iranian Rotary Club and a financial consultant at Merrill Lynch (which, like many other financial institutions, has recognized the benefits of hiring Persian-speaking specialists), speculates that up to $25 billion has been brought into the Los Angeles area by Iranians since the revolution. Lending support to such claims is the British embassy's estimation that in 1976, two years before the revolution began, $1 billion a month in private capital was already leaving Iran for other countries.

Even if these speculations are exaggerated, Iranians in Los Angeles, at least those who run the economy at the community level and thus publicly define it, have a negative reputation, particularly among their own countrymen throughout the world. Culturally, morally, politically, and financially, L.A.'s Persians have been stereotyped as those who profited from a corrupt economy, "got away" from Khomeini, and not only escaped with their money but also reestablished their opulent lives abroad. Many Iranians in Los Angeles continue to support the deposed Iranian monarchy. Ali Limonadi, the owner of the first Persian-language television station in Los Angeles, guesses that up to 70 percent of the Iranians in Los Angeles are, at least tacitly, pro-Shah.

L.A.'s Iranian businessmen have not done much for indigent Iranian immigrants or artists here. Cultural events in Los Angeles, including those featuring Iran's most famous exiled poets, artists, artisans, and intellectuals, usually draw no more than two to three hundred people. Abdullah Nazami, director of the local Pars National Ballet, has more than seven hundred Iranian artists in his Los Angeles registry, including singers, painters, and dancers well known in the homeland. Many must support

FIGURE 87. Rodeo Drive, Beverly
Hills, 1988.

FIGURE 88.   Woman at Sizdah Bidar
picnic in Irvine. April 1989.

FIGURE 89. Rodeo Drive, Beverly
Hills.

FIGURE 90. Rodeo Drive, Beverly
Hills, 1988.

FIGURE 91.  Rodeo Drive, Beverly
Hills, 1988.

FIGURE 92. Rodeo Drive, Beverly Hills.

FIGURE 93. Pro-Shah rally at the
Federal Building in Westwood.

FIGURE 94. Woman waiting in line to hear an address by Reza Shah Pahlavi at the Los Angeles Sports Arena. September 1989.

themselves with full-time jobs their culture would consider humiliating. Nader Naderpour, one of Iran's most acclaimed living poets, has occasionally taught classes of only twenty students at Beverly Hills High night school. Only a select group of local Iranian popular singers with wide followings and artists with almost mythic status who make rare visits to L.A. draw large audiences.

The most wounding criticism of L.A. Iranians by their fellow countrymen around the world is that many are not even Persian any more. This criticism is not a new one. It is rooted in the history of Iran's links to the Western world and was vigorously promulgated by the Ayatollah Khomeini, who railed against the Shah's dictatorial efforts to mold Iran along Western lines. The Shah's social engineers, themselves wealthy, stood to benefit the most from these changes. As the rich became richer, they further adopted Western tastes and fashions as emblems of social prestige, self-consciously underscoring their dissociation from the predominantly poor and illiterate Iranian masses. "Westernization" became the revolutionary Islamic Republic's symbol for everything the poor did not have. If he had nothing else, the poor man had at least his Iranian identity, unpolluted by Western imperialism. This social strata formed an important base of the Ayatollah's support.

The large-scale westernization of Iranian culture goes back to the late nineteenth century, when the aristocracy began sending their children to Europe, particularly France, for their education. More recently, educating a child in Europe—for those who could afford it—became the measure of dignity, refinement, respectability, and "high class." The deposed Shah himself spent much of his adolescence in European schools. The tastes of many Persians in Los Angeles—well-to-do or otherwise—often still run toward eighteenth-century rococo, as evidenced by the paintings, furniture, and trinkets in their homes.

Perhaps the most obvious example of European influence in Persian society is that the French word *merci* is used colloquially for "thank you." Used first by those who aspired to status and civility, this token of French chic was incorporated over time into speech throughout metropolitan Tehran.

In Los Angeles, wealthy and even middle-class Iranian exiles have continued their obsession with French and Italian fashions and European automobiles: Mercedes (a favorite choice), BMW, and Rolls Royce. More than ever before, they display their prosperity to affirm their high status. The tendency to emulate American consumerist values is best exemplified on a local Persian TV station, Channel 18, where most programming mixes elements of MTV, the *National Enquirer*, and local shopping guides.

FIGURE 95. Anniversary celebration for
*Iran News* at the Beverly Hilton Hotel.
1988.

The worldview of the Armenian members of this Iranian social stratum is described by an Iranian-born executive administrator who has worked for fifteen years in the Glendale Public School System:

In Iran they lived the European world. For Armenian Iranians who had a taste of flying from Iran to Paris to shop, it's very hard in America. The most difficult thing is having to accept a milder American format of life: shopping at Penney's and Nordstrom. One of the things that used to bother me was that my parents' friends would come from Iran and would say, "This is the house you live in?! And you shop at Nordstrom and Penney's? Why aren't you shopping on Rodeo?" For me, education and intellectual activity is far more rewarding. Yet I found what these people said affected me. And their BMW's and Mercedes affected my children. Right away the kids are into big-name cars. This is a strata-conscious community. Definitely. And so are the other Iranian communities here. You watch them in Beverly Hills. It's a stereotype. I'm sure I can find Armenians this isn't true for, but in general they do drive good cars; they make sure they dress well. Appearances are very important. The home. The education of the child. "Where is your child going to school?" UCLA.

I think it happened during the time of the Shah . . . the affluence and the opening of doors, the best of everything . . . The Jewish community from Iran is somewhat similar. They had far more access than the average Iranian, because of their business know-how, their education. They had access to all of Europe. And it's hard, you know, once you've skied Saint Moritz, which is where most of my Iranian Armenian friends skied. And I get so upset. I tease them. They say, "This is nothing compared to Saint Moritz." Well, I wouldn't know. Lake Tahoe is the best I've skied. Once you've skied Saint Moritz, once you've shopped Paris, it's very difficult to shop in downtown Glendale.

Class concerns are also manifested among Iranians in other ways, sometimes including an emphasis on racial purity. The tenets of Islam and other faiths notwithstanding, many Iranians are anti-Arab. The Shah's propaganda reinforced an Aryan national identity, and now, for some Iranians, the lighter a baby's skin, the better. When an African-American Muslim sought to marry a young Iranian woman in Los Angeles, her family hired a private detective agency to investigate his background. When the investigation cleared him, his prospective brother-in-law offered him a certified cashier's check for $50,000 to call off the marriage the day before the wedding was to take place. He declined.

FIGURE 96. Woman and dog at Pro-Shah rally.

Many Iranians, of all classes, have relied on marriage as a means of social mobility and a way to increase and solidify economic power. Inbreeding was long an institution in Iran, with the ideal marriage that of a young woman to her father's brother's son. Typically, the economic status of a suitor was, as it still is, an important criterion of eligibility. However, in Iran, the most powerful determinant of status was the extended family: a recognized "name." Historically, Iran has been controlled economically by families who traced their lineage back to feudal society. The most revered and respected individuals were descendants of this landed aristocracy. More recently, especially during the oil boom years, successful Iranians have literally purchased a "good name" for themselves and their families.

In social circles, familial status is often reflected in the lavishness of the parties given to celebrate engagements, weddings, and anniversaries. Often these are held in hotel ballrooms in upscale parts of Los Angeles. Hundreds of guests are served dinner by professional caterers as Persian pop singers provide entertainment. Once, during the eulogy for a deceased member at an Iranian Jewish synagogue, the presiding rabbi chastised the local Iranian community for its materialism, epitomized by women's casting off an expensive dress worn only once and by young women's obsession with finding rich husbands. Affectations among Iranian men, particularly the older ones, sometimes include stiffly strolling about in public on leisure days immaculately pasted into a suit and tie, one hand tucked into the shirt or vest in self-conscious emulation of Napoleon.

After the fall of the Shah in 1979, many wealthy Iranians came to Beverly Hills in search of a home, attracted by the city's prestige and, according to a prominent Persian banker in the area, its rejection of inner-city busing programs.

The Iranian impact upon business, residential, and other real estate in the Los Angeles area is significant, especially in Beverly Hills, Westwood, and other desirable West Los Angeles communities, as well as in Glendale. One gauge of the Iranian presence is Beverly Hills High School. Although the school's official policy is not to cooperate with outside researchers of their institution, it is common knowledge within the community (and verified by a BHHS teacher) that 20 percent of the school's student body is Iranian.

Most of these Persian students are Jewish. Jewish Iranians, as a group, have fared extremely well in Los Angeles, sometimes aggravating old anti-Semitic feelings of jealousy and resentment among non-Jews in the Persian community. They owe much of their success to the capital they brought from Iran and to shrewd business dealings here. But perhaps most important, Jewish Iranians have a tight network among themselves. One non-Jewish Iranian community leader insists that to say Iranian Jews in Los

FIGURE 97. Sizdah Bidar picnic in
Irvine. April 1991.

FIGURE 98.   Former secretary of state
Alexander Haig, after a fund-raising
speech, meeting an invited group of
Iranian Republican party supporters.
1990.

Angeles are related to each other five different ways exaggerates only mildly. Another piece of non-Jewish "folklore" ventured as a reason for Jewish success is that Israeli intelligence operatives in Iran warned the Jews of the impending collapse of the Shah's regime and recommended that they liquidate their assets and leave Iran while there was still time. For their part, Jews ascribe their success to hard work and an emphasis on education.

The Persian interest in real estate and other business opportunities extends beyond Beverly Hills to all parts of the metropolitan Los Angeles area, from Lancaster in the north to Irvine in the south. The late Shah's sister owns a home in Santa Barbara. In Santa Monica, Iranian landlords have often joined with their American counterparts in lawsuits against rent control. In Glendale, Iranian Armenians began purchasing homes in the most desirable mountain heights during the revolutionary era. They often ran afoul of the city's redevelopment department when the newcomers tried to turn existing structures into mansions.

Westwood (or Little Tehran, as it is known to some), an expensive and prestigious area near UCLA, is also increasingly Iranian owned, from the local Burger King to some of a growing corridor of high-rises along Wilshire Boulevard. Among the skyscrapers in Westwood is the new twenty-story Center West Building, owned by Kambiz Hekmat, a U.S. resident for thirty years and the former president of a local Chamber of Commerce; the building was constructed on the site of a Ship's Restaurant after efforts to declare it a historic landmark were thwarted.

The downtown Los Angeles garment and jewelry district is another area of Iranian real estate investment. Perhaps the concentration of Iranians in this area reflects their keen interest in fashion as the accoutrement of public prestige and their experience in the bazaar, as well as the need for only minimal skills and quickly garnered knowledge to market clothes and jewelry. Iranian developers have been prime players in redeveloping the garment district. Sia Kalhor, for instance, partner with a Canadian firm called Four Corners Properties (with assets of $50 million), recently constructed the L.A. Fashion Gallery on Santee Street. Future developments include an already purchased square block of prime downtown property in the same area.

Such high-level wheeling and dealing has its critics. An Israeli shop owner in the garment district bemoaned his inability to compete with Iranians. "Most of the buildings down here are being bought up by Iranians," he complained. "They have money to burn; they can afford to make business mistakes and learn as they go. Who can compete with that?"

Even on a small scale, the differences between Iranian and American business etiquette can cause tension. Iranians pride themselves on being great negotiators. In Iran, the marketplace has deep roots in the bazaar tradition of bargaining and bartering. In America, Iranians are as likely to haggle over the price of a bag of oranges at the Santa Monica Farmers' Market as over the development plans for a new skyscraper. Another cultural difference is that business deals in Iran were often secured by a handshake, a practice that in America could mean financial ruin. In fact, over the past twelve years, some Persians here have been cheated of hundreds of thousands of dollars by the unscrupulous—often other Iranians—who take advantage of the newcomers' ignorance of American laws and business practices.

Some Persian entrepreneurs, eager to "beat the system" whenever possible, have taken legal risks. Cottage industries exist for doctoring documents and creating false papers for immigration and visas. One distraught Iranian-born woman, disgusted with exploitative employment in the local Persian community, told of the small-scale fraud her boss initiated when she asked for a raise in her subsistence wages. Although the employer refused her request, he directed her to purchase office equipment each week at a local department store; when she brought him a copy of the receipt for the goods, he would reimburse her for them and write off the purchase as a business expense on his tax return. Meanwhile, the employee was left to return the unused goods on her own time, asking the same returns departments over and over again for refunds, which, unbeknownst to the stores, were a regular part of her income.

During and after the revolution, many affluent Iranians came to Los Angeles, intending, for the most part, to live abroad until the troubles passed in Iran. The years since the revolution, however, have offered most exiles no opportunity to return home. The Islamic Republic still persecutes political dissenters, bans opposition groups, targets anyone associated with the Shah, and enforces a strict Islamic lifestyle. More disturbing, during the prolonged Iran-Iraq war, any young Iranian males returning home would be subject to the military draft.

For many Iranian exiles, a decade passed and the possibility of returning to Iran remained remote. By the time the Iran-Iraq war ended, the exiles had roots in America. Their children had grown up here and become largely American in their values and attitudes. What did Iran offer these children? Thus most Iranians abandoned their dream of returning and began to realize that their stay in America could well be permanent. Increasingly, those who had invested their wealth here with an eye to a quick return began searching for deeper, more secure, more influential positions in the American marketplace.

FIGURE 99. Rancho Park Rotary Club,
an Iranian business club that meets
weekly at a hotel in Beverly Hills. 1988.

FIGURE 100.    Boutique in the Beverly
Center shopping mall. West Hollywood,
1986.

FIGURE 101. Rodeo Drive, Beverly Hills, 1988.

For years, residual anti-Iranian American sentiment forced local Iranians to keep a low profile. For all the economic power bases they were quietly building, they remained almost invisible to the American public. No more. Recently Iranian businessmen have organized to protect their rights, exercise their influence overtly, preserve their ethnicity, and develop a more positive image in the American public eye. Two Iranian-based Rotary Clubs in the Beverly Hills area have been established in the last five years. The Coalition of Iranian Entrepreneurs was recently created to facilitate Persian business networking in weekly meetings. And the Iranian Cultural Association, ostensibly an arts and humanitarian foundation, garnered congratulatory letters from Los Angeles Mayor Bradley, then-governor George Deukmejian, and then-congressman Pete Wilson on the occasion of the Persian New Year. Yet another new group to aid the community is the Iranian Assistance Foundation.

At the highest echelons, small groups of Iranian businessmen unite to influence local business. According to an American close to the Iranian community, one such "club" has twelve members, each worth $50 million or more. A few Persian business circles even have their own traditional judicial system to govern internal disputes, with a mutually respected businessman serving as judge and arbiter between opposing parties.

An important question is how all the economic clout will exert itself politically. Although Iranians identify with a wide range of positions in American politics, the L.A. Iranian community is top-heavy with people from Iran's upper classes, who are at least tacitly sympathetic toward the deposed monarch and often wistful about conditions under the Shah. How then might these people vote in the United States? Not necessarily at the ballot box, since many Iranians here are not U.S. citizens. The community can "vote," however, and effectively, with its wealth.

One of the newly formed Persian organizations is the Iranian Republican party, estimated to number a few hundred members and active supporters, many of whom are not yet American citizens. No Democratic party has yet been formed. Iranian Republicans are actively courting Governor Pete Wilson and other prominent Republicans and are even exploring the possibility of running their own candidates for Congress.

According to one source close to the proceedings, a group of Iranian businessmen went first to Los Angeles Mayor Bradley and the local Democratic party in their search for a political party in which to work for Iranian interests. Dissatisfied with the response they got from the Democrats, the Iranians turned to the Republicans, who embraced them. Arguments brewed among the Persians about this noncommittal approach to party politics and lack of concern with each particular party's agenda and principles. These mattered less to most Iranians than simply entering the American political process.

An American businessman, who has worked closely with the local Iranian community for eleven years, scoffs at this account. "Nonsense," he insists. "Of course, rich businessmen are going to become Republicans."

Aside from the Democratic party's traditional association with unions and labor (anathema to much of the Persian monarchist community), there remains considerable resentment among Iranians here toward the Democrats. Former President Jimmy Carter, beginning with his demands on the Iranian monarchy to improve its human rights record, is widely considered to have betrayed the Shah and handed Iran over to Khomeini.

The main danger with speculation on the subject of affluence and influence in the Iranian community is that of overgeneralization. The community is politically, ethnically, and religiously factionalized and diverse. But now that it has sunk deep roots in the area, Iranian-born individuals hold prestigious and influential positions in local business, scientific, and civic realms, from an estimated twenty to thirty Iranian scientists and engineers at the NASA Jet Propulsion Laboratory in Pasadena to an Armenian Iranian mayor in Glendale to the city manager in Santa Monica. However the Iranian community here asserts itself in future years, one fact is certain: few immigrant groups in American history have begun their stay with such widespread economic and educational resources.

# WOMEN ENTREPRENEURS: THREE CASE STUDIES OF SMALL BUSINESSES

*Arlene Dallalfar*

Nadia is a Jewish Iranian woman in her mid-fifties. In 1983, she converted two bedrooms of her home into a work area for a small clothing business. She offers a wide variety of clothing, catering to women thirty-five and older. Her specialty is evening wear and semiformal outfits, particularly beaded dresses sent to her by a sister living in Indonesia. Most of her customers are Jewish, but in the first year she had numerous Muslim clients as well.

Nadia guarantees her clients that no one else will be similarly dressed at the ceremonial occasions they attend. She sells her clothes selectively and makes sure that women who purchase similar outfits are not part of the same social circles, reducing the chance of two customers appearing in the same outfit at a party. Such an incident actually happened at a wedding in 1981 and was the source of much embarrassment and frustration for the women involved. That night Nadia started thinking about an evening wear business. A number of women had complained to her that it was difficult to find evening wear appropriate for them that was also original, not in all the department stores.

The cost of setting up this small business was close to $15,000; family savings covered the initial expenses. Unlike other trades that require a considerable investment for advertising, Nadia relied on her ethnic ties and on social networks to advertise her business. She had never worked outside the home in Iran, and starting a business at her age, with no previous experience, was a major challenge. "My daughters are getting all kinds of degrees, and I did not even finish high school," she said. "But I have other experience that will help me with my business."

Nadia has no established working hours, but she is available most weekdays and on evenings and weekends. Her home is conveniently located in Beverly Hills, and interested women come there to view her merchandise. In the beginning, two or three women—usually either members of her extended family or friends—made arrangements to go together to Nadia's house as both a shopping venture and a social visit.

When clients arrive, certain formalities are observed, including a period of socializing when Nadia serves Turkish coffee and sweets in the living room. During this time, no business is discussed. Topics include the latest news about husbands, children, and mutual friends as well as gossip about the community and news from Iran or Europe. The socializing lasts about twenty minutes, but it can last longer, if, for instance, one of the guests is asked to put her fortune-telling skills to work in reading the events foretold in the coffee grounds.

At an appropriate time, Nadia turns to business and suggests that they go to the rooms where she has hung up the clothes. She shows the merchandise available. Then she concentrates her attention on one of the visitors. She pulls out the appropriate size of outfits she feels suit her client and directs her to a dressing room behind a curtain. Then, one by one, she addresses the needs of the other women present. Nadia is extremely accommodating to her clients and will sometimes spend two hours with one person even if she doesn't make a sale that day. She knows that her client will return and that her investment of time will not be wasted.

If a guest is interested in purchasing an article of clothing, a sequence of events follows that differs slightly depending on the intimacy and the closeness of the family connection between Nadia and her customer. The sequence begins with *taarof*: Nadia offers her customer the merchandise as a gift. The client cordially thanks her but requests that she set a price for it. After Nadia names a figure, a period of bargaining commences. Invariably, the price comes down until it reaches a figure below which Nadia will not go, and the client must make a decision based on that final price. Often Nadia ends the bargaining by claiming that she is selling the clothing at her cost and that she simply cannot go any lower than the last price for anyone, not even her sister. Bargaining, which usually lasts about five minutes, is the most delicate time in the whole transaction. Nadia must be alert and careful not to offend her client. At the same time, however, she must be decisive and firm about her lowest price. The success of her entire operation depends on the satisfaction of her clients, not only with the quality of what they buy from her and the bargains they get, but with the social dynamics that must accompany these business visits.

Nadia requests that all transactions be in cash. Sometimes, if her customers are close friends or relatives who do not have the cash on hand, she allows them to take the clothing and pay her the next time they see her.

Thus far Nadia enjoys her business and takes pride in her autonomy and in her control of a profitable business. She is aware that an independently run small business that caters exclusively to the Iranian immigrant population in Los Angeles gives her the best chance of success. Given her limited education and skills, the only jobs open to her otherwise in Los Angeles would probably be blue-collar jobs.

### JALEH AND PARVIN

Jaleh is an unmarried Jewish Iranian woman in her late twenties. When she arrived in Los Angeles in 1979, she tried her hand at different jobs, such as selling cosmetics on a commission basis, before deciding to open a clothing business that she could operate from her apartment. Her fluency in English and a college degree allowed her to compete for jobs in white- and pink-collar occupations, but she was determined to maintain her ties with other Iranians and chose to pursue jobs where she would be involved with them. The complexity of beginning a business with no prior experience and attracting Iranian customers was lessened by the partnership she formed with a friend, Parvin, also Jewish and unmarried. Parvin has a high school degree and worked for a large import company in Tehran as the head secretary. In Los Angeles she had just quit her job in a travel agency and was looking for other employment.

The business partnership began in 1981, with each partner investing about eight thousand dollars, provided by their parents. Because of the convenient location of her Westwood apartment, Jaleh suggested that they use a room in it as the site of their business. This would allow them to sell clothes at lower than retail prices, since they could avoid some overhead costs, like rent. "These upper-class Iranian women go to a lot of parties and have a lot of parties," said Parvin. "They spend a lot of money on clothes, sometimes wearing a dress once and then not wearing it again."

After a year their business began making enough profit to justify their efforts and make up for the difficulties they had in handling some of their customers. Jaleh and Parvin both preferred not to see clients after five in the afternoon, especially on weekends, yet often they would invite women into the apartment who had not called first for an appointment. This was especially bothersome for Jaleh, who felt that her home was never free of clients and that she had to be hospitable and accommodating even when she didn't feel like it.

In 1983, Jaleh became engaged to an Iranian man, and it was no longer feasible to use the space in her apartment for the business. She looked for a site near Beverly Hills where she and Parvin could carry on the business. The rents there, however, were exorbitant and would consume the profits they had been making. They finally found a single room on the second floor of a building for five hundred dollars a month. The space for the store shrank when they converted a section of it into a changing area. Because it was uncomfortable for everyone if more than three clients at a time were in the store, their transactions changed drastically. Women visiting the store could no longer linger comfortably as they had in Jaleh's apartment, greatly diminishing the social component of the "visit" and underscoring the commercial transaction.

Even before they moved their business out of the apartment, Jaleh and Parvin had experienced difficulty with their customers' demands and expectations. The young women were not interested in offering tea, engaging in small talk, and maintaining other social rituals. Parvin, in particular, had difficulty with the bargaining (*chouneh-zadan*) that could stretch on endlessly after an item was selected for possible purchase. Because she was younger than many of their customers, it was often difficult and unpleasant to stand firm in resisting an unacceptably low price for a sale.

Jaleh and Parvin did not understand that such social interactions were intricately connected to the selling of clothes. Their inexperience with the social etiquette integral to business in the ethnic economy led to many difficult moments. They kept the business operating in the new location for an additional year, but the profit margin had become so low with the additional rent that they decided to close the business in 1984.

Nadia's ability to merge the economic and social spheres in her business ensured her a profitable return. Other older women with less education and English-language facility have also begun profitable labor-intensive small businesses in the informal and ethnic economy. They have succeeded where younger Iranian entrepreneurs have failed because the older women maintain the social niceties that are an essential component of such businesses.

## NILOUFAR

Niloufar is a Muslim woman in her late forties who works as a seamstress at a dry cleaning facility owned by an Iranian couple in the Fairfax district of Los Angeles. Her husband, a former colonel in the Iranian armed forces, has been retired since they fled Iran in 1979, and the family has had to rely on their sons for financial support. Niloufar was a homemaker (*khanedar*) in Iran and had only a high school diploma and no work experience when she arrived in America. Because she has little contact with Americans, she still speaks English with difficulty. In 1983, her sons bought her a sewing machine and other items she needed to start a business as a seamstress at home. She converted one bedroom of her condominium into a space where she could sew and meet her customers. She said, "I thought it would be hard to find customers, but sometimes I have more than I can handle. Some nights I have to stay up till ten or eleven to keep my promises. But thank God, even though I get tired, I'm happy that I have work to do and feel sorry for my husband who has time on his hands and can't find a job."

She is seriously considering quitting her job at the laundromat and taking on a new job, working for an Iranian woman who runs a small clothing business from her home. She would be able to make more money than at the laundromat. She would also be working in a home setting with Iranians, where there is increased social interaction between the seller and the buyer, and she could thus meet potential customers for her own business. She was uncomfortable about taking customers away from the dry cleaner, and she was tired of being secretive about working at home. Moreover, she was unhappy about her relationship with the family she worked for, always feeling *madun* (indebted) to them for giving her a job. Given that her elder son's wife had just had a baby boy, she also chafed at her set hours. "Sometimes there are no customers, and I just sit there. I could be at home instead preparing a healthy meal for the family or taking care of other responsibilities."

Two of the most appealing aspects of her recent job offer are that she could bring items home for alteration, and her salary would be fixed, regardless of the hours she actually spends at this woman's home. She is hoping to set up an arrangement whereby she can take care of her own domestic responsibilities in the morning and go to work around 10:30, when it is more likely there will be customers. Since her home is nearby, she could also come home around 2:00 for lunch with her husband and then go back and work a few more hours in the late afternoon.

Niloufar asserts that working has benefited her both psychologically and financially. Although she is now the primary breadwinner in the household, her duties and responsibilities as a wife and homemaker have remained intact. The social dynamics within her household have not altered dramatically as they often do in families where the wife has a job but the husband does not.

*Interview*

Roshan ("Roz") Kermani is a Century City businesswoman.

KERMANI:     I came to this country about three and a half years ago because of the situation in my country. I was going to Tehran University, studying dentistry. They didn't let me continue because I wore makeup. They upset me, and I called Khomeini something—something bad, you know? They took me to court and said, "You do not respect Khomeini, and you cannot continue studying at the university." They didn't even give me a transcript to prove I had enrolled there. They didn't give me anything.

   So I came here. My father sent me. When I came, I had nothing. I mean, really nothing. But after a week I started working. I couldn't even speak English. But I started working. And I didn't give up. I remember my brother telling me, "You can't work this fast, you can't start working. You must have patience." I said, "No, I have to live here and make money. I have to work." First I worked in a dentist's office. But I couldn't make much money. So I worked in retail for a couple years, without any experience. All the good stores wanted experience. But after a couple months I got a management position in a very good chain store.

RON KELLEY:     A Persian store?

KERMANI:     No, American. My supervisor loved me because I was so—I don't want to exaggerate—smart and a good salesperson. Every month I sold seventy to eighty thousand dollars worth of goods, by myself—the best sales in the company. I was the best. That's why I got a management position in the company after two months with no experience. About fifteen girls were working for me.

FIGURE 102. Roshan (Roz) Kermani, a
Century City businesswoman. 1989.

Then I thought about making more money, and many of my clients who knew me told me to go into real estate. So I took a job with Unified Financial Service. I was the office manager and executive consultant. I did very well. I brought them a lot of business. I thought then that I should go into business for myself. I was the person who brought in the most business. About two months ago I opened this company with Mr. Mir, my partner. We do very well. We pick up a lot of business.

Q: What do you do exactly?

KERMANI: We're a mortgage consultant firm. We help people who want to buy property. We help them get the loan. The bank gives them just two options, fifteen years and thirty years; they actually have four or five. We give people more options so they can pay off their loan instead of paying too much interest. They can pay less and save thousands of dollars.

Q: Is there any discrimination against women? Is it an advantage to be a businesswoman, or a disadvantage? How are you treated?

KERMANI: I have to be serious in business. Very. When I have an appointment, I wear very conservative clothes and I try to be serious with people, especially Persians, because they are not used to seeing women working.

Q: That's my point. Do they put as much faith in a woman businessperson?

KERMANI: To be honest with you, most women, here and in Iran, who are attractive don't go into business, at least serious business. They do something like modeling in my country. But most of them don't work. The husband doesn't let them work, because they are pretty, attractive, whatever. But here, I've had many clients. I have a client who is Persian; he's making his payments. He has nine thousand apartments. His payments are half a million a month, and he doesn't trust anybody. Any man even, Persian or American. But he just talked with me on the phone, and he sent all the original documents and asked me to do business with him because he feels I'm a serious businesswoman.

Q: Do you think that as a Persian woman you have to work any harder to prove yourself than a Persian man in the business community?

KERMANI: No. Why would we have to work harder than men?

FIGURE 103. Merchant in the downtown Los Angeles garment district.

FIGURE 104. *Opposite:* Store in the
downtown Los Angeles jewelry mart.
1988.

FIGURE 105.    Antique dealer in Century
City.

FIGURE 106. Lighting fixture merchants, who indicate that they sell most of their chandeliers to Iranians and Asians. West Los Angeles.

Q:      Could you do this job in Iran?

KERMANI:      Under Khomeini, no way. I had a lot of friends in Iran; they came to the United States, and they spent many years in universities. Then they went back to Iran. They thought they could get the best jobs in the country, but they couldn't.

Q:      Most of your business clients are Persians, I imagine. Do you have much American business?

KERMANI:      Oh, yes. I have American clients too. I prefer to deal with American people.

Q:      Why?

KERMANI:      Why? Because they're more serious in business.

Q:      What is the difference between the Persian and American business communities here?

KERMANI:      I prefer to work with Americans because if they're not serious, they don't waste my time. I've had bad experiences with Persians. They were wasting my time because, you know, I'm a woman. They think America is a free country, and they can use a woman and take advantage.

Q:      So you have had that problem in your business.

KERMANI:      Oh, yes!

Q:      With Persians and Americans?

KERMANI:      Just Persians. Not with Americans.

Q:      To be a businessperson here you must be assertive and directorial and confident, all qualities that are not traditionally associated with women in Iran. Must a Persian woman who wants to get into business here be very liberal?

KERMANI:      Strong or something? I never worked in my country, even one day. Never. I don't even remember if I worked one hour in my life. When I came here I didn't know I could do this much. When I started, I proved to myself that I can do many things. Not better than a man. I don't want to be a man. But I can do many things the same as a man. It's a discovery for Persian people. I know many Persian women who didn't work in Iran because they were married. They stayed at home, cooking, taking care of the children, and that's all. Shopping. They didn't work because Persian men—most of them in Iran—don't like the wife to work. Especially a beautiful or attractive wife.

Q:     Why did you stay in Iran until recently?

KERMANI:     Because I was married. I was fifteen years old when I got married.

Q:     Were you a religious person?

KERMANI:     No. My ex-husband was a very strong and powerful man. And very rich. And my father was a doctor. He completed his degree in Texas. And everything was perfect.

Q:     This was a family-arranged marriage?

KERMANI:     Yes. It was a family arrangement. No, I wasn't in love. Not at all.

Q:     There's a huge difference between your experiences at fifteen and what you're doing now.

KERMANI:     Exactly. It's totally different. I don't believe it myself. My family is still in shock. I was married at fifteen, and I have two children. My son is twelve, almost, and my daughter is five. And I just stayed home. Maybe once a week or twice a week I went out; that's all. I didn't see anything. I didn't work. I was totally different from who I am now.

Q:     Were you ever happy as a homemaker, living that life?

KERMANI:     No. Not at all.

Q:     You always knew that you wanted to escape it?

KERMANI:     At that time I didn't know. I didn't see. For example, if you live in a village, and you don't see the city, you accept the village. You know

FIGURE 107. West Los Angeles
hairdresser, 1988.

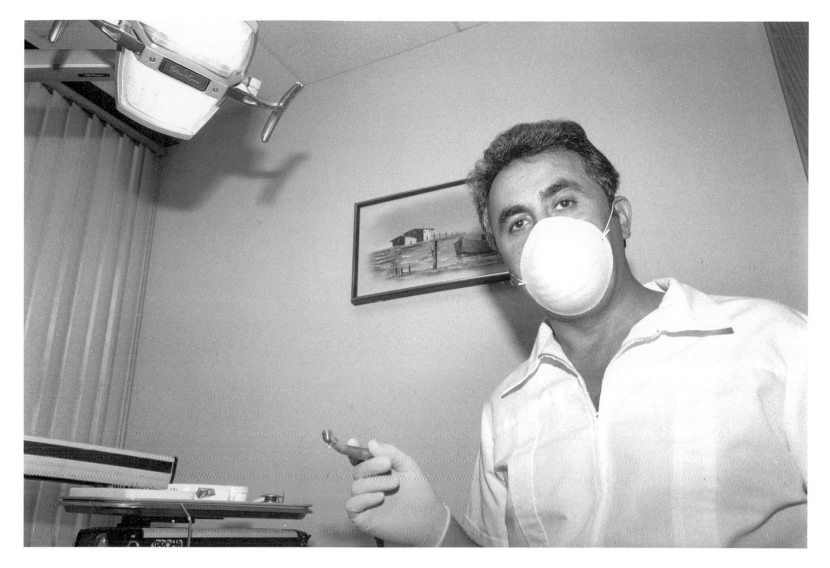

FIGURE 108. West Los Angeles dentist.

FIGURE 109. Taxi drivers in Beverly
Hills, 1986.

FIGURE 110. Behrooz Hashimi, Glendale policeman. According to Hashimi, the most common crime among Glendale Iranians is wife beating. 1989.

what I mean? I was like that. My ex-husband was really possessive, and he didn't want to even . . . It was 1978 when I came here to visit my family. I had one son. My family lives in San Jose, and my husband was scared to send me here to visit my family by myself. He wanted to come with me and watch me. Persian men are like that. Most of them, I think, love women in the chador. When I came here, I thought, some Persian men, here for fifteen, twenty, thirty years, will be more open-minded, different. But it's not true. They are not different. They want to go out with many girls—Persian girls. They really take advantage of girls here. And then they want to go back to the old country and marry a virgin. That's stupid, I think.

Q:     How did you escape your past? How did you come to realize that you could do a lot more than just stay at home?

KERMANI:     First of all, I didn't know what I could do, to be honest with you. I knew I had to work because I had to support myself. Nobody was supporting me. I had to make money. When I started working, I didn't know that I could be the best salesperson at the company. I thought maybe the others were stupid. I'm not special. You know what I mean? But then I found out, no, they're not stupid. They are good. But I am better than they are. I discovered myself, and that made me stronger. Now I'm talking with you. My goal is really high. Everything I said, I did. When I said I wanted to buy a fifty-thousand-dollar car, I made it. I bought it. I've told my friends I'm going to work, and next year I'm going to buy a million-dollar home. I know I can do it, because I have found myself. I know I can do it. You know what I mean?

# *Interview*

Interview with Fariba Khaledan, Part 2

RON KELLEY:     Are there any other Persians who work for the UFW (United Farm Workers)?

KHALEDAN:       No, I think I'm the only one.

Q:       What thoughts do you have about the relation of your own identity to social justice? Historically, Persians have nothing to do with Hispanics. In the broad range of issues that need social attention, how have you come to one in which you have no personal stake, rather than fighting for an Iranian-related justice?

KHALEDAN:       I do have a personal stake in it. I'm going to be eating the food that has carcinogens and pesticides and that's very much a personal issue. The food that I'm eating is poisoned food, not natural food. In Iran most food is not sprayed with pesticides. Fruit, after a couple days, goes rotten. Here it lasts two or three weeks because of the pesticides on it. I would much rather eat natural food. So there are some personal things at stake.

Not only that, but when you are helping people, the dispossessed, that's the most enriching kind of work anyone can do. Someone asked me, "How come you're doing this? How come you're not doing something for the Iranian people?" But is there much of a difference? All people are one. Many Iranians don't agree with that. They're nationalistic, very nationalist. They're proud to be Iranian. I'm proud to be Iranian too. But you know . . . I would rather do something with the UFW than have five credit cards and wear Gucci jeans.

FIGURE 111.  Santa Monica Farmer's
Market. This weekly open-air market,
similar to the bazaars of Iran, attracts
many Iranians. 1986.

Q:      What do you do for the UFW?

KHALEDAN:      Many different things. When Cesar Chavez was fasting, everyone
focused on that. We went to Delano, California; we would try to get
people to boycott grapes. And we helped organize the end of the fast,
which attracted a lot of media coverage. I worked on pickets. I went to
different universities, schools, churches, synagogues, and consumer
organizations and showed our video, gave a presentation. I went on
marches. Did you hear about the marches? We had some in Malibu, with
Martin Sheen and some actors. We had a march in East L.A., and we
had a march in the Silverlake area. The fast brought a lot of people's
consciences up in this country. A lot of people who would otherwise
have done nothing. The whole question is much broader than the UFW;
it's a question of social justice. That's what's really important to me. It's
an ideal I've always had and will always fight for.

PART V

POLITICAL LIFE

FIGURE 112. Demonstration in support
of the Iranian revolution. Federal
Building, Westwood, 1980.

# IRANIAN PROTEST DEMONSTRATIONS IN LOS ANGELES

*Ron Kelley*

The political demonstration is an important part of the Iranian social landscape in Los Angeles. In the late 1970s large numbers of Iranian students in the United States, a diverse coalition of ideologies, took to the streets against the Shah's regime. Pro-Shah counterdemonstrations—often at the very site of pro-Khomeini rallies—were staged in an attempt to dilute the growing perception in the United States that the Shah was under popular siege.

When the American hostages were seized in Iran in 1979 and the American mass media focused relentlessly on President Carter's inability to secure their release, American popular opinion toward Iran and Iranians turned increasingly ugly. Although some Iranian revolutionaries sought to distinguish their protests against the U.S. government from their attitude toward U.S. citizens, most Americans never saw the distinction. In Los Angeles, passing American motorists jeered at all Iranian demonstrators, pro-Shah as well as pro-Khomeini.

In 1979 a California state senator attempted to plug into the American frustration, ignorance, impatience, and media-induced hysteria surrounding the hostage situation and organized a counterdemonstration against the entire nation of Iran. Disgusted with images of burning American flags coming out of that country as well as with Iranians chastising the U.S. government, the senator rented the Los Angeles Coliseum and called on patriotic Americans to send a "message" to Iran. In a facility equipped to hold a hundred thousand people, only five thousand showed up—a vocal and animated group including members of unions, churches, and motorcycle gangs. As if the event were a sports spectacular, they gathered in sections of the stadium to burn effigies of Khomeini and to implore the U.S. government to "nuke" Iran. They waved American flags at the news cameras and burned a large makeshift Iranian flag with the lion, sword, and sun emblem—the flag most Iranians perceive as the symbol of the overthrown Pahlavi regime. Khomeini himself, no doubt, would have been happy to put a match to that particular icon.

Local civic groups organized other, considerably less sensational, media events. The Los Angeles City Council held a candlelight vigil for the hostages in Iran, and Hollywood held a "Welcome Home Hostages" ceremony on Hollywood Boulevard when the U.S. embassy workers were finally released.

In the late 1970s the largest demonstrations by Iranians in the United States, predominantly students, were anti-Shah. More recently, however, as most pro-Khomeini supporters have returned to Iran, exiles here have become increasingly factionalized, apathetic, and disillusioned.

Few demonstrations in Los Angeles since the revolution have captured either media attention or American sympathies. In fact, few political events in the Iranian community have been attended by non-Iranian journalists. Hence, although leftist and rightist demonstrators have little in common politically, they agree that the U.S. government has intentionally blacked out news of political activity among Iranian exiles. According to this widely held view, the U.S. government, for years before and after the exposure of Oliver North's gunrunning escapades, was covertly in league with the Islamic Republic—as the lesser evil—against encroachment by its former nemesis, the Soviet Union.

Today most of the political demonstrators, and certainly the wealthiest, support the Shah's son, Reza Pahlavi, and "constitutional monarchy." Every February a few thousand of them demonstrate at the Westwood Federal Building to protest the Islamic government in Iran. Unlike all other protest demonstrators, many participants arrive in Mercedes and other fine automobiles, dressed to march in fashionably expensive clothing.

In recent years, the highly fragmented Iranian Left has been able to bring together no more than a few hundred people for their Los Angeles rallies because of difficulties in organizing numerous and often mutually hostile factions—including Maoist, Islamic, and, formerly, pro-Soviet groups. These demonstrators have often found themselves marching with placards in a circle downwind from a larger pro-Shah contingent. In the late seventies, this situation sometimes resulted in fistfights and other violence, but these days, the two groups, both disempowered, rarely interact, even when marching in close proximity.

One of the most active Iranian opposition organizations is the Mojahedin, the group usually associated with planting the bomb that killed scores of the Islamic Republic's parliamentary leaders in 1981. After this attack, the government ruthlessly purged all political opposition in Iran. The Mojahedin—typically branded "Islamic socialists," to their dismay—has maintained some presence in Los Angeles. However, the most dedicated members, calling themselves the "National Liberation Army," fought the

FIGURE 113. Rally celebrating the death of Khomeini. Westwood, 1989.

Khomeini regime during the Iran-Iraq war. Their links with Saddam Hussein have impeded their struggle to regain broad support in Iran.

Mojahedin seminars, meetings (often featuring communal marching and singing), and rallies have been held occasionally at local colleges and universities. Every year, the Mojahedin has sponsored a major march against the Islamic Republic in Washington, D.C.

Yet another political network in Los Angeles is pro-Khomeini. Their number is too small (and they are too vulnerable to harassment) to mount effective counterdemonstrations at royalist and leftist rallies, but they surface publicly when international events leave them particularly outraged. Although most are Iranian, Lebanese, Iraqis, Pakistanis, and other nationals sometimes demonstrate with them. After the killing of Iranian pilgrims at Mecca in 1987, a contingent of Islamic Republic supporters made their way to the Saudi embassy in Westwood to memorialize those killed and vent their anger. After the U.S. Navy shot down an Iranian airliner, with the loss of hundreds of lives, an entertainer popular on Iranian TV, Rafi Khatchetorian (well known for his satire of Khomeini and the Islamic Republic), crossed paths with supporters of the Khomeini regime. After a harsh exchange of words, Khatchetorian was so savagely beaten with sticks that he lost the sight in one eye.

The Kurds represent still another, ethnic, political faction in Los Angeles. Many are political refugees, and some are former Pesh Mergas, "those who face death," who consider themselves Kurds first and citizens of a nation second. Small demonstrations mounted by Kurds (from Iran, Iraq, Turkey, and Syria), usually against Iraq, have protested gas attacks and the massacre of Kurdish civilians. Some non-Kurdish Iranians (mainly leftists) join their ranks in solidarity with their plight.

In the wake of the Desert Storm war, even local Assyrians protested in August 1991. Concerned that the international media were only focusing on the Kurdish refugees from Iraq, Assyrians from a range of countries gathered at the Westwood Federal Building to call public attention to Assyrian refugees of that same war.

In September 1987 when both royalists and leftists demonstrated at the Westwood Federal Building against the impending speech of the Iranian president at the United Nations, Neusha Farrahi, a self-described leftist bookseller, set himself afire to protest the Islamic Republic, pro-Shah royalists, and U.S. foreign policy. His death a week later threw the local Iranian community into turmoil. Was Farrahi a despondent artist, a self-destructive lunatic, a political martyr, or a national hero? Whatever the answer, Farrahi's act galvanized local Iranian public opinion. Even many who did not support his cause sympathized with his actions. As exiles, they

FIGURE 114. Anti-Iranian rally at the Los Angeles Coliseum during the "hostage crisis." 1979.

could fathom the depth of his frustrations here in Los Angeles. Some of his friends even complained that his ideological enemies in the Persian community were appropriating his sacrifice for a campaign to unify Iranian exiles. Over the years, for many of L.A.'s Iranians, safe from revolution and war, political passions had softened, and many had become resigned about the affairs of their homeland. Whatever the effect of Farrahi's disturbing death on the local Iranian population, it generated heated debate, attention, and introspection, causing many observers to reflect on their own political inertia and disillusionment in America.

Within a few months of the Farrahi incident, as the random bombing of population centers in both Iran and Iraq escalated, local Iranians joined in a rare unified protest against the Iran-Iraq war and, particularly, this ruthless "war of the cities."

With calls to abandon political dogmatism, as many as ten thousand Iranian immigrants and exiles of all persuasions lined busy Wilshire Boulevard in front of the Westwood Federal Building for days on end in an attempt to focus U.S. media attention on the events in Iran that had generated their own outrage. Iranian students at local colleges used the Persian media to spread the word about other demonstration sites across town. A group of people set up camp and began a hunger strike sit-in at the Federal Building. (Reza Pahlavi reportedly stopped by to encourage those who were inclined to receive him.) Iranian businesses throughout the city closed for a day to protest the war. The Persian New Year, which fell within this protest period, was marked at the Federal Building in a ceremony that emphasized, not New Year's joy, but rather sorrow, moral responsibility, and mourning. To elicit U.S. media attention, about two hundred Iranian surgeons, general practitioners, dentists, optometrists, and other medical professionals mounted a "doctor's protest march" at the CBS television facility on Beverly Boulevard.

Advertisements urging the Persian community to demonstrate suggested that they leave flags and ideologies at home. But fundamental disagreements continued to exist about even such matters as the meaning of the traditional Iranian flag, with its green and white and red stripes and a yellow lion wielding a sword against a rising sun. More than once at these rallies some demonstrators protested that the flag represented only the former Shah's regime; others proudly insisted on waving it for this very reason; still others maintained that the flag motif predates the Pahlavi "dynasty" and hearkens back to the glory of ancient Iran. At least one man took matters into his own hands and proudly waved a generic green, white, and red-striped flag—the lion, sword, and sun design entirely missing.

FIGURE 115. Prayers at the Federal
Building, Westwood. This gathering
was held both to mourn the death of the
Ayatollah Khomeini and to protest Saudi
Arabian responsibility in the slaying of
over four hundred Muslim pilgrims in
Mecca in 1987. July 1989.

FIGURE 116. Reza Shah Pahlavi, the late Shah's son and heir to the Peacock Throne, taking the stage at the Los Angeles Sports Arena to address twelve thousand supporters. February 1989.

FIGURE 117. Audience for Reza Shah
Pahlavi. The women in the foreground
include his wife and other relatives.
Los Angeles Sports Arena, February
1989.

FIGURE 118. *Opposite, above:* Pro-Shah rally on the seventh anniversary of the Iranian revolution. Westwood, February 1986.

FIGURE 119. *Opposite:* End of pro-Shah march along Wilshire Boulevard. Westwood, February 1986.

FIGURE 120. *Above:* Demonstration against the United States government for giving sanctuary to the Shah. Westwood, May 1980.

FIGURE 121.   Pro-Shah rally at the
Federal Building, Westwood. February
1988.

FIGURE 122. Prayers following a
demonstration against Saudi Arabia
held in Westwood Park near the Saudi
embassy. July 1988.

FIGURE 123. Passersby at an Iranian
demonstration. Federal Building,
Westwood. October 1980.

FIGURE 124.   Americans rally against
Iran during the "hostage crisis." The
makeshift flag being burned replicates
the Shah's symbols of the lion and rising
sun. Many Khomeini supporters would
probably have lit a match to it themselves. December 1979.

FIGURE 125. Cotton-candy vendor at
anti-Iran rally, December 1979.

FIGURE 126. Mass media at anti-Iran rally, December 1979.

FIGURE 127. Culmination of a hunger
strike against the Iran-Iraq war on the
night of No Ruz (the Iranian New Year).
Federal Building, Westwood, March
1988.

FIGURE 128. Rally of Iranian doctors and medical practitioners at the Los Angeles CBS television studio to draw attention to their protests against the Iran-Iraq war. March 1988.

FIGURE 129. The self-immolation of Neusha Farrahi. Farrahi left documents describing the rationale for his protest against the Islamic Republic, pro-Shah monarchists, and United States foreign policy. Friends here frantically try to extinguish the fire. Federal Building, Westwood, September 1987.

FIGURE 130. Neusha Farrahi, waiting
for an ambulance.

FIGURE 131. Farhang Farrahi, Neusha's father, mourning the death of his son at the site of the immolation. Federal Building, Westwood, October 1987.

PART VI

POPULAR CULTURE

FIGURE 132. The tradition on Chahar Shanbeh Suri, the last Wednesday of the Persian year, is to leap over a fire for good luck. Santa Monica beach, March 1988.

FIGURE 133. Sizdah Bidar. Traditional Iranian picnic held thirteen days after the Iranian New Year. In Los Angeles, the day of celebration has been shifted to a convenient weekend. Sites for communal meeting places are announced throughout the Iranian media. Griffith Park, April 1989.

FIGURE 134. Iranian pop star Fataneh
(the name means "Desire") at a concert
in the Bonaventure Hotel. Noted for her
sensual performances, Fataneh appears
not only in concerts, but also—like
many Iranian pop stars—at private
parties. 1987.

# POPULAR CULTURE OF IRANIAN EXILES IN LOS ANGELES

*Hamid Naficy*

Through popular culture Iranian immigrants and exiles in Los Angeles create a symbolic community. In it certain representations of home and the past are repeatedly circulated and reinforced—thus, for the moment, unifying and preserving their cultural and ethnic identity and protecting their own subculture from the seemingly hostile dominant culture. At the same time, however, this immigrant popular culture is helping to create "cultural capital" (Bourdicu 1977, 187–189) for the dominant culture by reproducing its consumerist ideology. Immigrants, as consummate consumers, consent to the ideological and economic domination of the host country. In this symbiotic process, popular culture both furthers assimilation and sustains alternative values that can be a source of vitality for the mainstream culture as well as the ethnic subcultures.

The exile's popular culture changes constantly in response to both the host society's economic fluctuations and the rapid shifts and transformations in the immigrant community itself. Many exile media have been short-lived; those that have survived owe their continued existence to their adaptability to such fluctuations and transformations. The elements of Iranian popular culture in the analysis that follows are those of a particular moment in Iranian exile culture, reflecting the forces at work and the content of the media at the time of writing.

## PERIODICALS

Since 1980 nearly eighty periodicals have been published by Iranian immigrants in Los Angeles alone, almost all of them in the Persian language. A few have experimented with an English-Persian bilingual format, but the English-language text in them usually constitutes less than 10 percent.[1] Of the dozen or so Armenian-language periodicals in Los Angeles, only *Kajnazar* is printed in the Eastern dialect used by Iranian Armenians.

The frequency of publication and the content of the periodicals vary.

Two newspapers, *Sobhe-Iran* and *Asr-e Emruz*, are published daily while others are published weekly, biweekly, monthly, quarterly, yearly, or only occasionally. Most of the periodicals contain a mixture of news and commentary, entertainment news, and features, with the primary focus depending on the target audience. For example, the weekly magazines *Javanan* and *Tamasha* highlight entertainment and news about performers in exile. News-oriented periodicals concentrate primarily on events in Iran. *Seda-ye Shahr*, a periodical distributed on audiocassette, contains classical Persian music, poetry, short stories, essays, and commentary.

Special magazines for women, children, and physicians have emerged, along with others focusing on such specific interests as earthen architecture, mysticism, literature, sports, astrology, and real estate. Although not all periodicals are political, the majority stand firmly against the Islamic government in Iran. A number of the periodicals published in Southern California are official organs of religious minorities or political parties and factions operating against the Islamic Republic (Naficy 1990a).

Some periodicals receive direct financial support from political organizations. In some cases, the subsidy is sufficient to allow the paper to be distributed free to customers (for example, *Jebhe-ye Hamgam* and *Jebhe-ye Jam*). When organizational support is insufficient, the periodical may solicit advertisements (for example, *Payam-e Iran*). Some periodicals receive enough advertising income to survive without charging for newsstand sales in Los Angeles. The two daily newspapers operate this way.

During the past decade periodicals have competed ruthlessly for enough advertising from Iranian businesses to survive. The effort to attract advertisers colored the content of the periodicals, which engaged in political labeling, mudslinging, personal attacks bordering on slander, and loaded language. Since September 1989, however, these weeklies have begun to seek income both from advertisers and the sale of individual issues. This new source of income has cooled their discourse and toned down their shrillness as they have become less beholden to advertisers and more motivated to attract paying customers.

Since this shift, the contents of the periodicals have changed. They are becoming less politicized and less focused on domestic politics in Iran; they have turned from their emphasis on news, since current news is readily obtainable from other sources, both Iranian and American; they are censoring their own contents to obtain commercial rather than political sponsors; they emphasize culture, literature, and the arts more than partisan politics; and they pay attention to the conditions of living in exile.

A number of the Iranian periodicals published in Los Angeles are owned by companies with two or more media outlets. Such companies are able to reach larger and more diverse audiences and, as a result, can theoretically charge steeper advertising fees (or undercut the smaller companies), generate higher income, and be bolder in experimenting with new contents and formats. The affiliated media owned by such companies can promote each other through advertising or links in content. For example, a radio call-in show might pick up the topic discussed on a TV program earlier in the day, or the edited transcripts of radio programs may appear in affiliated journals. Such links expand not only the readership of the journals and the audiences of the radio programs but also the dominance of the media conglomerates.

Iranian intellectuals have attacked the popular media, especially TV, for being shallow, spurious, and a threat to both morality and Iranian "authenticity." For their part, the popular media generally ignore Iranian high culture or relegate it to pages and sections devoted to poetry and literature. The intellectuals' own periodicals have limited circulation and irregular publication schedules. During the recession of the 1990s a number of them folded.

TELEVISION PROGRAMS

Although relative newcomers, Iranians have been one of the most prolific ethnic minorities in this country in producing television programs. In fact, with the exception of Hispanic programming, Persian-language television broadcasts top all other locally produced ethnic programs in the Los Angeles area. Even though more Chinese- and Korean-language programs are shown on television here, most of them are imported from China and Korea.

Since 1981, when the first regularly scheduled Iranian television program, "Iranian," began in the United States, some thirty-nine regular programs have been aired.[2] Currently twenty two shows are scheduled, lasting over twenty hours per week. All are produced in Los Angeles. "Assyrian," "Iran," "Shahr-e Farang," "Javanan va Nowjavanan," and "Negah" are cablecast, "Sobh Bekhair Iran" is aired on KVEA-TV (Channel 52), and all other current programs are broadcast by KSCI-TV (Channel 18). Many of these are syndicated. The two daily live morning programs, "Simay-e Ashena" and "Jong-e Bamdadi," are telecast by satellite to the entire United States.

Both existing and now-defunct programs are secular, opposed to the Islamic Republic in Iran, and, for the most part, royalist. As such they reflect the composition of the exile community in Southern California, which also tends to be against the Islamic Republic and in favor of the

FIGURE 135.   Man in a ghost costume
passing an Iranian family on Halloween
night. Westwood, 1986.

FIGURE 136. Woman dressed for
Halloween in the traditional Iranian
chador. Westwood, 1986.

FIGURE 137. Viguen, kissing his wife at
the Cabaret Lido in Reseda. Variously
acclaimed as "the Persian Elvis Presley"
and "the Persian Frank Sinatra," he was
one of the first performers to incorporate
Western influences into Iranian popular
music. 1987.

return of some type of monarchy to Iran (Naficy 1990a, 176–185). There is little precise information about the demographic profile of audiences watching the so-called ethnic television programs. The standard rating services compile no regular statistics on the viewing habits and preferences of ethnic viewers, with the exception of Hispanic audiences. Individual stations, however, conduct their own research. According to the latest figures released by KSCI-TV, in 1987 the weekly Iranian viewing audience in Los Angeles encompassed approximately 70,000 households and 240,000 viewers. The producers of "Jonbesh-e Iran" claim over two million viewers worldwide (Ketab Corp 1991, 442), and copies of "Jam-e Jam" and "Iranian" are purportedly seen in Canada, Western Europe, Persian Gulf countries, and Iran itself (Naficy 1990b). The national or international viewership, however, is difficult to substantiate.

Iranian ethnic and religious minorities have a choice between these Persian-language programs and those produced by non-Iranian minorities, which include Armenian-language programs ("American Teletime" and "Horizon"), Arabic and English programs ("Islam," "Arab-American TV," "The Good News"), and Hebrew and English programs ("Phil Blazer Show," "Jewish Television Network," and "Israel Today"). Iranian minorities, such as the Baha'is and the Jews, have occasional television broadcasts but no regularly scheduled programs. Certain programs, such as "Jam-e Jam" and "Iran va Jahan," seem to cater more than others to the needs and concerns of Jewish Iranians. In 1981, "The Spiritual Revolution," a series of programs sponsored by the Baha'i Center in Illinois on the Baha'i community and its beliefs, was aired in Los Angeles in English (Naficy 1984, 116).

During the initial phase of exile, between 1978 and 1986, much experimentation with program form and format took place. The discourse of exile TV, however, remained relatively stable and homogeneous. The magazine format, which dominates, typically consists of political news reports, chiefly from Iran; news about Iranian entertainers in Los Angeles and their concerts; anti-Khomeini news commentary; a brief comedy sketch, usually satirizing the Islamic government or life in exile; one or two musical numbers; and sometimes part of a serial imported from Iran. Interspersed are numerous commercials for Iranian-owned insurance companies, furniture stores, restaurants, and nightclubs; for services by Iranian physicians, lawyers, real estate brokers, and auto mechanics; and for such products as cars, beauty supplies, fresh vegetables, fruits, and other foodstuffs.

During this first phase of exile, while a constant stream of commercials acculturated Iranian viewers to the consumerist values of American society, the programs shut out the host society and its institutions, consolidating an Iranian ethnic identity. Images of pre-Islamic Iran were frozen into icons and fetishes, which circulated and recirculated in television titles, logos, and programming (Naficy 1991). Ideologically and psychologically, audiences could identify with this unchanging symbolic construction of Iran. With programming focusing on the homeland, Iranian nationalism, racial difference and cultural authenticity, and secularism and the monarchy, viewers could disavow the loss of Iran, the current Islamic government at home, the fact of their exile, and the periodic waves of anti-Iranian sentiment emanating from their U.S. hosts. Until the 1988 cease-fire, reports on Iranian politics and the Iran-Iraq war dominated the newscasts. Offering a strictly Iranian point of view, untainted by Western reactions or perspectives, the newscasts gave viewers the impression that they were living and watching the news in Iran—not today's Iran but pre-revolution Pahlavi Iran. Classical and popular music recorded prior to the revolution was also featured. Since the cease-fire, however, the emphasis on the politics of Iran has given way to an examination of the lives of Iranians abroad.

The pervasiveness of male authority and patriarchy on Iranian television reflects traditional Iranian culture. Until late 1988, when "Didar" appeared, all programs were produced by a single man, whose vision, connections, financial resources, and personality dominated the discourse, and, since most producers also appeared as on-camera talent, the same man dominated the screen itself. Between 1988 and 1991, three programs, "Didar," "Ma TV," and "Sima va Navay-e Iran," were produced and hosted by women, and a female discourse began to emerge. These programs were presented more informally than those produced by men and were marked by experimentation with program formats. Unfortunately, none of the three has survived.

While programs have helped to create and consolidate an Iranian identity for viewers, commercials have depicted a culture offering as consolation for the pain of loss products ranging from esoteric herbs to BMW's. For over twenty minutes every hour, commercials parade luxuries as well as services to help the exiles re-create themselves and their lives: cosmetic surgery, interior decorating, the legal transformation of their immigration status. The economics of exile television and its consumerist ideology are evident not simply in the advertisements themselves but in the development of an advertising-driven schedule, which positions the audiences to receive advertisers' messages at all times, from morning to the wee hours of the night.

FIGURE 130. Persian rock-and-roll
concert, featuring Hatef, at the
Hollywood Palace. 1988.

FIGURE 139. Children's dancing school performance at the Scottish Rite Auditorium. Los Angeles, 1988.

FIGURE 140. Arman graduation ceremony in an Irvine hotel.
Rooted in the tenets of an assertive humanistic psychology, Arman
and Bunyon, another local group, are distinctly Persian and very
popular offshoots of the American Lifespring self-help organization.
Whatever their intended purposes, such groups provide an
environment where predominantly secular Iranian men and
women can meet one another in Los Angeles. 1991.

FIGURE 141. Shahrdad Rohani, a
conductor and composer, rehearsing an
orchestra for a concert. 1990.

FIGURE 142. Morteza Varzi, a teacher
of traditional Iranian music, in his
Westwood apartment giving lessons to
an American student on the *kamancheh*,
one of the oldest Iranian musical
instruments. The student's husband
passes, in a blur, in the background.
1988.

FIGURE 143. *Top of page:* Ahmed Shamloo, considered by many to be Iran's greatest living poet, waiting to give a poetry reading at UCLA. 1990.

FIGURE 144. Mohammad Reza Shajarian, considered one of Iran's most accomplished and knowledgeable singers of traditional Iranian music, preparing for a benefit concert for Iranian earthquake relief efforts. 1990.

FIGURE 145. Hossein Alizadeh, a composer and master instrumentalist specializing in the *tar* (a lute) and other classical Persian instruments, at a 1991 concert at UCLA. Alizadeh has led the movement to make traditional music more accessible to the younger generation of Iranians living in Iran and abroad.

FIGURE 146.   The poet Esmail Khoi
reciting his work at a memorial for
Neusha Farrahi.

FIGURE 147   Parviz Sayyad, an actor
and film and theatre director, at a
rehearsal for one of his plays at the
Westwood Playhouse. 1987.

FIGURE 148.  Payman at his studio in
Westwood. He was working on an
oversize painting commissioned to
depict the Shah's lavish coronation when
the monarch was overthrown. 1988.

FIGURE 149. Jalili Sussan-Abadi, a
renowned painter of Persian miniatures,
at his home. April 1989.

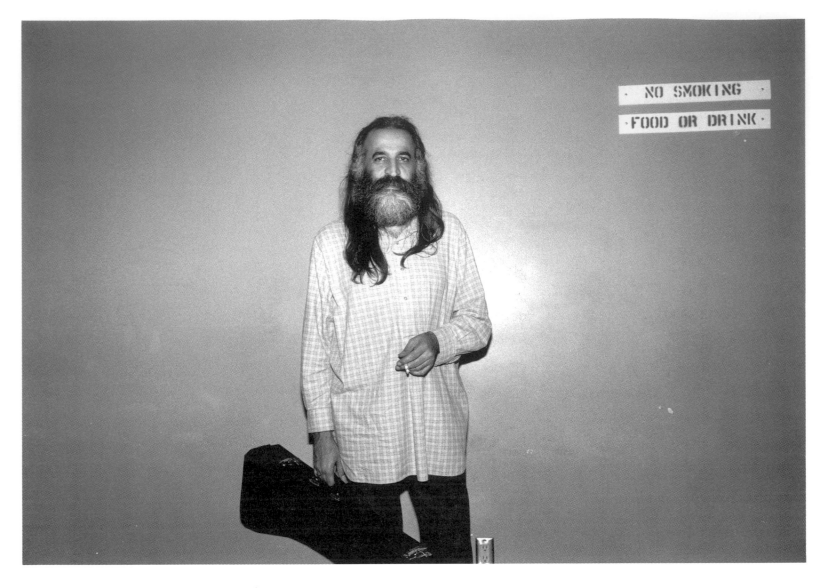

FIGURE 150. Mohammad Reza Lotfi, a
virtuoso on the *tar* and *setar* (a lute with
a pear-shaped body) and a composer
and teacher of traditional music. 1987.

FIGURE 151.   Actors in an Iranian play
by Parviz Sayyad. Westwood, 1987.

The money that Iranian businesses spend on advertising and that Iranian producers spend on airtime and production costs totals several million dollars a year; Iranian exile television is thus an example of an "ethnic economy" at work (Naficy 1991, 93–94). Competition among the stations prods program producers to engage in counterprogramming and theoretically reduces the cost of airtime as one station plays against another. More important, competition among stations can help to preserve political and ideological diversity. "Sima-ye Azadi," an entirely commercial-free program underwritten by the Mojahedin, was taken off the air by KSCI-TV, only to resume broadcasting on KDOC-TV (Naficy, forthcoming).

### RADIO PROGRAMS

Radio has been an integral part of exile media, not only because of the number of programs but also because of the number of hours these programs have aired.[3] "Omid," the first regularly scheduled program, began its broadcasts in the early 1980s. From that time to 1991 "Omid" and "Iran" together accounted for some three hours of programming nightly; "Seda-ye Iran" has aired around the clock. With the exception of "Seda-ye Iran," all programs have been broadcast on FM frequencies by a commercial radio station (KFOX) on a lease-access basis; that is, program producers leased their airtime from the station and in turn sold spot advertisements to Iranian businesses. In 1991 Korean broadcasters took over much of the programming of KFOX, forcing Iranian programs like "Omid" and "Iran" off the air. Subsequently, "Iran" was integrated into "Seda-ye Iran." To hear "Seda-ye Iran," transmitted on a sideband frequency inaccessible to regular radio receivers, listeners need a special receiver. This program generates revenues from advertisements and the fee it collects from the sale of receivers.[4]

Although most of the Iranian radio programs in Southern California have been in the Persian language, some have also been in Armenian, especially Eastern Armenian, a dialect used by Armenians from Iran and the former Soviet Union.

Like television programs, most of the radio shows have used a magazine format, usually including news, commentary, poetry, music, interviews, and advertisements. "Omid," which for years was an authoritative voice of Iranian culture in exile, used interviews, on-location reports, and call-in formats more regularly than most. "Iran," in contrast, became a reliable source of international and Iranian news. The mix of entertainment programming has also been varied: "Omid" and "Iran" were more serious and intellectual than "Rangarang," whose intended audience was Iranian youth.

Because of its extended airtime, "Seda-ye Iran" is able to target the entire family as well as different social strata with its diverse approach. Each day, "Seda-ye Iran" airs over ten hours of live call-in shows that appeal to both popular and intellectual tastes. These call-in programs have become a potent medium for expressing the tensions of exile and acculturation.

Again like Iranian television programs, all radio programs have been secular and opposed to the Islamic government in Iran, with royalists particularly well represented among radio producers and personalities at "Seda-ye Iran." Although there has been more diversity in radio programs than in the larger number of television programs, in general these two media have reinforced each other. In the past dozen years, a number of highly political radio programs, some acting almost as official voices of anti-Islamic and leftist factions, have emerged and disappeared; their failure is attributable to ideological shifts or the disbanding of the faction sponsoring them or a loss of audience, as listeners became depoliticized or disenchanted with their ideological bent. The political programmers failed to recognize their audience's need for entertainment and for guidance and information on living in exile. Like some periodicals, these highly politicized radio programs became ideological dinosaurs. The stations that survived the longest were those willing and able to reformulate and vary their programming in response to the evolving needs of the Iranian exile community.

Popular culture and media programs produced by the exile community have not only played an important economic role in immigrants' lives but have also helped link a population dispersed over a wide geographic area. Thus with the demise of Iranian broadcast radio in 1991—particularly the program "Omid"—many Southern California exiles experienced a sense of loss and discontinuity.

TELEPHONIC PROGRAMS

In 1971, a sociologist complained of "ninety-odd years of scholarly neglect" of the telephone as an agent of modernization and of social change (Aronson 1971, 301). According to him, the telephone creates a "psychological neighborhood" that compensates for the fragmentation of industrialization and urbanization. The same can be said of the telephone's role in exile, where the direct-dial international telephone system has helped to bridge the gap between exiles and their homeland. Such an electronic bridge has existed between the United States and almost all major Iranian cities, even during the "hostage crisis." This bridge helped form an electronic neighborhood whose residents were physically apart but psychologically near.

This two-way medium of communication was turned into a one-way medium for news and information by the highly volatile political situation in Iran and the intensely politicized factionalism in the United States, both of which demanded information rather than communication. During the revolution and immediately after, the telephone became an important source of news as Iranians dialed local telephone numbers to hear taped "newscasts" produced by political organizations. These newscasts, typically lasting up to five minutes, were available at all hours of the day and night.

Changes in the individual sponsoring organizations have affected telephonic as well as radio programming. Currently, only two political factions continue to offer telephone newscasts: Anjoman-e Daneshjuyan-e Mosalman-e Emrika va Kanada (Society of the Muslim Students of America and Canada), affiliated with the anti-government guerrilla group Sazman-e Mojahedin-e Khalq, and Anjoman-e Eslami-ye Daneshjuyan dar Emrika va Kanada (Islamic Society of Students in America and Canada), which represents the views of the Islamic Republic of Iran.[5] The news of both is strictly limited to Iran and is usually heavily slanted. It focuses on discord, disasters, and disarray or on positive achievements in Iran, depending on the sponsoring faction's point of view. These recorded microprograms begin with music, a voice logo identifying the sponsoring agency, and a greeting; after a single voice reads the news, there is a farewell and more music.

Although the telephone cannot easily be classified as a mass medium because it does not reach a large audience at once, the audience that it addresses individually can be quite large. As a result, it is a good example of what Wilbur Schramm (1977) called a little medium, one whose production and transmission are inexpensive and require little overhead, capital expenditure, or administrative infrastructure and few technical personnel. Its programs, recorded on inexpensive and reusable audiotape, are available twenty-four hours a day and cost the audience only the price of a local telephone call. As a little medium, the telephone has proved to be one of the few alternatives for disseminating the points of view of groups too small or marginal for radio, television, and film.

### FILM SCREENING AND FILM PRODUCTION

The cinematic activity of Iranians in exile comprises the showing of films made in Iran before and after the revolution and the production and exhibition of new films made in exile.

FIGURE 152. Iraj Gorgin, in his Hollywood studio. Gorgin was the founder of Radio Omid-e Iran, which went off the air in late 1991.

*Films Made in Iran* Over 130 feature films made before the revolution have been shown in Los Angeles commercial theaters.[6] Many were smuggled out of the country; some arrived with their producers, who had emigrated; others were obtained from foreign distributors, particularly those operating in the Persian Gulf states. For years, the now-defunct company Khaneh-ye Film was the most active distributor of Iranian features in Los Angeles. The reasons for its demise are largely economic. Like many other motion picture distributors, Khaneh-ye Film suffered from competition with the videocassette industry. Most pre-revolution films can be rented for one or two dollars a night from Pars Video, the chief distributor, but also from many Iranian groceries. Pars Video's latest catalog lists nearly two hundred Iranian feature films available for purchase or rental. As the video market grew, Khaneh-ye Film's only available copy of each of its films was deteriorating. The color gradually faded, the image became scratched, and the sound track developed more noise. Khaneh-ye Film found it impossible to compete.

Most of the pre-revolution feature films available in the United States would probably be categorized as B-grade films. Comedies, melodramas, and *luti* (tough guy) films predominate, along with a sprinkling of new wave films and documentaries.[7] The ready availability of B-grade films might be explained by the source of their financial backing. Whereas new wave films were often cofinanced by the government of Iran and production companies and housed in government film archives, B movies were made by the private sector, and copies were less strictly controlled. Like many television programs, these B-grade films and videos freeze images of Iran in the pre-revolution period, rekindling viewers' nostalgia for their homeland and helping them relive, perhaps, their first viewing of the same film in an Iranian theater.

Anti-Iranian sentiments and policies in the United States and the Iranian government's policies discouraging film exports have prevented most feature films made since the establishment of the Islamic Republic from entering this country. Since the mid-1980s, when the Farabi Cinema Foundation was set up in Iran, Iranian films have appeared at international film festivals in increasing numbers and have met with generally high acclaim. Because of the antagonism between successive U.S. administrations and Iranian authorities, however, few films have been shown at U.S.-based festivals, and post-revolutionary Iranian cinema has remained largely unknown in this country (Naficy 1987; 1992a). The few exceptions, including *Dar Mohasereh* (Under Siege), *Fasl-e Khun* (Season of Blood), *Noqteh Za'f* (Weak Point), *Otobus* (The Bus), and *Towbeh-ye Nasuh* (Sincere Repentance), were shown only once. Preceded by a low-key advertising campaign, they received a lukewarm response from an audience largely antagonistic to the Islamic government and its products. The only exception was the visually stunning *Davandeh* (Runner), directed by the new wave filmmaker Amir Naderi, which audiences received enthusiastically.

Beginning in the late 1980s the situation changed, thanks to the cease-fire with Iraq, the gradual acculturation and depoliticization of the exiles, the less strident political rhetoric of both the U.S. and Iranian governments, and a major film festival at UCLA in 1990. This festival, "A Decade of Iranian Cinema, 1980–1990," screened eighteen feature films and a number of short films. Although royalist groups and media protested against the festival and called for a boycott, it was a great success. Iranian exiles came from as far away as New York and Washington, D.C., and waited in lines for over eight hours to see the films.[8]

*Iranian Fiction Feature Films Made in Exile*  Iranian filmmakers in the United States and Europe, all of them independent of the major studios, have produced over twenty feature films on Iran and other subjects. The following have been shown in Los Angeles, often with the director present: *Cat in a Cage* (Tony Zarrindast, 1985), *Checkpoint* (Parviz Sayyad, 1987), *Face of the Enemy* (Hassan Ildari, 1989), *The Guests of Hotel Astoria* (Reza Allamehzadeh, 1989), *The Guns and the Fury* (Tony Zarrindast, 1980), *The Mission* (Parviz Sayyad, 1983), *The Nuclear Baby* (Jalal Fatemi, 1990), *The Suitors* (Ghasem Ebrahimian, 1989), *Veiled Threat* (Cyrus Nowrasteh, 1988).[9]

The films about Iranians tend to portray a community under siege and a mind-set that closes off the host society not only physically but also symbolically and spatially (*The Nuclear Baby*, *The Guests of Hotel Astoria*, *Checkpoint*). Claustrophobia, obsessive relationships, and the intensity of the hunt or the chase are common themes (*The Mission*, *The Suitors*, *The Nuclear Baby*).

Another feature of exile cinema is the strong representation of women. Exiled women's newly elevated status and the shift away from traditional patriarchal family structures are reflected in the strong roles for women in such films as *The Mission*, *The Guests of Hotel Astoria*, and *The Suitors*. In these films, the major female characters have a significant impact on the outcome of the plot: in the first a woman prevents a political assassination by intellectually and emotionally disarming the assassin; in the second a woman sacrifices her virtue and ultimately her life to ensure the survival of her husband and child; and in the third the woman is transformed from the victim (cutaway to a sheep about to be slaughtered) to the murderer of her overzealous suitor.

FIGURE 153. Discussion after a film
screening by a local Iranian women's
group. UCLA, 1988.

FIGURE 154. Iranian-sponsored sympo-
sium focusing on Hafez, the greatest of
Persian lyrical poets. His poetry is
often studied for its esoteric, mystical
content. After the Quran, the poetry of
Hafez is the literature most commonly
found in traditional Iranian households.
UCLA, 1988.

In general, exile cinema foregrounds Iran and pushes the host society into the background. But the host society hovers at both the psychic borders and the cinematic frame edges—a threat barely held at bay. In this case, television and cinema in exile resonate *with*, not against, each other. In both media, the Islamic Republic is portrayed as a "terrorist" state and Iran as a wasteland. This political stance, reflecting the dominant view of Iranians in the United States, is encoded either in the plot (*The Mission, Veiled Threat, Face of the Enemy*) or in the dialogue and narration (*Checkpoint, The Guests of Hotel Astoria*). Such partisan and unrealistic views of Iran tend to suppress differences and the contradictions within the country. They may comfort exiles, but they also blind them to the full force of the changes occurring both in Iran and in the exile community. For filmmakers an obsession with home can become a serious impediment to development, restricting them to a narrow range of provincial themes and a largely Iranian audience (Naficy 1990c).

## THEATER

Iranian directors have staged many plays in Los Angeles, most dealing with life in the Islamic Republic or in the liminal and transitional phases of exile.[10] But Iranian theater has not flourished in Los Angeles. To be sure, all elements of the popular culture in exile must struggle to survive, but the exile theater seems to be losing in its struggle. Plays produced in Southern California suffer from multiple ills, including poorly conceived and written scripts; meager financial resources; inadequate sets, stage properties, and wardrobe; technical problems; and inexperienced actors. Whereas Iranian periodicals, radio, and television support some full-time employees, exile theater has been unable to do so. As a result, Iranian stage actors, directors, and technical people must support themselves outside of theater, making it difficult for them to meet rehearsal and performance schedules.

A number of very small theater companies exist, but these tend to be loose associations of like-minded individuals with irregular and insufficient financial backing and no permanent home in which to practice and perfect their art.[11] Because of this provisional existence, Iranian exile plays typically run for only a few weekends.[12] These inadequacies assume an additional importance because of the temporal nature of the theater. Live performances have their own aesthetics and expectations of immediacy, intimacy, and spontaneity that cannot be realized when productions are burdened with financial, technical, and artistic problems.

The plays performed in Los Angeles, whether comedies or tragedies,

FIGURE 155. The funeral of Hayedeh, one of Iran's greatest popular singers. She is buried in Westwood, at the same exclusive cemetery as Marilyn Monroe.

examine certain common themes: (a) life and politics in the Islamic Republic, usually viewed with a condemnatory eye; (b) the often painful daily life of Iranians in exile, particularly their first days in refugee camps or hotels or on the streets; and (c) the conditions that drove the Iranians out of their country and justify their continuing exile.[13] Both the radio programs and the plays produced in exile offer a window on the pain and ambivalence exile engenders.

## SEMINARS, CONFERENCES, AND SALONS

Since their rapid and massive emigration to the United States in the late 1970s and early 1980s, Iranians have been organizing seminars and conferences about Iran throughout Southern California. Both the revolution that caused most Iranians to leave Iran in the first place and the fact of exile itself have caused a profound physical, psychological, spiritual, and intellectual dislocation. Deep pessimism and self-doubt can result, but also intense curiosity, seemingly insatiable passion for knowledge, and cultural dynamism that fosters great intellectual and artistic achievement.

I have shown how some elements of popular culture work with or against each other. There is a further tension between the exile mass media (television, radio, cinema, the press) and the discourse of intellectuals in their private *dowreh*s (salons) and in their public seminars, lectures, and conferences. In a sense, the conflict is between the mass media, concerned with daily life and commerce, and the "republic of scholars" pursuing knowledge (Naficy 1990a, 134–141).

Iranian organizations sponsor professional and cultural events throughout Southern California. Cultural and academic organizations aim to propagate and reevaluate Persian culture. At UCLA, the most popular site in Southern California for exilic intellectual discourse, most of the functions sponsored by Iranian organizations are cultural and intellectual.[14] They usually take place on weekends and often include prepared Iranian meals; entertainment (films, slide-tape presentations, plays, or dance or music performances); lectures and poetry readings; and the sale of books, audiocassettes, and periodicals. The atmosphere is congenial rather than combative. As a general rule, the films shown are short subjects, either fiction or documentaries, about Iran. Directors are often invited to participate in a question-and-answer session.

In addition to regularly scheduled meetings and celebrations of national holidays such as No Ruz, organizations may plan gatherings in response to events in Iran, such as executions and earthquakes, or to commemorate historic developments, such as the rise of guerrilla movements during Shah

Mohammad Reza Pahlavi's reign. Most of the sponsoring associations have been left-wing, working against the Islamic Republic. A large number of the associations are student based, many focus on women and feminist issues, and a few support ethnic and minority causes.

With few exceptions, these associations have been ephemeral. They come into being because of the personal and political needs of their members, and they undergo transformations as those needs and conditions change. Some have disbanded altogether, a few have merged with other organizations, many have reconfigured their ideology and membership, and some have "shed skin" by merely changing their name. Organizations, particularly the most radical, may undergo a number of these changes in their lifetime. The women's organization Anjoman-e Farhangi-ye Zanan (Cultural Society of Women), for example, has undergone a series of metamorphoses. It started as Komiteh-ye Defa' az Hoquq-e Demokratik-e Zanan-e Iran (Committee for the Defense of the Democratic Rights of Women) affiliated with the Feda'iyan-e Khalq organization. It soon dropped the affiliation and later split into two groups: Anjoman-e Defa' az Hoquq-e Demokratik-e Zanan (Society for the Defense of the Democratic Rights of Iranian Women) and Tashakkol-e Mostaqqal-e Zanan dar Jonub-e Kalifornia (Independent Formation of Women in Southern California). After a while, the former group adopted its current name, Anjoman-e Farhangi-ye Zanan. In this series of transformations, the organization moved away from the political sphere and toward the cultural domain. The evolution of organizations thus has not been cosmetic but transformational, involving ideological, political, and theoretical as well as personal struggles among the members. In general, cultural associations like those discussed here are both dynamic responses to change and agents of change.

These associations and their events focus on the collection and dissemination of information about Iran, the education and enlightenment of their members, and the provision of opportunities for companionship and long-term personal relationships. In some cases, they also promote the mutual interests of participants, serve as means of political and ethnic empowerment, and plan such political activities as demonstrations. The events also provide opportunities for participants to express conflicting opinions and to practice democratic procedures of debate and parliamentary discourse. Finally, many events function as entertainment.

Perhaps the most important goal of these organizations is to gain culturally the ground lost politically by the Left during and after the revolution. In exile, leftist intellectuals became aware that culture, even popular culture, is an arena for political struggle (perhaps the only one) that must not be yielded to supporters of the monarchy. This is a radical reorientation, from the Left's previous monolithic theories of mass culture critique and cultural populism to the present Gramscian conception of culture as an active arena for the struggle over hegemony (Gramsci 1988). The Left has realized that hegemony cannot be imposed politically but must be won in the larger civil society. It is to that end that these intellectual and cultural gatherings are organized, and it is in this light that the shift of the Feda'iyan's women's organization from a political to a cultural focus must be seen.

The discourse produced both in these gatherings and in the intellectual publications is marked by questions about self, group, ethnic and sub-ethnic, national, gender, and linguistic identities; the theoretical approaches to be adopted; and the proper political actions to be taken. The days of imposing imported formulas—leftist or rightist—are gone. This is one of the most positive outcomes of the soul-searching engendered by both revolution and exile.

In addition, the intellectual and professional voluntary associations and the events they sponsor produce cohesiveness, routine, and security for the exiles, who lack the traditional social structures of the homeland. Former jobs, professions, contacts, and support from extended families may be lost, the practice of religion and customs may be disrupted, and a new language must be learned. In a way, these intrafamilial, occupational, and intellectual associations replace missing family networks. As the familial self gives way in exile to an increasingly individuated self, such group affiliations help the exiles meet new professional and occupational needs. Finally, in the absence of traditional courting institutions, the new networks help the exiles find love and life partners. In all these ways, the *dowreh*s and the professional, religious, and intellectual associations are engaged in aiding acculturation and in managing the conflicts and the interests of the exiles through what Georg Simmel has called "the web of group-affiliations" (1955).

MUSIC AND MUSICAL PERFORMANCES

Music, one of the earliest modes for ethnic communication, preservation of cultural heritage, and retention of popular memory among exiled Iranians, is also the one most favored. Immediately after Iranians began to arrive in the United States, the classical and pop music recorded in Iran prior to the 1978–79 revolution was duplicated and distributed. As exile wore on, however, first the established artists who had emigrated and later a new crop of emerging talent began recording music here, turning Southern California into the world mecca of Iranian pop music. In fact, Pars Video, Los Angeles's foremost recording and distributing agency for Iranian music, claimed in an article in *Jam-e Jam* weekly (June 1987, 28–29) that although it rarely produces more than six thousand audiocassettes, its audience exceeds a million. The size of the audience is especially large in Iran, where pirated copies of exile-produced cassettes are duplicated freely by local entrepreneurs and individuals. The popularity of exile pop music inside Iran is due in part to the banning of the genre by the Islamic authorities. Here exile produces a reversal: home at first nourishes exiles; then those in exile feed those who have remained at home.

The availability in Iran of the music videos, television programs, and musical cassettes produced in exile, however, does not constitute a deep penetration into the dominant culture of the Islamic Republic. Some researchers doubt the relevance or the influence of exile media on the culture or politics of the homeland (Sreberny-Mohammadi and Mohammadi 1991).

Exile pop music is most often performed at concerts, where thousands of Iranian teenagers and adults bask in the tumult and, sometimes, the nostalgia and allure of the music. Mainstream stars perform in half a dozen nightclubs that cater to Iranians in Southern California. Some are no more than dingy, dimly lit restaurants with sound systems where dinner and alcoholic drinks are served and even children are allowed. The "shows" themselves consist of performances by individual singers, backed up often by the nightclub's resident band. Both the concerts and the nightclubs are heavily promoted on Iranian TV and radio programs and in the popular press.

The rituals and events of popular culture in exile such as concerts, seasonal festivals, and nightclub acts mark the boundary between the exiles and the host society. By staging indigenous rituals and performances in a foreign country, the exiles play their private, ethnic, and national symbolic forms of culture against those of the host society. Moreover, these cultural events not only reduce isolation and loneliness but also promote ethnic solidarity and integration, helping the exiles find new friends, companions, lovers, and especially future spouses.

Following the U.S. model, Iranian music celebrities, especially pop stars, have begun producing and distributing their music on audiocassettes, laser compact disks, and music videos. Music videos, in particular, have turned tragic and nostalgic representations of home and the past into celebratory commodities for those in exile (Naficy 1992a). The videos, catchy dance numbers or nostalgic songs, are shown repeatedly on exile TV. In addition, film clips from concerts and music videos; news reports about pop concerts and new albums; interviews with pop singers; and television ads for concerts, new albums, and new videos are incorporated into Iranian television shows.

Exile music and television are so closely intertwined that it can be difficult to distinguish programs from commercials. A producer, for example, may make and distribute music videos and television programs and audiocassettes as well as having a financial stake in the revenues generated from concerts. As a result, this producer uses music and music videos on his TV shows intertextually: each use of a video (as a program segment, advertisement, news report, or promotion for a concert or a new album) promotes another enterprise in which he has an interest. It is these links that account for the royalists' virtual monopoly over important segments of Iranian popular culture in exile.

CONCLUSION

John Fiske has noted, "There can be no popular dominant culture, for popular culture is formed always in relation to, and never as part of, the forces of domination" (1989, 43). Popular culture in the United States is a constellation of competing minicultures, which are themselves no more monolithic, authentic, or hermetic than the popular culture as a whole. The popular culture of exiles is formed in relation to that of the host society; that of the Iranians is varied, interconnected, and in constant flux. Imposed neither by host nor home society, it embodies many contradictions and hybrid forms. The fluctuations in the Iranians' popular culture reflect and are a constitutive part of the exiles' ongoing negotiation of new identities and authentic cultural forms.[15] Of course, no culture is "authentic" in the sense either of being pure and uncontaminated by other cultures or of having a moment of origination, and Iranian popular culture is no exception. As the host country's popular culture acculturates exiles, the exiles develop their own popular culture, which enables them to resist the dominant culture by consolidating and maintaining their own ethnic and national identity. To remain vital, popular culture—that of a nation as a whole and that of each population in the nation—depends on novelty, change, and mutual influence. By incorporating these elements from each other's popular cultures, both U.S. and Iranian-exile cultures are enriched and renewed. In the end, however, the national popular culture tends to co-opt the ethnic and exilic subcultures.

1. The following Iranian periodicals have been published in Los Angeles since 1980 (those still appearing in May 1991 are marked by an asterisk): *A'ineh, Andisheh, Arya, Asa, Asqar Aqa,\* Asr-e Emruz,\* Ayandegan, Baray-e Azadi, Barresi-ye Ketab,\* Bazar,\* Chesmandaz,\* Donia-ye Yahud,\* Elements, Elm va Erfan, Farman-e Panjom,\* Fogholadeh, Forugh,\* Hafteh Nameh, Iran-e Emruz, Iranian Recycler,\* Iran Life, Iran News,\* Iran Post, Iran Report, Iran Tribune, Jahan-e Pezeshgi,\* Jahan-e Varzesh,\* Jam-e Jam, Javanan,\* Jebheh-ye Hamgam,\* Jebheh-ye Jam, Jelveh, Jonbesh-e Iranian-e Banitorah,\* Jong, Kabobnameh, Kajnazar, Khabarnameh-ye Zanan, Khandaniha,\* Khaneh va Zamin,\* Kurosh-e Bozorg,\* Mellat-e Bidar, Mowj,\* Nasl-e Now, Niazmandiha,\* Nima,\* Omid, Pardis, Pars,\* Payam-e Ashena,\* Payam-e Azadi, Payam-e Iran,\* Payk-e Aramesh,\* Payman, Payvand, Payvand Nameh,\* Pey-ke Ketab,\* Pol, Qalam dar Khedmat-e Jahad,\* Rah-e Zendegi,\* Rahavard,\* Rayegan, Sarnevesht,\* Seda-ye Shahr,\* Shahr-e Farang,\* Shakhsar, Shofar,\* Simorgh,\* Sobh-e Iran,\* Sosialism, Sowgand, Sufi,\* Tamasha,\* Tamashabazar,\* Tamasha 64, Tofigh-e Ejbari,\* Touka,\* Vauli-Vaul, Zan.\**

2. The following Iranian television programs have aired in Los Angeles (those marked with an asterisk were on the air in May 1991): "Arya in L.A.,"\* "Assyrian TV,"\* "Chesmandaz," "Cheshmak," "Didar," "Fogholadeh,"\* "Iran,"\* "Iranian A.M.,"\* "Iranian Music TV," "Iranian P.M.,"\* "Iran va Jahan,"\* "Jahan Nama," "Jam-e Jam,"\* "Javanan va Nowjavanan,"\* "Jom'-eh," "Jonbesh-e Iran,"\* "Jong-e Bamdadi,"\* "Khaneh va Khanehvadeh,"\* "Khorus-e Bimahal," "Ma TV," "Mehr-e Iran," "Mellat," "Melli," "Melli-e Pars," "Midnight Show,"\* "Mikhak-e Noqreh'i," "Negah,"\* "Omid-e Iran," "Pars,"\* "Parsian," "Shar-e Farang,"\* "Sima va Nava-ye Iran,"\* "Sima-ye Ashena,"\* "Sima-ye Azadi," "Sobh Bekhair Iran,"\* "Sobh-e Ruz-e Jom'eh,"\* "Tamasha," "Tapesh TV Show,"\* "Zendegi-ye Behtar."\*

3. The following regularly scheduled radio programs targeted at Iranians have aired in Southern California (those with an asterisk were on the air in May 1991): "Happy Harry," "Iran," "Nayiri," "Omid," "Omid-e Iran," "Payam," "Payam-e Enqelab-e Eslami," "Purang," "Rah-e Shab," "Rangarang," "Seda-ye Afghanistan,"\* "Seda-ye Arameneh," "Seda-ye Azadi," "Seda-ye Hezb-e Komonist," "Seda-ye Iran,"\* "Seda-ye Iran-e Javid," "Seda-ye Nehzat." Another program, "You're on the Air,"\* is aimed, not at Iranians, but at all Muslims living in Southern California. It is a live program focusing on current topics and featuring a call-in segment. "Seda-ye Afghanistan" is produced by and for the Afghan exiles, but because its language is understandable to Iranians, it is included here.

4. Interview with Ali Reza Maibodi, a program director of "Seda-ye Iran," September 1989.

5. Two other telephone newscasts that have not survived were sponsored by Anjoman-e Daneshjuyan-e Irani dar Jonub-e Kalifornia (Society of Iranian Students in Southern California), which was affiliated with Feda'iyan-e Khalq (majority faction) and the Tudeh party, and Sazman-e Daneshjuyan-e Irani (Iranian Student Organization), which was affiliated with the Confederation of Iranian Students (CIS) and Feda'iyan Khalq (minority faction).

6.   The following feature films produced in Iran prior to the revolution were shown in Los Angeles commercial cinemas during the 1980s: *Ajal-e Mo'allaq, Alafha-ye Harz, Ali Baba, Aludeh, Aqa-ye Halu, Aramesh dar Hozur-e Digaran, Asrar-e Ganj-e Darreh-ye Jenni, Baba Shamal, Bandari, Bar Faraz-e Asemanha, Bedeh Dar Rah-e Khoda, Biganeh, Biqarar, Bita, Bonbast, Bot, Charkh va Falak, Cheshmeh, Dalahu, Dar Emtedad-e Shab, Dash Akol, Dashneh, Doroshgehchi, Ehsas-e Dagh, Emshab Dokhtari Mimirad, Farar az Taleh, Faryad-e Zir-e Ab, Faseleh, Ganj-e Qarun, Gav, Gavaznha, Gharibeh va Meh, Ghazal, Gholam Zhandarm, Haft Shahr-e Eshq, Hamkelas, Hamsafar, Hasan Kachal, Hasan Siah, Hashtomin Ruz-e Hafteh, Hasrat, Havas, In Goruh-e Mahkumin, Javanmard, Jenjal-e Arusi, Kajkolah Khan, Kalaq, Kandu, Khak-e Sar Behmohr, Khakestari, Khaneh Kharab, Khashm-e Oqabha, Khastegar, Khaterkhah, Khodahafez Tehran, Khoda Qovvat, Khorus, Khoshgel-e Mahalleh, Khoshgeltarin Zan-e Alam, Ki Dasteh Gol Beh Ab Dadeh?, Kineh, Laili va Majnun, Mah-e Asal, Malek-e Duzakh, Mamal-e Emrika'i, Man ham Geryeh Kardam, Mard-e bi Setareh, Mard-e Sharqi Zan-e Farangi, Marg dar Baran, Marsiyeh, Mehman, Mi'adgah-e Khashm, Mogholha, Mohallel, Mo'jezeh-ye Eshq, Moslakh, Moshgel-e Aqa-ye E'temad, Mowj-e Tufan, Mozzafar, Naqs-e Fanni, Nazanin, O.K. Mister, Panjereh, Pashneh Tala, Pol, Qafas, Qaisar, Qalandar, Qasr-e Zarrin, Ragbar, Ranandeh-ye Ejbari, Raqqaseh, Reza Motori, Salomeh, Samad Artist Mishavad, Samad beh Madreseh Miravad, Samad Darbehdar Mishavad, Samad dar Rah-e Ezhdaha, Samad Khoshbakht Mishavad, Samad va Qalicheh-ye Hazrat-e Solaiman, Samad va Sami Laila va Lili, Saraydar, Say-eh ha-ye Boland-e Bad, Sazesh, Sehta Bezanbahador, Shab-e Ghariban, Shab-e Yalda, Shahrashub, Shazdeh Ehtejab, Showhar-e Kerayeh'i, Showhar-e Pastorizeh, Showharjunam Asheq Shodeh, Sutehdelan, Tabi'at-e Bijan, Takhtehkhab-e Seh Nafareh, Taksi-ye Eshq, Tangsir, Tavalodat Mobarak, Topoli, Towqi, Tufan-e Nuh, Usta Karim Nokaretim, Yaqut-e Seh Cheshm, Yek Del va Do Delbar, Yek Esfahani dar New York, Yek Esfahani dar Sarzamin-e Hitler, Yeki Khosh Seda va Yeki Khosh Dast, Zabih, Zanburak, Zir-e Bazarcheh.*

7.   New wave films shown in exile include the following: *Aramesh dar Hozur-e Digaran, Asrar-e Gang-e Darreh-ye Jenni, Bonbast, Cheshmeh, Dash Akol, Gav, Ghazal, Khak-e Sar Behmohr, Marsiyeh, Mogholha, O.K. Mister, Ragbar, Saraydar, Shazdeh Ehtejab, Sutehdelan, Tabi'at-e Bijan, Tangsir, Topoli.* For details on the new wave films and the Iranian feature film industry prior to the revolution, see Naficy, 1979; and Issari, 1989.

8.   For details of festival showings see the catalog *A Decade of Iranian Cinema, 1980–1990,* prepared by the author. As a result of the success of the festival, a number of Iranian films such as *Ejarehneshinha* (The Tenants), *Bashu, Gharibeh-ye Kuchak* (Bashu, the Little Stranger), and *Hamun* were picked up for commercial exhibition; they have received both critical and popular acclaim. For details on Iranian post-revolutionary cinema, see Naficy, 1987, 1992b.

9.   In addition to these films with Iranian themes, Iranian directors have produced the following feature films in exile: *Destination Unknown* (Sohrab Shahid Saless, 1983), *Escape* (Tony Zarrindast), *L'Etat de crise* (Mamad Haghighat, 1984), *Far from Home* (Sohrab Shahid Saless, 1975), *Heaven Can Help* (Tony Zarrindast, 1989),

*House beyond the Sand* (Tony Zarrindast), *Kill Alex Kill* (Tony Zarrindast), *Night-songs* (Marva Nabili, 1984), *Revolt* (Jim Sheybani, 1985), *Le Tablier de ma mère* (Arbi Ovanesian, 1988), *Terror in Beverly Hills* (Moshe Bibian, 1989), *The Time of Maturity* (Sohrab Shahid Saless, 1976), *Treasure of the Lost Desert* (Tony Zarrindast), and *Utopia* (Sohrab Shadid Saless, 1982).

10.   The following list includes most of the plays staged by Iranians in Los Angeles: *A'ineh*, *An Safarkardeh*, *Ansu-ye Marz*, *Aqay-e Gandi*, *Baz ham Yek Ruz-e Digar*, *Chamedan*, *Cheshm dar Barabar-e Cheshm*, *D.Z. Shame and Cat*, *Falgush*, *Faseleh-ye do Darvazeh*, *Gomshodeh dar Bad*, *Haft Rang*, *Hameh-ye Pesaran-e Iran Khanom*, *Jan Nesar*, *Khaneh-ye Rowshan*, *Khar*, *Kuti va Muti*, *Mah va Palang*, *Marg-e Yazd-e Gerd*, *Mas'aleh-ye Kuchak-e Haleh*, *Mashinnevisha va Olaq*, *Matarsak*, *Mina-mata*, *Mohakemeh-ye Sinema Rex*, *Mohallel*, *Nan va Eshq va Green Card*, *Qarantineh*, *Samad az Jang Barmigardad*, *Samad beh Jang Miravad*, *Shahr-e Qesseh*, *Talaq*, *Tehran-geles Press*, *Tehran O' Tehran*.

11.   The major exile theater companies that have staged plays in Southern and Northern California are: Kargah-e Namayesh (headed by Zoya Zakarian and Reza Zhian), Parviz Sayyad and his groups, Darvak (headed by Farhad Aiesh), and Tandis (headed by Manijeh Mohammadi and Mohammad Eskandari). In addition to those mentioned, prominent theatrical producer-directors active in Southern California include Ali Pourtash, Mas'ud Assadollahi, Parviz Kardan, Hushang Towzi, Shohreh Aghdashlu, Mahmud Hashemi, Naser Rahmaninezhad, Bahman and Ardavan Mofid.

12.   Parviz Sayyad's productions (such as *Khar*, *Mohakemeh-ye Sinema Rex*, *Samad beh Jang Miravad*, and *Samad az Jang Barmigardad*) and Farhad Aiesh's plays (such as *Chamedan* and *Marg-e Yazd-e Gerd*) are the exception; each has had a run of several weeks in Los Angeles and in San Francisco. Moreover, Sayyad has taken a number of his plays on tour to cities in the United States, Canada, and Europe.

13.   For more on exile theater, see Karimi-Hakak, 1991.

14.   The following exile associations have held academic and cultural functions at UCLA since the 1978–79 revolution: Iranian Association of America, Radio Omid, UCLA Iran Education & Research Group, UCLA Center for Near Eastern Studies, UCLA Iranian Student Group, Anjoman-e Azadi-e Zan, Anjoman-e Daneshjuyan e Irani, Anjoman-e Daneshjuyan-e Mosalman-e Emrika va Kanada, Anjoman-e Defa' az Hoquq-e Demokratik-e Zanan-e Iran, Anjoman-e Eslami-ye Daneshjuyan dar Emrika va Kanada, Anjoman-e Farhangi-ye Zanan, Anjoman e Farhangi-ye Nima, Boniad-e Kian, Havadaran-e Cherikha-ye Fada'i Khalq, Hezb-e Demokrat-e Kordestan, Hezb-e Komonist-e Iran, Kanun-e Andisheh, Kanun-e Farhangi Siyasi-e Iranian, Kanun-e Hambastegi-ye Zanan-e Irani, Komite-ye Bainolmelali-ye Defa' az Hoquq-e Demokratik-e Mardom-e Iran, Komiteh-ye Demokratik-e Zanan-e Iran, Majalleh-ye Iranshenasi, Sazman-e Havadaran-e Hezb-e Tudeh-ye Iran.

15.   Fischer and Abedi, 1990 (253–332), provide an ethnographic analysis of the dialectics of identity and authenticity as played out in the arena of the Iranian exile culture.

REFERENCES

Aronson, S. H. 1986. "The Sociology of the Telephone." In *Intermedia: Interpersonal Communication in the World*, edited by G. Gumpert and R. Cathcart, 300–310. 3d ed. New York: Oxford University Press.

Bourdieu, P. 1977. *Outline of a Theory of Practice*. Translated by R. Nice. New York, Schocken Books.

Fischer, M. J., and M. Abedi. 1990. *Debating Muslims: Cultural Dialogues in Postmodernity and Tradition*. Madison: University of Wisconsin Press.

Fiske, J. 1989. *Understanding Popular Culture*. Boston: Unwin Hyman.

Gramsci, A. 1988. *An Antonio Gramsci Reader: Selected Writings, 1916–1935*. Edited by D. Forgacs. New York: Schocken Books.

Issari, M. A. 1989. *Cinema in Iran, 1900–1979*. Metuchen, N.J.: Scarecrow Press.

Karimi-Hakak, M. 1991. "The Struggle for a New Identity of Iranian Theater in America." *Jong* 4 (January 1): 3–5.

Ketab Corporation. 1991. *Yelo Paij-e Iranian*. Los Angeles.

Mowlana, H. 1991. "Oppositional Media outside National Boundaries: From Constitutionalism to the Islamic Revolution." In *Iranian Refugees and Exiles since Khomeini*, edited by A. Fathi, 37–54. Costa Mesa, Calif.: Mazda Publishers.

Naficy, H. 1979. "Iranian Feature Film: A Brief Critical History." *Quarterly Review of Film Studies* (Fall): 443–464.

———. 1984. *Iran Media Index*. Westport, Conn.: Greenwood Press.

———. 1987. "The Development of an Islamic Cinema in Iran." *Third World Affairs 1987*, 447–463.

———. 1990a. *Exile Discourse and Television: A Study of Syncretic Cultures: Iranian Television in Los Angeles*. Ph.D. diss., University of California at Los Angeles.

———. 1990b. "From Liminality to Incorporation." In *Iranian Refugees and Exiles since Khomeini*, edited by A. Fathi, 228–253. Costa Mesa, Calif.: Mazda Publishers.

———. 1990c. "The Aesthetics and Politics of Iranian Cinema in Exile." *Cinemaya* (Fall): 4–8.

———. 1991. "Exile Discourse and Televisual Fetishization." *Quarterly Review of Film and Video* 13, nos. 1–3:85–116.

———. 1992a. "The Poetics and Practice of Iranian Nostalgia in Exile." *Diaspora*, no. 3.

———. 1992b. "Islamizing the Film Culture." In *Iran: Political Culture in the Islamic Republic*, edited by S. Farsoun and M. Mashayekhi. London: Routledge.

———. 1993. *The Making of Exile Cultures: Iranian Television in Los Angeles*. Minneapolis: University of Minnesota Press.

Schramm, W. 1977. *Big Media, Little Media: Tools and Technologies for Instruction*. Beverly Hills, Ca.: Sage.

Simmel, G. 1955. *Conflict and the Web of Group-Affiliations*. Translated by K. H. Wolff and R. Bendix. New York: Free Press.

Sreberny-Mohammadi, A., and A. Mohammadi. 1991. "Iranian Exiles as Opposition: Some Theses on the Dilemmas of Political Communication Inside and Outside Iran." In *Iranian Refugees and Exiles since Khomeini*, edited by A. Fathi, 205–227. Costa Mesa, Calif.: Mazda Publishers.

PART VII

THE PHOTOGRAPHY OF *IRANGELES*

FIGURE 156. Neusha Farrahi in his
bookshop holding a photograph of
himself and his father, with his grand-
father's photo on the back wall. This
photograph was taken three months
before his public immolation. June 1987.

# *IRANGELES*: PHOTOGRAPHIC CONTEXTS

## *Ron Kelley*

The most interesting photograph I ever "saw" in the Los Angeles Iranian community is not in this book; I wasn't permitted to record it. In July 1989 I learned that the Moslem Student Association, Persian Speaking Group, was holding the customary Shi'i memorial forty days after death for the Ayatollah Khomeini. I showed up at the University of Southern California and sought permission to photograph the event.

The man in charge refused my request, insisted that no one there cared to be photographed, and, alluding to the highly politicized context of Shi'i Islam, asked how he could know that I wasn't a U.S. government agent. Explaining my project, presenting letters of introduction, cajoling, begging, and arguing with him were to no avail. I was allowed to witness the event but forbidden to photograph it.

Later, browsing in the lobby at a display of books extolling the Islamic Republic, I glanced up to see a woman covered by a long black chador pulled tight around her face. Although this itself is an unusual sight in Los Angeles, more strikingly, beside the woman was her young son, come to mourn the death of Ayatollah Khomeini in a black Batman costume. As little Batman's fluttering cape approached me, I was struck by the ironic repetition of black shapes, the merging of similar forms and conflicting contents. In this visual paradox, contesting cultures were consolidated, mother and son mirroring each other, Los Angeles style.

Although I took no photographs, that night was far from wasted. Sitting in a darkened auditorium with two hundred people, the only non-Muslim Westerner present, I listened, entranced, to an eerie chorus of mourners weeping and wailing in communal sadness and suffering. Nothing I've experienced in Western culture compares to that night, although later that year I would experience similar feelings at nightly gatherings of Muslims in an Orange County high school during the holy month of Moharram. Although the weeping this time was for the death of the martyr Husain in the year 680, I found myself again engulfed by the emotion around me. It was not the death of the ancient hero—or of Khomeini—that affected me but something far less foreign. I couldn't help feeling linked to the agony of those around me; it lapped against me in the dark like a wave of human suffering: a brother dead, a mother in the hospital, each person's own frail mortality—the universal predicaments of loss and frustration.

I found the dramatic outpouring of emotion cathartic and in some odd way beautiful. I watched as groups of mourning men stood up and began striking their chests rhythmically, filling the room with a thunderous drumming. I didn't weigh, those nights, the alleged injustices of the Islamic Republic. And I still can't prove what I knew then instinctively: that if you want to understand Iranians, you've got to start here.

I dwell on this story to foreground some of my interpretive biases and to note the energy and fascination—intellectual and emotional—that led me to explore the Iranian community in Los Angeles. I understand the images of this book as both artistic (self-expressive, interpretive) endeavor and ethnographic research; their full meanings grow out of the Los Angeles Iranian community, my studied experiences of it, and my own life and worldview. The images were neither taken nor intended to illustrate the written text; they have their own life and make their own subjective statement. Neither are they "art photos" isolated from the Iranian experience in America, decontextualized, ahistorical.

The photographic image is always a paradox: it implies the existence of irrefutable evidence (the one-to-one point mapping of the physical world—the visual "facts" that the camera lens transferred to the negative plane). At the same time, it is a subjective product of continuous decision making. Toward what has the photographer decided to point the camera? From what vantage point? At what precise moment is the image taken? Which of the many frames of exposed film is selected for use? And where will the resultant images be presented? Photography is a process of continual editorializing, and each choice involves endless possibilities. No matter what the struggles and claims to objectivity, the photographer is always standing somewhere, both literally and ideologically. Photography, then, is always an active construct, never a passive record.

Photography, too, is an implicitly appropriative, objectifying medium. It takes the transient, the elusive, and the ephemeral and makes them concrete. As part of this appropriative dynamic, the camera represents a power relationship between subject and photographer; the photographer does not merely observe but defines the camera-less other, acting as an arbiter between subject and visual history. In this process of mediation, the image maker inevitably gives the objectifying of experience priority over experience itself. The photographer interrupts the flow of life to establish a

Pour un IRAN libre et éternel

REZA SHAH II

FIGURE 157. Pro-Shah demonstrator.
February 1986.

conceptual framework within which the proceedings become a visual object. In raising the camera to the eye, the photographer steps out of the immediate environment, placing a wall between observer and subject. This wall can last but a few seconds or can remain as an alienating barrier between the photographer and the subject community.

In a photograph objects before the lens are transformed, forever changed. They have left the context of their origins to merge into the complex syntactical systems of photomechanical replication. Even if an image maker focuses on the unmanipulated purities of a cultural scene, the connotative range of any fact is not absolute; it is subject to a range of interpretations based on viewers' personal and cultural decoding strategies. Any viewer mediates the "truth" of a given image according to his or her own beliefs and perceptions.

From the beginning I realized that this project on Iranians would be formidable—not just because of the large and varied Persian community I was photographing but also because of the sometimes opposing forces at work in this volume. I wanted to assemble a series of photographs reflecting my studied opinion of the Iranian community here, structured to my own standards of visual quality. But I also felt obliged to reflect accurately the diversity within Iranian culture and the exile predicament, regardless of the intrinsic visual interest of a particular scene. I had to compromise between an artistic/aesthetic venture, which would feature the most visually interesting images and those whose highly personalized meanings had little to do with the Iranian community per se, and a social science approach, which would present the images that best represent social and cultural phenomena: a catalog of cultural information. (The best social science data might be the unedited contact sheets, which underscore the frame-by-frame sequence of events and reveal some of the decision making of the photographer.)

An awareness of the theoretical currents and practical stratagems of the photographic medium informs my own day-to-day picture taking. Although I prefer the spontaneity of recording whatever evolves before me, I know that this kind of image making is no more purely objective than positioning people in the frame to my liking. In any case, the simple strategy I often used for this project was to photograph a person or scene from different angles and at different moments, and sometimes in juxtapositional contexts. Later I would decide which image was the best.

The "best" image for me is one in which the arrangement of elements reinforces the photo's rhetorical and interpretive statement. Often such an image includes paradox and irony. In such a paradigm, the ideal photograph is an epitome, an aggregation of syntactic elements that highlights a

FIGURE 158. Mojahedin march against
the Islamic Republic of Iran. Washington,
D.C., June 1988.

latent truth. This summation is based on denotative facts but foregrounds their connotations. In this sense, a good image might simply be one in which the metaphoric and symbolic elements convincingly supersede the literal in making a critical point.

A related photographic methodology is the unposed, unrehearsed excerpting from the transient "chaos of life" that the photographer Henri Cartier-Bresson called the search for the "decisive moment." For Bresson, anticipating the fortuitous accident was a lyrical concern: the orchestration of undirected visual events into fluid interrelational forms. Although it can be argued that any image is a decisive moment in the sense that every instant entails a decisive change, lyrical or not, the deeper implications of Bresson's strategy are that image makers weave a structural paradigm and anticipate, like spiders with their webs, the world falling into it. That is the nature both of photographic recording and of human perception, of consciousness.

I spent parts of the five years from 1986 to 1991 and shot a thousand rolls of film in an attempt to fathom, and depict, the complex Iranian community in Los Angeles—from Muslims to Baha'is, from Sufis to belly dancers. I went to cabarets, religious centers, poetry readings, political demonstrations, private homes, and business establishments. I even took beginning courses in Persian. But these images, for me, are not only about Iranians in Los Angeles. They are also linked to others I have taken that comment on the values and mores of American society. That work reflects my fascination with visually exploring, interpreting, and commenting on the icons and mythologies of American social life, including the political foundations of social interaction that have become ideologically naturalized—as people, for example, become so used to the ethnocentric norms governing their daily lives that they no longer see that these are not the only guidelines for behavior. The images in this volume from anti-Iranian demonstrations in 1979–81 were recorded before I knew much about Iran or its revolution. At the time, I was interested in the spectacle of re-emergent American nationalism, the influence of the mass media in constructing public opinion, and the application of visual strategies to the critical interpretation of such phenomena.

The subjective tradition of Robert Frank and his seminal photographic work *The Americans* have strongly influenced me. Frank, a Swiss Jew, journeyed through the United States in the 1950s to make his broad critical statement about American culture, to "define" it visually. Critics of his era complained that he could hardly have explored all of America in his ninety photographs and accused him of wallowing in some of the worst of the

American social scene. His pictures weren't pretty, nor were they gratuitously flattering. His was not a lovely coffee-table book. Frank had no social science agenda, nor did he intend to represent fairly, diplomatically, and categorically the entire United States. He simply wandered in with his nebulous poetic intuitions and some strong passions and gravitated toward what he thought was important—jukeboxes, bars, automobiles—American icons of the era. Although Frank inevitably failed to depict a broad-based sample of American people and social life, he triumphantly succeeded in something far more important: he mapped the demise of the American spiritual and moral character.

My intention in the photographs of this project was not to satisfy all elements in the Los Angeles Iranian community. Some will be disappointed that the photographs are black and white, not color. Others will have difficulty fathoming the images. "No airbrushing? No rhapsodic lyricism? And you photographed the lesser of the two holy ceremonies? Why did you photograph the pro-Khomeinis so much when they represent such a tiny community here? Why so many pictures on Rodeo Drive? And why did you photograph this musician who is not as important as the ones you overlooked?"

In the complex photographic process, with its illusory ease, nothing can be taken for granted. Once, an Iranian college student, after seeing a selection of this book's photographs in an exhibition, questioned the use of the wide-angle lens. It was, I explained, part of a conscious aesthetic and strategy, part of my self-expressive repertoire. This lens expands space, accentuates juxtapositional relationships, and forces me to confront the subject matter from only a couple steps away. It can also be preset for a wide depth of field with no recurring need to focus. The student continued to object, however, to the "distortion" of the 28mm lens. Surprised, I argued that of course the subjects were distorted, as was anything ever depicted in a photograph. Wasn't the three-dimensional world always profoundly transformed when it was represented on a two-dimensional plane? Never mind that these images are black-and-white replications of a color world. Wasn't it strange, I asked my critic, how the many conventions of photographic distortion had become culturally naturalized, invisible to the viewer immersed in them? What system of visual depiction is not involved in distorting real-life experience?

Los Angeles Iranians, who will actively criticize and comment on this volume, will inevitably reflect both Iranian and American values. Many Iranians here are more American than I am: they endorse, as important extensions of personal pride and identity, the very American values I reject.

My own views are deeply rooted in the counterculture values of the 1960s, including anti-materialism, dissatisfaction with consumerist values, and a belief in the sanctity of the individual. Many Iranians here are model corporate consumers and some, like Bijan (who promotes himself as well as his perfume in elaborate marketing campaigns) are even active shapers of consumerist values. Ironically, many of the Iranians living in Los Angeles have more in common, in terms of aspirations and hence self-identity, with Filipino, Nicaraguan, Chinese, and other immigrants of their own socioeconomic strata than they have with their own compatriots in Iran, who at last report were still largely illiterate.

Most Iranians here have absorbed both the values of Western popular culture and its strategies for decoding photographic images. (In Iran, support for the visual arts expanded only in relatively recent history beyond traditional genres such as miniature painting and geometric design.) Many Los Angeles Iranians praise Roloff Beny's color photographs in his books *Iran: Elements of Destiny* and *Persia: Bridge of Turquoise*. Beny depicts butterflies, fields of flowers, sunsets, scenic vistas, folk costumes and classical architecture in lavish coffee-table volumes replete with clichés of transcendent beauty. Other images—equally romanticized—highlight the institutions of a dictatorial society, including military marches, tank columns, jet fighters, technological icons, and industrial complexes. His two books are extravagant testaments to the myths of the Shah's era, celebrating the monarchist past and anticipating a glorious technological future. They have little to do with the day-to-day realities of the people of Iran.

A similar photographic formula has been used in *National Geographic*, which has long rendered the cultural Other in exotically beautiful terms, typically juxtaposed with strange fish, insects, weird plant life, and other curiosities of the natural world. In March 1968 the magazine published twenty-one color photographs of the Shah's self-coronation, with laudatory commentary.

In contrast, from both a social and an aesthetic perspective, Gilles Peress's *Telex: Iran. In the Name of Revolution* is an extraordinary visual rendition of the Iranian revolution and an important predecessor of this volume. (The look of the people who populate his images is planets away from the collective image of those here.) Peress, a photojournalist by trade, portrays the chaos of the revolution not only symbolically but also in the structure of his images, whose form follows their content. His visual aesthetic (hybridized from Lee Friedlander and Henri Cartier-Bresson, among others) is a carefully concentrated orchestration of disjointed fragments into a unified whole. Often Peress's frames break, like shattered glass, into scattered and contesting—or seemingly chaotic—elements, their very structure rendering the tensions of the revolution. Jagged, disjointed shapes and forms in careful juxtaposition reaffirm the images' symbolic content—riotous revolutionary upheaval—as the French photographer struggles to make sense of the seething social earthquake around him.

That a photograph can function simultaneously as fact and metaphor is part of its fascinating power. It is at once specific and generalized. The image in this volume of a line of women in Islamic veils standing under a parallel line of American flags (Fig. 122) depicts a moment, after a protest march at a U.S. government building, when the women bring their hands to their ears in prayer. The metaphor I recognized as I took the image is sociopolitical. Clothed in the traditional Islamic veil, the women allude to the current political milieu of Islam. They appear to be shielding their ears from the "sound" of the American flags above them, the flags symbolizing everything that the Ayatollah Khomeini condemned as morally corrupt.

Such juxtaposition can be an important rhetorical device along with irony. Another image (Fig. 97), of a woman in a polka-dot dress juxtaposed with a polka-dot dog, suggests an infatuation with fashion so intense that the woman treats her dog as an accessory to her clothing. Of course, the literal truth of the juxtaposition remains unknown. Did the woman consciously construct her polka-dot relationship to the dog? Was it coincidence? Was the dog even hers? No matter. The transient situation has been appropriated for the photograph, and its literal meaning has faded in importance. The photograph, after all, is not the subject itself but merely its reconstruction. The form of the image enhances its content: a zigzag of water, blanket, and other lines serves as compositional backdrop to the center attraction of the polka-dots, pulled taut with the line of a leash. The woman leans down, touching—metaphorically joining—the animal; the dog is an extension of her, or she of it. True to this particular woman or not, the resultant photo is metaphorically true for an image-conscious segment of the Iranian exile community. In another context, the fact that the woman is Iranian would be unimportant. The photo would remain an ironic commentary on, among other things, those obsessed with appearances.

Among the most difficult scenes to render creatively in this project were those set in the various religious communities. The Jews wanted no pictures on the Sabbath. Some Shi'i Muslim groups resisted being photographed too, sometimes because they suspected my political motivations. But most religious communities were open to me. Even with access, however, facing highly controlled routines and environments, I had little room to maneuver and interpret. It was difficult to comment visually on a religious scene—and by extension, the faith itself—in situations that physically limited angles to the proceedings. It was also a challenge to diplomacy to search out ironic juxtapositions in a religious milieu.

One visually interesting image among those of the religious communities (Fig. 67) depicts a veiled Muslim woman looking into a mirror. Like other pictures, this one functions as both record and metaphor. As the young woman seems to assess her own image, the photograph suggests metaphorically a self-reflection of her religious identity. Such a subjective inference rests entirely on her fleeting expression—one of apparent doubt, disdain, or uncertainty—at the image she sees in the mirror, as well as its American context. This inference may contradict the literal reality. Is a photographer's interest in what a photograph implies rather than what it is a betrayal of the "truth"? I would argue that it is not. Photographic truth is always relative. Ten exposed frames in a row are ten different realities. Which one is most important?

These images are not intended as a comprehensive catalog of the Los Angeles Iranian community. Rather, they are a deeply considered impression. I have sought to reveal something elusive, dynamic, and highly subjective about the Persian character here—visually manifest through body language, male-female relationships, power relationships, public personas, and affectations—that reflects both a studied and intuitive sense of it. My strongest interest has been in the nebulous poetic "truths" of the Persian character as I perceived and experienced it. I am moved by the great warmth, deep passions, generous hospitality, rich cultural tradition, profound grief, tormenting melancholy, and paradoxical sensuality of the Iranians. I am repulsed by their conspicuous materialism, obsession with status, and pretense. I have attempted—among other things—to deconstruct their public presentations of the self.

The interviews in this book allow a multi-ethnic blend of Iranians to "speak for themselves." The very fact that I am not Iranian has helped me photograph the many subcommunities for this project. Being Iranian could well have kept me from gaining access to all the ethnic, religious, and political factions that make up the community. As it was, I found most groups eager to share their traditions, histories, and ideologies with me.

To explore a "foreign" culture always involves the investigator's struggle not only to understand—and represent—the psychosocial dimensions of that culture but also to come to deeper terms with his own culture and hence, ultimately, himself. Iranians in Los Angeles are particularly intriguing in this regard: the exiles, refugees, and immigrants, as they become culturally assimilated, themselves join in the self-reflective process, weighing—sometimes by painful trials—the relative merits of their old and new values. To maintain their sense of dignity and balance, some Iranians have affected a level of affluence they no longer possess, an important element to this photographic study.

In this context, I would argue that coming to terms with the communal mourners of the Ayatollah Khomeini's death is critical to an understanding of the many Iranians here who have fled the Islamic Republic. Whatever their socioeconomic and religious background, a subtext of suffering runs like a dark river through the Iranians' psychosocial terrain. The loss of Imam Ali's rightful caliphate and the martyrdom of Imam Husain at Karbala echo through a long history of foreign invasion, political repression, and disillusionment. Strains of melancholy can be found throughout much of Iranian culture, from the impassioned poetry of ancient Hafez, Rumi, and modern Shamloo to traditional music that wails with grief and lamentation. In recent political history, the homeland has shaken in the throes of violent revolution and suffered over a million casualties in the terrible Iran-Iraq war, an anguishing backdrop for most Iranians during their first decade in America.

Not long ago I ventured to an Iranian acquaintance that hauntingly beautiful eyes are Iranians' most noticeable physical feature. This compliment, familiar to the community, didn't faze him. "Of course Iranian eyes are beautiful," he said. "But it is not necessarily their physical shape that is so striking. It's how expressive they can be. All the hurt and repression. Through those eyes you can see what is inside of them."

FIGURE 159.   The funeral of Neusha
Farrahi. Glendale, October 1987.

# ABOUT THE CONTRIBUTORS

MEHRDAD AMANAT

Mehrdad Amanat is a Ph.D. candidate in the UCLA Department of History. His doctoral research deals with educational reforms in modern Iran.

MEHDI BOZORGMEHR

Mehdi Bozorgmehr received his Ph.D. in sociology from UCLA, where he currently teaches. He was project director of a study of Iranians in Los Angeles funded by the National Science Foundation. He is a post-doctoral fellow at the UCLA Institute for Social Science Research.

ANITA COLBY

Anita Colby is associate director of the ERIC Clearinghouse for Junior Colleges at UCLA.

ARLENE DALLALFAR

Arlene Dallalfar received her Ph.D. in sociology from UCLA. She is currently a research fellow at the Center for Middle Eastern Studies at UC Berkeley and teaches in the Department of Sociology. She is completing a book on immigrant women, entrepreneurship, and emerging ethnic identity.

CLAUDIA DER-MARTIROSIAN

Claudia Der-Martirosian is a Ph.D. candidate in sociology at UCLA. She is in charge of data management for a study of Iranians in Los Angeles funded by the National Science Foundation.

JONATHAN FRIEDLANDER

Jonathan Friedlander is the Assistant Director of the UCLA Center for Near Eastern Studies. He is the writer and producer of a television documentary on Arab immigration to the United States and the editor of *Sojourners and Settlers: The Yemeni Immigrant Experience* (University of Utah Press, 1988). An associate of UCLA's International Studies and Overseas Programs, his current work deals with religion and identity in Brazil, India, Israel, and the United States.

SHIDEH HANASSAB

Shideh Hanassab is completing her doctoral work in counseling psychology at the UCLA Graduate School of Education. Her dissertation study examines mate selection among young Iranians in Los Angeles.

RON KELLEY

Ron Kelley holds a degree in anthropology from Michigan State University and an MFA in photography from the Department of Art at UCLA. He is the recent recipient of an Artist Grant from the Cultural Affairs Department of the City of Los Angeles and a Fulbright research grant for continued work on immigration to and from the Middle East. He is currently concluding a volume of his photographs and interviews concerning Muslims in Southern California as well as a book of images on American culture entitled *Mythologies*.

HAMID NAFICY

Hamid Naficy is currently teaching at the UCLA Department of Film and Television. Naficy has written widely on media, culture, and society. His latest book, entitled *Exiled Cultures and Minority Television*, will be published by the University of Minnesota Press in 1993.

GEORGES SABAGH

Georges Sabagh is professor of sociology and director of the UCLA Center for Near Eastern Studies. Sabagh has written extensively on the immigration of Middle Easterners to the United States. He was co-principal investigator of a National Science Foundation–funded study of Iranians in Los Angeles.

NAYEREH TOHIDI

Nayereh Tohidi is currently a lecturer and research scholar at the UCLA Center for the Study of Women. Tohidi received her Ph.D. in educational psychology from the University of Illinois at Urbana-Champaign. Her recent published research examines identity politics and the woman question in Iran. She is a recipient of a Fulbright grant to study women and *perestroika* in the former Soviet Republic of Azerbaijan.

# INDEX

Nowrasteh, Cyrus, 351
*Nuclear Baby,* 351

Occupations: of Iranians in Los Angeles,
  62, 73–76, 102, 156, 187–91, 233–48,
  274–92; of Iranian subgroups in Iran, 25,
  62, 99, 100, 115–16; of Iranian subgroups
  in Los Angeles, 62, 73–76, 102, 156; of
  Iranian women in U.S., 187–91, 274–92;
  self-employment, 62, 74, 102, 186–90,
  274–78. *See also* Business; Professional
  class
Oil, Iranian, 9, 13, 16, 17, 24, 65
Organizations: Armenian, 70, 77, 121–23;
  Assyrian, 132–39 passim; Baha'i, 65, 70,
  77, 89; business, 272; cultural, 210–11,
  212, 356–58, 363n. 14; intellectual, 356–
  58; Iranian advocacy groups, 14; Jewish,
  65, 70, 77, 89, 102; Moslem Student Association, 83; Muslim, 65, 70, 77, 89;
  mutual assistance, 49, 121–23; professional, 356–58; refugee resettlement, 47,
  70, 248–49, 251; secular self-help, 335;
  student, 83, 189, 193, 205, 210, 357,
  361n. 5; women's, 210–12, 357;
  Zoroastrian, 23, 140–48 passim, 160. *See
  also* Leftists; Political parties; Religions
*Otobus* (The Bus), 350
Ottomans. *See* Turkey

Pacific Palisades, Temescal Canyon Park,
  Kurdish picnic (1988), 150
Pahlavi, Mahmoud Reza, 247
Pahlavi, Mohammad Reza Shah, xiii, 8–21,
  24, 35–36; Baha'is in government of,
  126; brother's arrest, 247; Carter and, 13,
  20, 34, 35, 273; corruption under, 245,
  251; death (1980), 21; demonstrations
  against, 16, 299, 300, 309; demonstrations for, 3, 26, 258, 263, 299; history of
  regime (1941–79), 8–21; and industrialists, 28; and Kurds, 154, 155; marriage,
  207; *National Geographic* on, 374; Payman
  painting of coronation, 342; sister, 267;
  torture under, 12, 31, 32, 34, 37, 38, 40;
  and wealth of Iranians in U.S., 247, 251,
  272; westernization under, 9, 12–13, 260;
  and Zoroastrian monarchies, 142. *See
  also* Pahlavi, Reza Shah (Mohammad's
  son); SAVAK

Pahlavi, Reza Shah (Mohammad's father),
  8, 9, 12–13, 16, 100, 207
Pahlavi, Reza Shah (Mohammad's son), 25,
  94, 300, 304; demonstrations for, 169,
  300, 308, 310, 369; at Los Angeles Sports
  Arena, 259, 306–7
Pahlavi era (1925–79), 5, 9, 12–13, 16–17,
  20–21, 24, 25, 28; chronology of, 8–20;
  flag, 304, 313; and Kurds, 154, 155; mod-
  ernization during, 9, 183–84, 190, 210
Painters, 225, 251, 342–43
Pakistan: Iranian refugees to, 55, 56, 108–
  13; and Rushdie, 28
Pakistanis, in Los Angeles, xii, 84, 90, 302
Palestinians, in U.S., xii–xiii
Palms, Muslims in, 76
*Paris Match,* 42, 151
Parliament, Iranian, 12, 21, 23
Parliamentary government, Iran, 8–9, 13,
  21
Parsis, Zoroastrian, 144, 145–48
Pars National Ballet, 251
Pars Video, 350, 359
Pasadena, NASA Jet Propulsion Labora-
  tory, 273
Pasdaran Enqelab (revolutionary guards),
  Iran, 20, 35, 43, 44
Passover, 100, 103, 104
Patriarchy, 180, 183–84, 332
Patriotic Union of Kurdistan, 155–56
*Payam-e Iran,* 326
Payman, 342
Pentateuch, 111
Peress, Gilles, 374–75
Periodicals: Assyrian *Shotapouta* magazine,
  139; *Ettelaat* in Tehran, 16; Iranian popu-
  lar culture, 325–27, 361n. 1; *Iranian
  Yellow Pages,* 251; *Javanan,* 248, 326; *Los
  Angeles Times,* xii; *Al-Shiraa* in Lebanon,
  28; *Time* magazine, xi–xii; women's con-
  cerns, 212; *Zoroastrian* newsletter, 147
*Persia* (Beny), 374
Persian Gulf war/Desert Storm, 81, 136,
  151, 302
Persian language: Armenians and, 77; Assyrians and, 139; Baha'is and, 77; Jews
  and, 77; Kurds and, 156, 157; Muslims
  and, 77, 83, 84, 168; nationalism in Iran
  and, 13; periodicals in, 325; radio programs in, 346; television programs in,
  251, 260, 327–46

Persian nationalism, 12–13

Persian New Year (No Ruz), 89, 142, 145, 272, 304; candy serving, 66; concerts, 22, 27, 197; *haft seen,* 222; hunger strike, 316; Jews celebrating, 102; Sizdah Bidar after, 323

"Persian Night" at nightclubs: San Fernando Valley, 11; West Hollywood, 7

Persian traditions, 168–70; Assyrians and, 139; Mehregan folkdance (October 1988), 23; tea serving, 66. *See also* Persian New Year

Persian Zoroastrian Association, San Francisco, 142

Pesh Mergas ("those who face death"), 154, 155, 302

Photography, 365–77; Beny's, 374; "best" image, 370–72; Frank's, 372–73; *National Geographic,* 374; Peress's, 374–75; process, 368–70; wide-angle lens, 373

Pico-Fairfax area, Jewish business in, 102

Pico Rivera, East African mosque, 84

Plays, 341, 345, 354–56, 363

Poets, Iranian, 84, 225, 260, 338, 340, 353, 377

Police: Iranian *komitehs,* 18; SAVAMA, 35. *See also* SAVAK

Political asylum, 47, 69–70. *See also* Refugees

Political parties: in Iran, 13, 20, 21, 24, 43–44; in U.S., 210, 266, 272–73

Politics: in Iran, 9, 13, 16–28, 31–36, 43–44, 45, 126; of Iranians in U.S., 210, 242, 266, 272–73, 299–320; Kurdish, 155–56; Los Angeles Muslims and, 85–86; and marriage, 207; periodicals and, 326; and telephonic programs, 348; in television newscasts, 332; women's, 9, 185, 210–12. *See also* Demonstrations; Hostage crisis; Islamic Republic; Leftists; Pahlavi era

Population: Assyrians in Southern California, 136; Baha'i in Los Angeles, 73, 128; Census, 60–62, 73, 186; Jews in Los Angeles, 73, 102; Kurds in Iraq, 154; Kurds in Middle East, 153; Kurds in U.S./Southern California, 153; Los Angeles foreign-born, xi–xii; Los Angeles forty-sixth district, xiii; Los Angeles Iranian, xii, xiii, 70–73, 102, 128, 234, 247; religious subgroups in Iran, 60, 62, 126, 136, 142; Southern California Iranians,

251; television audience of Iranians, 331; U.S. immigrant, xi, 65; U.S. Iranian, 73; Zoroastrians, 142, 145

Professional class, 243, 250; cultural organizations, 356–58; "doctor's protest march" (March 1988), 304, 317; Iran, 5, 9, 17, 20–21, 24, 25, 51–52, 69; refugee, 51–52; Zoroastrian, 142

Proselytizing, Zoroastrians and, 146–47

Protests. *See* Demonstrations

Psychiatry/Psychologists, 162–72

Purim holiday, 99, 106

Qadiri, Mahvash, 182–83

Qajar dynasty (1796–1925), 5–8

Qom, holy Iranian city, 84

Qotbzadeh, Sadeq, 25

Quran, 81, 82, 84, 353

Race: Aryan, 9, 148, 262; in Los Angeles forty-sixth district, xiii. *See also* African-Americans; Ethnic identity; Racism

Racism, 130, 262, 264. *See also* Ethnicity

Radio programs, targeting Iranians, 327, 346–47, 349, 356, 361n. 3

*Rahezendigee* magazine, 165

Raja'i, Iranian President, 24

Rajavi, Mas'ud, 24

Rallies. *See* Demonstrations

Ramadan (month of fasting), 80, 85, 213

Rashidian, Farhad, 42, 43–45

Rashidian, Hassan, 45

Rashidian, Shahyar, 45

Rastakhiz (Resurgence) party, Iran, 13

Razzazi, Nasir, 156

Reagan, Ronald, 24, 28

Real estate, 102, 281–86; construction, 62, 74–76, 251; investment, 233–40, 243, 251, 267; Iranians as tenants, 248

Refugees, 5; Armenian, 116, 117; Baha'i, 130; Jewish, 108–13; Kurdish, 43–45, 151, 155; to Pakistan, 55, 56, 108–13; resettlement organizations, 47, 70, 248–49, 251; to U.S., xi, 43–56, 69–70, 116, 117, 130, 151, 155, 248–49; U.S. arrangements for, 47, 54

Regency Council, Iran, 17

Registry for documents and property, Iran, 9

Religio-ethnic groups. *See* Armenians . . . ; Assyrians; Baha'is . . . ; Jews . . . ; Kurds; Muslims . . . ; Zoroastrians

Designer:     Janet Wood
Compositor:   Keystone Typesetting, Inc.
Text:         11/14 Bembo
Display:      Onyx
Printer:      Malloy Lithographing, Inc.
Binder:       John H. Dekker & Sons